PALESTINE SPEAKS

PALESTINE SPEAKS

VOICES FROM THE WEST BANK AND GAZA

COMPILED AND EDITED BY

CATE MALEK AND MATEO HOKE

Research editor
ALEX CARP

Creative assistant
TIMOTHY FAUST

VOICE OF WITNESS

Additional interviewers
ABEER AYYOUB, JENNY BABOUN

Transcribers
ALESSANDRA BAUTISTA, KYLIE BYRD, TYLER DOYLE, MARIE DUFFIN,
LOUISA DUNNIGAN, ANN-DERRICK GAILLOT, RUBY GOLDBERG, WILL GRAY,
KAYE HERRANEN, MAGGIE HUANG, MARIA LATTANZI, JESSICA MCHUGH,
CAYLA MIHALOVICH, JOEY NARGIZIAN, NAOKI O'BRYAN, SORAYA OKUDA,
ANN READING, ALEXIS SATTLER, ABIGAIL SCHOTT-ROSENFIELD, VALERIE SNOW,
ROSANNA STEVENS, ILARIA SABINA VARRIALE, SALLY WEATHERS, KEZIAH WEIR

Translators
MJAD ALAWI, IYAD ALI, ABEER AYYOUB, JENNY BABOUN, GEORGE GHANTOUS,
WASSIM GHANTOUS, NIDAL HATIM

Copy editor
VICTORIA ALEXANDER

Fact checker
HANNAH MURPHY

Additional assistance
KYLIE BYRD, KAYE HERRANEN, MARIA LATTANZI, NAOKI O'BRYAN

*This book goes out to everyone fighting to be seen, heard,
or simply recognized as human. Yalla to the people.*

VOICE OF WITNESS

McSWEENEY'S BOOKS
SAN FRANCISCO

For more information about McSweeney's, see www.mcsweeneys.net
For more information about Voice of Witness, see www.voiceofwitness.org

Map and illustrations by Julien Lallemand

Front cover photo by Mateo Hoke

ISBN: 978-1-940450-24-7

VOICE OF WITNESS

Voice of Witness is a non-profit organization that uses oral history to illuminate contemporary human rights crises in the U.S. and around the world. Its book series depicts these injustices through the oral histories of the men and women who experience them. The Voice of Witness Education Program brings these stories, and the issues they reflect, into high schools and impacted communities through oral history-based curricula and holistic educator support. Visit www.voiceofwitness.org for more information.

CONTENTS

INTRODUCTION

BETWEEN US
BREAD AND SALT

by Cate Malek and Mateo Hoke

Crossing into the West Bank generally requires passing through a series
of obstacles. For example, to get from Jerusalem into neighboring
Bethlehem means navigating a twenty-six-foot concrete wall that spans
the horizon. To pass through on foot, individuals must walk through
a maze of security screenings known as the "300 Checkpoint," one of
numerous heavily guarded checkpoints set up along the 440-mile-long,
partially constructed barrier that separates Israel from the West Bank.

As one approaches the 300 Checkpoint from Jerusalem, the landscape is green, almost idyllic, filled with olive trees, wild flowers, and the
occasional grazing sheep. But closer to the wall, in a militarized no-man's-
land, trash and barbed wire litter the sides of the road. The checkpoint
itself is marked by a concrete and metal structure, stark despite a fresh
blue-and-white paint job. At the entrance to the checkpoint is a red sign
warning Israeli citizens that entering Area A—the small portion of territory within the West Bank controlled by Palestinians—is against the law.

Beyond the simple entryway, travelers enter a narrow maze often filled to capacity with foot traffic.

There is a grated metal walkway above the screening corridors of 300 Checkpoint. Looking up, pedestrians will find soldiers peering down at them, guns in hand, boots directly overhead. The first screening station is an ID check. Here, Palestinians must electronically record their thumbprints to prove they haven't overstayed day-long work permits. International travelers need only show their passports. Pedestrians then go through a long passageway, a monitored turnstile, a large empty parking lot, one more ID check, another monitored turnstile, and another long passageway before finally spilling out into the outskirts of Bethlehem.

Compared to the eerie austerity of the checkpoint, the city of Bethlehem is pulsing with life. Taxi drivers, dwarfed by the wall behind them, offer rides to the people coming through the crossing. Vendors call out the prices of fruit and sweets. People stop to greet friends or buy cups of coffee at nearby cafés. The wall itself is coated on this side in layers of colorful graffiti.

The contrast between the grim realities of the wall and the brisk, verdant liveliness on either side was one of the things that struck us when we first visited Bethlehem and the West Bank in 2009. At the time, Cate was working for a non-profit tourism group organizing walking trips across the West Bank. For her work, she traveled on foot through both major cities and rural villages, meeting people from all walks of life and hearing their stories. Her work gave her an extraordinary introduction to Palestine, where she found a sense of hope and humor she would have never expected when first passing through the checkpoint to Bethlehem. Mateo arrived not long afterward to begin work on this book, and he too was struck by the charisma of the city on the other side of the wall and the people working to make a life throughout the West Bank. It's hard to remember now precisely what we expected when we set out to explore the lives of Palestinians in the West Bank and Gaza. But we've found surprises at every turn.

Beyond the news stories of failed negotiations, protests, and armed clashes, there are millions of stories of ordinary life. Many of those lives have been difficult. Aside from the checkpoints and barrier walls, life in Palestine has many hard edges to it. A feeling of insecurity permeates nearly every facet of existence. It's difficult for the average Palestinian to find a job, and most of the jobs that are available are low paying, menial, or dangerous. It's not unusual to meet taxi drivers or street vendors with Ph.D.s. In the West Bank, thousands of men cross into Israel every day to find work. If these men cross legally with required permits, it means waking up at one a.m. in order to make it through crowded checkpoints to arrive at work in time. If they go illegally, they risk being arrested or shot as they walk long distances in order to cross the gaps in the barrier wall between the West Bank and Israel. In Gaza, the situation is even more dire. Its border with Israel and Egypt is tightly sealed. Because of an Israeli blockade of trade goods into and out of the region, meeting day-to-day needs of survival often means reliance on humanitarian aid rather than gainful employment.

It often seems impossible to take day-to-day stability for granted in Palestine. Israeli Defense Force soldiers come in the middle of the night to arrest family members. People lose their residency rights and homes with little or no warning. School is often canceled because of strikes, protests, or clashes with soldiers. Palestinian governance is often corrupt, ineffective, and suspicious of signs of dissidence. Sanitation workers often go on strike, leaving mountains of trash on the streets. Basic necessities such as clean water and electricity are in short supply. This is especially true in Gaza, but it's also common for Palestinians in the West Bank to run out of water toward the end of hot, dry summers, which means weeks without the ability to shower, do laundry, or flush the toilet.

Some simple pleasures taken for granted in other parts of the world aren't possible in Palestine. In the West Bank, it's almost impossible to get a permit to go to a beach, and in Gaza, miles of coastline are often choked with pollution. Israeli settlements and closed military zones in the West Bank have taken over much of the open space, making it difficult to spend time outdoors in nature. Moving between cities is difficult because of bad roads and military checkpoints, so people stay home. And in Gaza, rolling blackouts due to a blockade of energy supplies often means there are only a few hours per day to run washing machines or space heaters, let alone computers or televisions.

But these restrictions are not the end of the story. Despite the hardships and increasing restrictions, life goes on, much as it has for generations. Despite pessimism among Palestinians regarding the future of the Palestinian state, individuals continue to dream of a better life for themselves and their families. Education is extremely important. Palestine has the highest literacy rate in the Arab world at more than 95 percent. Religion is also important for both Muslims and Christians. Weekends are devoted to large family meals and weddings. There's an easy intimacy among friends and strangers alike. And, as we quickly discovered, Palestinians pride themselves on their hospitality, welcoming guests extravagantly. There's a deep connection to the land and to nature that comes across in the details of daily life, from appreciation for the local produce to the unabashed pride people display for the natural beauty of the region.

All the narrators in this book felt it was deeply important to tell their stories and to share a sense of their homes with those outside the region. An example is Muhanned Al-Azzah, one of the first people we interviewed. When we headed into the Al-Azzah refugee camp to meet Muhanned on a cold morning in January 2011, we knew little about him. We'd heard from our contacts in the city that he was an artist, that he had a history of political activism, and that he'd been arrested by Israeli Defense Forces for his association with a political party that Israel considered a terrorist organization. We'd heard Muhanned had been tortured while in prison. We also knew that the refugee camp where he lived was named for his grandparents, who had led their community in a flight to Bethlehem after their village was razed during the Arab-Israeli War in 1948. But we didn't know how much of his personal story he'd be willing to share with a pair of journalists from the United States.

Arriving at Muhanned's house, we climbed an outdoor staircase—past socks and towels hung to dry on a railing—to the third floor. Muhanned's mother answered the door.[1] She ushered us into the living room and cheerfully explained that Muhanned was still asleep. A few minutes later, he came in, a man in his late twenties with a lean face. He shuffled around the room searching for cigarettes, wearing black sweats with fuzzy pink slippers on his feet. A tiny Chihuahua strutted just behind him. Muhanned was not exactly our preconceived idea of a political prisoner. Still, he took time warming up to us, speaking in short, vague answers to start. We asked a few ice breakers, seeking to make him comfortable—and us a little more comfortable as well. It went on like this for a while. Then, Muhanned's mother brought in a tray of cookies and instant coffee with plenty of sugar and milk. The coffee was a welcome addition to our conversation. Not only did it keep us warm, it relaxed us. Muhanned's answers started to flow more easily. Soon he was eagerly sharing stories of his childhood in a refugee camp, his harrowing arrest, and his time in prison.

Those cups of Nescafé were the first of hundreds of cups of coffee, glasses of lemonade, and plates of rice we would share with people over the

---

[1] In Palestine, it's typical for adult children to continue living at home until they get married.

course of putting this book together. There is a saying in Arabic, *baynatna khubz wa milah*, which means, "between us bread and salt." It is a nod to the deep tradition of hospitality in this region and means that once two people share a meal together, they have a foundation for friendship.

We started this project expecting to have a difficult time convincing Palestinians to talk to us about experiences that were often deeply traumatic. But most of the people we talked to said it was vitally important to them to record not only their history as a people or nation but also the troubles and triumphs of their own individual lives and the lives of their family members.

One reason it was so important for our narrators to share their stories was that Palestinians have reached a particularly desperate time in their history. As negotiations with Israel remain deadlocked, the situations in the West Bank and Gaza continue to deteriorate. Every day, Palestinians lose access to more land to Israeli settlements in the West Bank. Meanwhile, Gazans experience higher unemployment and more restricted access to necessities such as clean water and housing every year.[2] Even as we write this, the West Bank and Gaza are experiencing mass arrests and military strikes following the reported kidnapping of three Israeli teenagers in the West Bank. A proposed reconciliation between Palestine's two rival powers—the Palestinian Authority and Hamas—seems on the brink of collapse. The people we spoke to for this book wanted a record not only of their lives as Palestinians, but also what they'd hoped Palestine would become, even if those dreams seem more and more remote.

This book can be little more than a glimpse into Palestinian life and culture. In an area of land smaller than the state of New Jersey, Palestinians

---

[2] According to a report released in 2012 by the United Nations Country Team (UNCT) in Palestine, population growth coupled with contamination of local fresh water supplies and restrictions on goods into and out of the country will make the Gaza Strip "unlivable" by 2020.

have more than 200 dialects. The landscape itself is extremely variable, moving from deserts, to green hill country, to the Mediterranean coast. To say that Palestinians are a diverse people would be a vast understatement. But for what this book lacks in breadth, we hope we make up for in depth, immersing readers in lives that are rarely noticed or read about outside the Middle East.

During our nearly four years of interviews, we spoke in depth with more than fifty individuals. From that pool of interviews, we chose fifteen stories that we believe offer a diverse, challenging look at the past and present of Palestinian life. We focused our attention on those living in occupied Palestine—here defined as the West Bank, Gaza, and East Jerusalem—though in doing so we've left out numerous important stories from Arab-Israeli citizens, Palestinian refugees living in Syria, Lebanon, and Jordan, and the fascinating stories of many international aid workers who pass through Palestine each year.

Many of the people we interviewed are from the area near Bethlehem. This is not only for practical reasons (Bethlehem was our base throughout the project) but also because the city offers a glimpse of the complexity of Palestinian life and is a convergence point for much of Palestine's rich history and culture.

We have also included two Israeli citizens living in the West Bank. We have *not* sought to provide equal representation of Israeli and Palestinian voices in this collection, because our concern here is delving deeply into the experience of growing up and making a life under a military occupation that spans generations. We decided to include our Israeli narrators for two reasons. First, Israeli citizens living in settlements and cities in the West Bank make up a substantial portion—perhaps as much as 10 percent—of the total population of the occupied territories. Second, we thought it important to give a face to some of the surprising, complex attitudes that Israelis in the West Bank have to the land they inhabit. Still, our narrators only represent themselves, and our two Israeli citizens are not meant to stand in for the lives, attitudes, or opinions of other Israelis.

In this book, we also want to offer a sense of how Palestinians still see themselves as Palestinian, as a single people separated by physical and historical boundaries. Passing between Bethlehem and Jerusalem, ancient cities connected by a well-traveled pilgrimage road, once took minutes. But with the construction of the wall in the late 2000s, the journey can now take hours. This sense of isolation is even stronger for those wishing to visit Gaza—just fifty miles from the West Bank, but almost impossible for any but a persistent few to enter. The walls surrounding the West Bank and Gaza do more than serve as physical barriers between the two territories—they also serve as psychological barriers. More and more, residents of the West Bank and Gaza feel cut off from one another and know of each other's lives more through news reports than any firsthand contact.

We were able to enter Gaza for a two-week period in 2013 and spoke with as many residents as we could during that time. We've conducted follow-up interviews through contacts in the region. One message that came through from many of our interviewees during that brief stay was the longing to travel to the West Bank, to be part of something larger than Gaza once again—and to rejoin the world after years of isolation.

There is a psychological barrier between Palestine and much of the outside world as well. Many outside the region see Palestine as violent and unstable, too complicated for anyone but an expert in political science to understand. Palestine is the global poster child for intractable conflict, a symbol of hopelessness. Palestine has become one of the most reported on yet least understood regions of the world. Our aim is to show that these stereotypes are far from the reality.

Cate Malek and Mateo Hoke

May 2014

EXECUTIVE EDITOR'S NOTE

The narratives in this book are the result of extensive oral history interviews with more than fifty men and women from across the West Bank, the Gaza Strip, and East Jerusalem, conducted over the course of nearly four years. These recorded interviews—over 250 hours of audio—were conducted by Cate Malek and Mateo Hoke as well as a team of interviewers and translators, and then transcribed by a small corps of dedicated volunteers. Managing Editor Luke Gerwe and I helped the interview team shape and organize those raw transcripts into first-person narratives.

With every Voice of Witness narrative, we aim for a novelistic level of detail and a birth-to-now chronologized scope in order to portray narrators as individuals in all their complexity, rather than as case studies. With *Palestine Speaks*, we did not set out to create a comprehensive history of human rights in Palestine. Rather, our goal was to compile a collection of voices and experiences that would offer an accessible, thought-provoking, and ultimately humanizing and intimate window on what can often seem like an impenetrable topic.

The stories themselves remain faithful to the speakers' words (we seek final narrator approval before publishing their narratives), and have been edited for clarity, coherence, and length. In a few cases, some names and details have been changed to protect the identities of our narrators and the identities of family and acquaintances. The narratives themselves have been carefully fact-checked, and are supported by various appendices and a glossary included in the back of the book that provide context and some explanation of the history of the region.

We thank all the men and women who generously and patiently shared their experiences with us, including those whom we were unable to include in this book. We also thank all the frontline human rights defenders working to promote and protect the rights and dignity of all

men and women throughout Israel and Palestine. Without the cooperation of these human rights advocates, this book would not be possible.

We make available additional interviews, audiovisual materials,
and news articles on the Voice of Witness website: voiceofwitness.org, and
on the Voice of Witness Tumblr: voiceofwitness.tumblr.com.

mimi lok
Executive Director
& Executive Editor
Voice of Witness

MAP OF THE WEST BANK AND GAZA

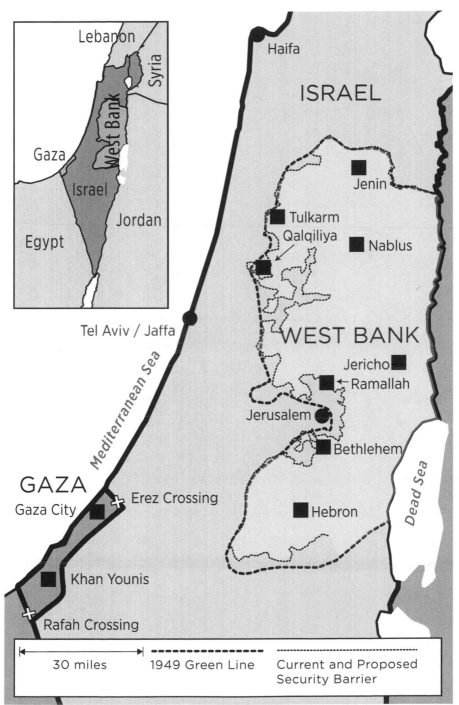

ISRAELI MILITARY ROADBLOCK, WEST BANK

IBTISAM ILZGHAYYER

Director of cultural center, 52
Born in Battir, West Bank &
interviewed in Bethlehem, West Bank

Ibtisam Ilzghayyer is the director of the Ghirass Cultural Center, which she helped found in 1994. Ghirass, which means "young trees" in Arabic, serves more than a thousand youth annually in the Bethlehem region through enrichment programs in reading, traditional Palestinian arts, and more. The center also provides literacy programs for women—generally mothers who want to learn to read, in part so they can take a more active role in their children's education.

Ibtisam speaks English with a distinct British accent, which comes from her time studying at Newcastle University in northern England. She smiles easily, unless she's talking seriously about the children at her center or the difficulties of being Palestinian in the West Bank. When she stands, she adjusts a clamp on a knee brace in order to walk. This is due to a childhood bout with polio, which she contracted when she was two years old.

The walls of Ibtisam's office are decorated with awards and framed drawings by children who have passed through the center. Throughout her day, children stop by to share their successes—an improved test score or a list of books read during the month. Ibtisam takes time with each one to congratulate and encourage them and to laugh with them. She spends most of her time at the center—she works six days a week, though she can often be found at the center on her day off. When she isn't at the center, she is likely to be at home with her elderly mother, tending a large garden of fruit trees, flowers, and vegetables.

ALL MY LIFE I HAVE
LIVED UNDER OCCUPATION

I was born in 1962, in Battir.[1] Life in the village was simple. Most of my neighbors were farmers, and when I was a child, people from Battir would all travel into Jerusalem to sell produce in the markets there. My parents had some land that they farmed, and my father was also a chef. When I was very young, he worked at a hotel in Amman, Jordan, and we'd see him on the weekends. Then, after 1967, he began working as a chef at the American Colony Hotel in Jerusalem.[2]

My mother stayed home and raised me and my siblings—there were nine of us. We didn't have TVs, no computers of course, and no plastic toys to keep us distracted. I think we were lucky to not have those things. Instead, we used nature. We'd play in the fields, climb trees, make toys ourselves out of sticks and stones. I remember that it seemed like there weren't divisions then between neighbors, despite religion or other

---

[1] Battir is a village of around 4,000 people located four miles west of Bethlehem and a couple of miles southwest of Jerusalem.

[2] The American Colony Hotel is a luxury hotel in the Old City of Jerusalem. It was built in the 1950s on the site of a former utopian Christian community started by an American couple from Chicago in 1881. The hotel is well known as a gathering spot for influential people from diverse political and religious backgrounds, and was the site of some of the earliest negotiations between the Palestine Liberation Organization (PLO) and Israel during the First Intifada. For more on the First Intifada, see Appendix I, page 267.

differences. It seemed as though we were all part of one culture in many ways. I remember playing with many Christian neighbors, and I remember my mother coloring eggs every Easter. It was something that had been passed down for generations—it wasn't a Christian thing or a Muslim thing, it was a Palestinian thing to mark Easter that way.

I must have joined in all the games when I was very young, but then I developed a disability as an infant. When I was two and a half years old, my mother was carrying me past a clinic in town one day. A clinic nurse stopped us and told my mother she should come in, that she should get me the vaccine for polio. So I was given a vaccine. That night I had a fever, and I couldn't move my right arm and left leg. Over the next few years, I was able to regain function of my limbs, but my left leg grew in shorter than my right. At age four, I started wearing a brace to help me walk. It was just bad luck that we walked past that clinic.

I had to get used to people treating me differently because of my disability. Even people's facial expressions when meeting me were different—they didn't react to me as if I were a normal child. When I was at school, I was excluded from many activities. That was really difficult.

I also had learning disabilities. My teachers labeled me as disabled and treated me like I was stupid. My teacher beat me once in fourth grade because I was nearly failing all subjects. Education was important to my parents, so they were unhappy that I was struggling. My father had only gone through fourth grade, so he could read and write a little. My mother had never been to school. But they wanted more for their kids. Especially me. Because I had a disability, they wanted me to do well in school so that I'd have some confidence when I grew up.

Then in the fifth grade, I succeeded on an exam, and the feeling was very strange. The teacher handed back the paper and said the work was "excellent." I couldn't believe I'd done anything that would make him say that. I couldn't believe that it was my paper that was excellent. I thought he'd made a mistake. I think that's common for children who aren't used to success—they don't realize it's their effort that leads to excellence. They think it's by accident. But I tasted success just that one time, and I realized I loved it. I just had to convince myself it wasn't a mistake! Then I continued to try hard at school, and I started to realize my potential.

In 1977, I was accepted into a boarding school in Jerusalem. It was actually right next to the American Colony Hotel, so I could see my father sometimes. I'd also go home on the weekends and on holidays. It was still relatively easy to travel into and out of Jerusalem then.

I did well enough in high school that I got accepted into the University of Jordan in Amman.[3] I started there in the fall of 1979, and I studied economics. I loved school, and I wasn't lonely. Other than college students who became friends, I had a lot of family living and working in Amman. But I still felt homesick sometimes, and I started to understand what made Palestine feel special. In my last year at university, the Palestinian poet Mahmoud Darwish came to read at a theater on campus.[4] I got tickets to go, but when I arrived, the theater was absolutely packed. And the streets outside were full. There were so many Palestinians in Jordan, and we all wanted to hear this poet remind us what it meant to be Palestinian.

IT RAISED A LOT OF EMOTIONS FOR ME

I returned home in 1984, and I had one of the hardest years of my life. I had just spent many years working extremely hard to make something of myself, to become independent from my parents—economically,

---

[3] The University of Jordan in Amman, Jordan, is considered one of the most prestigious universities in the Arab world. It was founded in 1962 and currently serves over 30,000 undergraduates.

[4] Mahmoud Darwish (1941–2008) was considered Palestine's leading poet, and helped lead a movement to promote Palestinian cultural heritage.

emotionally, socially—so that I wouldn't be a burden to them. Then I returned to Palestine and found I couldn't get a job. Because of my economics degree, I wanted to work in a bank, but there weren't any jobs in that field available, and I couldn't find any other sort of work. So I lived with my parents for a year and they supported me. I was very depressed during that time.

Then one day in 1985, I read a classified ad put up by the BASR.[5] They were offering to train workers in a field called community-based rehabilitation, which was about helping people with disabilities overcome them by working with the whole family—the whole society, really—to integrate the disabled into daily life. At first, I wanted nothing to do with that sort of work. I had an economics degree, and I had spent my whole life trying to get away from any limitations imposed by my own disability. I simply didn't want to think about disabilities. But I desperately wanted a job, so I applied.

I trained with the BASR for a year. It was hard. I worked with children who had hearing issues, blindness, mental health issues. The work brought up a lot of emotions for me, and it took some time to become comfortable around the children. But I kept getting praise from my supervisors, and they made me feel like I was useful.

In 1986, I began working in some of the refugee camps in Bethlehem as well, and that helped open my eyes. I got to see some of the real trauma that was happening in the community. That same year, BASR opened a community center for people with mental health disabilities, and I helped to run it. It was a very busy time for me.

---

[5] The Bethlehem Arab Society for Rehabilitation was originally founded in 1960 as part of the Leonard Cheshire Disability project, a major charitable organization in Great Britain dedicated to global disability care.

Then the following year, in 1987, the First Intifada began.[6] I remember it started just after I got my driver's license. I bought an old used car in November of that year, and I was really proud of myself. I was starting to feel quite independent. Then I set out to drive to work for the first time on November 30, and I ended up driving through streets littered with stones and burning tires. There had been a protest marking the fortieth anniversary of the partition of Israel and Palestine, one of the first organized protests of the Intifada. I couldn't make it to work that day—there was too much happening in the streets. So I spent the day listening to the news with my family.

THINKERS BEFORE FIGHTERS

The idea of starting a community center came to me in 1990. It was the middle of the First Intifada, and the streets were dangerous places to play for children. Aside from the threat of getting caught in fighting, children were sometimes targeted by soldiers. Sometimes children threw stones at soldiers, but other times soldiers would find children simply playing traditional games with stones. Many children, even young children, were arrested by soldiers who saw them playing these games. So the idea of the center started as a way to give children a safe place to play.

Also, at that time many schools were frequently closed by military order, so many children had to stay at home for long stretches of time. Sometimes the Israeli military would even use schools as checkpoints to control the area. The school in Battir was used as a military camp. These realities came together to make us want to start the center.

The BASR was able to establish the Ghirass Cultural Center in

---

[6] The First Intifada was an uprising throughout the West Bank and Gaza against Israeli military occupation. For more information, see the Glossary, page 276.

Bethlehem in late 1993, early 1994. In the West Bank at that time—
in schools before '95—the school curriculum was Jordanian. In Gaza,
it was Egyptian.[7] When I went to school, I studied a Jordanian curriculum. We never studied anything about Palestine or its history. We never
saw a Palestinian map. We studied the history of Jordan, of China, of
Germany, of England—I remember learning about all the families who
ruled England—but nothing connected to our history, nothing connected
to our geography, nothing connected to our culture.

When we started the center, we wanted to educate children about
Palestinian culture, Palestinian music, Palestinian poetry. We have famous
poets like Mahmoud Darwish, but it was forbidden for us to read from
them or read other Palestinian writers. If the Israelis caught us with a book
from certain Palestinian writers, we might end up in jail. We couldn't
have Palestinian flags, political symbols, anything considered propaganda
for a Palestinian state—everything could get us into trouble. My family,
like most in the West Bank, had a hiding spot at home. For us, it was at
the back of the cupboard. When we heard there were going to be raids
on houses, we'd quickly hide our forbidden books of poetry or flags or
whatever behind a false wall at the back of that cupboard.

With these restrictions in mind, one of our first goals at the center was
to provide a sense of Palestinian culture to children. We wanted the center
to be inclusive, so we didn't allow any religious symbols or symbols of
any specific political parties in the center. We had children from Christian
communities and Muslim, urban and rural, from refugee camps and from
relatively well-off neighborhoods. I also continued to work with children

---

[7] Jordan administered the West Bank and Egypt partially administered Gaza until 1967.
Textbooks developed during those administrations were used even during the Israeli occupation after 1967, but when the Palestinian Authority assumed administrative control of
the West Bank in Gaza after the Oslo Accords, it develop its own educational texts. For
more information on the Oslo Accords and the Palestinian Authority, see the Glossary,
page 276.

who had disabilities, but we integrated them with other kids in the classroom, whether they were blind or hearing impaired or had learning disabilities. They were all integrated.

After working this way in the cultural center, I even began to forget my own disability completely. I had other things to worry about or work on. One day, I saw myself in a reflection in a window while in the street, and I remembered I didn't walk as other people do— I had simply forgotten for a time that I had any disability at all. And I was happy for myself! Overcoming my own disability was no longer my focus.

In the center, I tried to make students thinkers before fighters. Sometimes, I would find them at demonstrations and bring them back from the street. We lost some children—some had a strong feeling that they wanted to fight. It was very difficult. Of course, they didn't always understand what they were doing. They were just imitating other people who were fighting in the streets.

Not long after the center was established and I had begun working there, I had the chance to travel abroad for the first time. I went with a friend to help her apply for a scholarship offered by the British consul to study in England. While there, I applied myself, sort of on a whim. But it turns out I won the scholarship. When I got the call that I had won, the consular office gave me two weeks to get ready for travel. So for the first time, I got to leave Palestine—other than my college years in Jordan.

I studied for a year at Newcastle University and learned administration and counseling. It was a good experience, even though it was hard. I felt homesick from the moment the plane took off. I was away from home from the fall of 1994 to the spring of 1995. I got to travel a lot throughout England, and that was interesting, but I wanted to go home the whole time. I remember I had very little money, and what I had I'd use to call my family. I'd spend hours asking my brothers about neighbors I barely knew—old men who hung out on the street that I never talked to, for instance—just because I wanted to know everything that was happening at home. When I completed all my coursework, I was expected to stay for the graduation ceremony and some parties. But I told the school administration I didn't want any parties, I just wanted to go home and see my family!

CHILDREN SEE THAT THEIR PROTECTORS ARE SCARED

The Second Intifada began in 2000.[8] During that time, I had to get around a lot of crazy obstacles just to continue my work. From 2001 to 2003, I used to practically live in this office because I couldn't always go back home. I remember the first time I tried to go home to Battir from Bethlehem in 2000, just after the Intifada started. It was just a couple of miles, and the checkpoint was closed. Nobody could cross to or from the five villages on the other side of the checkpoint. The soldiers refused to let anyone go back home. Children, old men, workers—imagine, all these normal people who wanted to go back home at four p.m., the end of the working day. Hundreds of people! We were surrounded by soldiers, and I remember thinking that nobody had any place to hide if shooting started. I waited that day from four p.m. to seven p.m. At seven p.m., I was so angry and depressed I started talking to myself. I said, "God, are you there? And if you are there, are you seeing us? And if you are seeing us, are you satisfied with what is happening to us?" Finally, a little after seven p.m., I gave up and came back to Bethlehem and stayed at the center.

Another time that same year, I tried to walk home past the checkpoint. The Israelis had blocked the road with rocks and stones. I wanted

---

[8] The Second Intifada was also known as the Al-Aqsa Intifada. For more information on the Intifadas, see the Glossary, page 276.

to go around the stones, because I couldn't climb over them with my leg problems. It was also slippery, because it was wintertime. But a soldier, a man less than twenty-five years old, stopped me from going around. When I tried to explain, the soldier said bad things to me—nobody in my life has said these things to me. He called me a prostitute. I can't repeat all the things he said. I became angry and I started to argue, and at that moment, a young man, Palestinian, tried to calm me down and asked me to stay quiet. He took my hand and helped me pass the checkpoint. At that moment I couldn't talk. I passed the checkpoint, and my brother was waiting for me on the other side. He took me by my hand and led me to his car, where my nephews and nieces were waiting. Normally I would talk to them, but I couldn't say a word. I knew that if I spoke, I'd start crying, and nobody would be able to stop me. I reached home and I threw myself on the bed. I felt I was paralyzed completely.

I saw the soldier the next day. I had a feeling that if I'd had a gun, I would have killed him. You know, I can't kill an insect, but in that moment, I felt my anger was more than it's been at any time. When he saw me, he began swearing at me again. It was very humiliating. I saw that soldier many times—usually soldiers would stay one week or ten days before they changed the group of soldiers at the checkpoints. I had to see him every day. And every day I looked at him and wished that someone would kill him in front of me. I wanted him to suffer.

One more occasion stands out from that checkpoint during the Second Intifada—I'm not sure exactly when. I remember a little girl was crying. She needed to get to school to take exams, and the soldier wouldn't let her. It's not guaranteed that a child is able to go to school. And it's not guaranteed that the child will be able to come back. Of course, this kind of helplessness has a psychological impact on kids as they grow up. Many parents have told us that their children have nightmares and achievement problems. Children look to us adults as people who can protect them, and when we can't—in many situations, we're scared! To see the child recognize that his mother is scared, his father is scared—it's not an easy thing.

When you move around Bethlehem, it's very restricted. We don't travel long distances. When you face a checkpoint or a wall, it's not more than a couple miles as the crow flies, but it's far away behind the wall. The children don't have the concept of distance. They might say they live "far away," and I'll ask, "How far?" And it's a fifteen-minute car ride away, if not for checkpoints. That's far for them, because that fifteen minutes might actually be an hour or two most days.

Sometimes I try to put all the obstacles in the back of my mind— the checkpoints, the harassments—to try and keep up my energy for my work, to keep my optimism for the future. But when I'm waiting at checkpoints, I have to face the hard realities of our lives. And the children I deal with—they also have to face these realities, and before they're even fully grown they have to face them without guidance, without someone to protect them.

THE SIGN JUST SAID "OTHERS"

Back in 1994, just after we'd started the center, we used to take students to Jerusalem for trips, to spend the day in the city. It was possible then. Since the Second Intifada, it's not possible.

I think this is the first generation of Palestinians that isn't able to see Jerusalem easily. Now we only talk about Jerusalem. At the center, when we ask the children, "What is Jerusalem?" they only know about the Dome of the Rock.[9] That's all Jerusalem is for them. They've never

---

[9] The Dome of the Rock is an Islamic shrine built on the site of the former Second Temple of Jerusalem. For more information on the Dome of the Rock and the Second Temple, see the Glossary, page 276.

experienced the city—to see it with true senses, to feel it, to smell it. They only know it through photos. I think it's really demoralizing that this experience, something that used to be essential to being Palestinian, has vanished. I think the Israeli government wants other parts of Palestine—Gaza, Jerusalem— banished from our minds. The new generation, these children might never come to Jerusalem. After years, how will it be in their mind? They won't think of it as Palestine.

Here in the center, we try to keep students connected with the different parts of Palestine, even if it's only through photos, movies, films—anything. For instance, I want our students to understand that Gaza is part of Palestine. This is my hope for all Palestinians in the West Bank, that if they have the opportunity, even if it takes a lot of effort, to go and visit Gaza. I think it's our duty. Many people lost their lives because of it. I'm not losing my life, but I have put in some real effort to go there.

In 2010, I went to Gaza to facilitate an outreach program. I was with a German colleague who worked for a German NGO that addressed international development projects. The German NGO was trying to fund a cultural center in Gaza that used our center as a model.

The Israelis keep a tight control on who gets into Gaza, so the permits to visit were not easy to get. I had to go through a lawyer and the court to get the permit. First, the Israeli military rejected my request for the permit, but I was able to appeal and get permission from the court to go for one night. It took me some time to get permission. But even then, I had to go through checkpoints—a checkpoint to get out of the West Bank, and then another checkpoint to get into Gaza.

To get to Gaza, we took the car of my German colleague. When Palestinian workers in Israel talk about the checkpoint, you can't imagine—you hear about it, but you need to live the experience to understand it. We went through the checkpoint nearest Hebron, because from

Bethlehem it is the most direct route to Gaza.[10] It was the first time I was at that checkpoint. I can't imagine the mind that designed that checkpoint. It's a kind of torture. We tried to pass through the checkpoint in her car, but we were not permitted, as I am a Palestinian. They don't let Palestinians pass through the checkpoint like they do internationals. Actually, she passed right through in her car at first, but then a soldier stepped into the road and stopped us. They checked my ID, and I was made to get out of the car and walk back to the checkpoint building—a fifteen-minute walk! It was difficult for me to walk all that way with my brace. When I got back to the checkpoint, I was put in line with the rest of the Palestinians. It was around seven a.m., so most of the people there were workers. We were herded in lines through cages, and all around us were young soldiers with guns. There were only three or four other women in line, and they all passed through with no extra delay. But not me.

All the Palestinians have to pass through metal detectors. I failed the detector because of my metal leg brace. The soldiers had to examine me personally because I couldn't just take off the metal and pass through the detector. Soldiers behind security glass told me that I'd need to be taken to a special cell. The whole time I was at the checkpoint, I hardly ever talked to a soldier directly—it was always through microphones, since they were always behind glass.

I was taken to a cell with no chairs. The walls were all metal with no windows, and I couldn't see anyone. I stood waiting for half an hour. I thought they might have forgotten about me. Because of my disability, it's difficult for me to stand for long periods of time. I knocked, and nobody came. Later, I knocked several more times, to remind them that there was somebody here.

---

[10] Likely the Turqumiya border crossing. For more on checkpoints and border crossings, see the Glossary, page 276.

Then I was taken to another room, also like a cell—just five feet by five feet. Here there was a soldier behind security glass. She was young, in her twenties. Otherwise I was alone in the room. The soldier was dealing with me as if I didn't exist. She ignored me and didn't bother to explain what would happen next. She just sat there behind the glass. From time to time I would knock, or ask her to please search me so I could leave the cell, and she'd say, "I'm just waiting for someone to come." For an hour she left me standing there.

Then another soldier joined her behind the glass. They told me to undress. I said, "I can't, there's a camera." She looked at it and said flatly, "Yes, there's a camera in the room." Every checkpoint has a Palestinian mediator, someone to translate and calm down tense situations, and I made them get him for me. This took a long time. Eventually, he arrived and I talked to him. He put his jacket on the camera and then brought me something to put on. I got undressed and then the soldiers told me how to move so they could examine me. Then I put on the clothes the mediator brought while he took my other clothes for them to examine. More waiting. After everything was over, the mediator took his jacket and left, and then I was taken to pass through the metal detector again.

The whole time, my colleague was outside in the car waiting for me. It had been hours. Then, once we made it to the Gaza border, it was the same procedure. My German colleague was allowed to pass quickly through the checkpoint, while I had to go through procedures strictly for Palestinians, not for foreigners. At the Gaza checkpoint, we were not in the car. We had to park, and after you pass through the checkpoint, everyone has to walk through a mile-long tunnel to where the taxis are.

At the start of the checkpoint, I saw the two signs—one for "Israelis and Foreigners," and the other just said, "Others." You know, it's like they want us to feel that we belong to nothing. They could write "Palestinians," they could write "Arabs," but "Others?"

The tunnel was an open-air tunnel, with fencing on both sides. It was narrow—not big enough for a car to drive through. Outside the fence was a barren, treeless security area. My colleague had waited for me so we could walk the tunnel together, but a mile is very far for me to walk. I had to sit on a luggage cart of another Palestinian who pushed me the whole way. It was a struggle for me. I'm strong, independent. I do things on my own. It's not easy for me to sit on a luggage cart and be pushed!

Going through the tunnel, there were open-air cells along the way. They were more modern than the Hebron checkpoint, but the same principle. The soldiers were all on high scaffolding with guns. They looked down on us from up high and talked into microphones. They would say things like, "Open gate number 2. Open gate number 10." And they'd tell us to move along. The whole time, we could see soldiers on the scaffolding, but we could never see exactly who was talking to us and ordering us onward to the next cell.

The last cell had a ceiling and a grated floor. A soldier behind the glass was there. She asked me to take off my clothes. We negotiated what I could take off and leave on. I took off my trousers and my brace and put them on the conveyor belt. She checked them and then put my things back on the machine to send back to me. I waited for them to contact the people who got me a permit. It took a long time. I thought I had already negotiated all the permits I needed, so it would be fine, but no. They made me wait anyway.

We finally made it to Gaza after hours going through the checkpoints. We went directly to the organization because we couldn't waste time. They only issued me a permit for one day! It's ridiculous, not to be able to visit your own country. We can move freely in other countries, but not in our own country.

I've spoken with some friends and some people at the Bethlehem Arab Society for Rehabilitation. They go through the same thing, the same conditions. They have the same procedure. It's not because of me—they target Palestinians anyway—but they could show more understanding. They could not make me wait so long, or bring me a chair to sit on, to be humane. I understand they need to check, but they could do it without humiliating the person. If this were just about security, they wouldn't need to humiliate Palestinians and not others. It's to show that we're a lower class of people. The Israelis and foreigners are first-class, the Palestinian people fifth-class. And people don't understand why we are fighting. I want to be equal! Equality! Not one of us is better than the other!

I want to go back to Gaza to keep working on this project, but I will plan to go through another way other than the Hebron checkpoint. I'm happy that I passed that experience, really. Now I know what it's like.

ALL THINGS INDICATE THAT THE FUTURE WILL BE MORE DIFFICULT

I am very proud of being Palestinian. I have never thought of living in another country. I've traveled across Europe, but I prefer to live in Palestine. When I was abroad and something bad happened in Palestine, it would be very difficult for me to sleep. If people I love die, then I want to die with them; if they live, I want to live with them. If they face a difficult situation, I want the same thing to happen to me. I want to be a member of this society. When I think of Palestine, I think of the struggles. We have to keep struggling for our rights, and there's no end to the struggling for me—some days it's for rights, some days it's to improve education. We are all fighters. When I do work with these children, that's fighting. When I work to improve their quality of life, that's fighting. And working against the occupation, that's fighting as well.

Day by day, it becomes more difficult. All things happening in Palestine indicate that the future will be more difficult. Ten years ago we did not have the wall, the settlements were fewer, the harassment was less. Everything bad is increasing. Usually I avoid going to the checkpoints, because it makes me sick—physically, emotionally, all kinds of sick. It usually takes me time to come back to normal.

My goal now is to expand the center—to extend it and spread it to other places. We're working on outreach programs, to reach schools and other communities that are struggling just to continue to exist. Some villages are surrounded by Israeli settlements and are cut off from important resources. We are looking to support these communities and improve the quality life through education. I believe a lot in education if you want to rebuild the nation.

At the cultural center, we try to keep our students as children as long as possible, to protect them. When they reach a certain age, we can't protect them anymore, they have to face the reality of the streets by themselves. And this is very sad. I can think of many times I've been out walking with my nephew, or with other young boys and girls who are nearing the end of childhood. Suddenly I would get very sad, because when they reach fourteen, fifteen years old, they are children under international and national law, but the soldiers don't think of them as children. They deal with them as adults. And it doesn't matter if they're following the law or not. How they're treated depends on soldiers' moods.

I use many strategies to manage. My strategy is that I love life. I want to protect my life, and the lives of others, as much as I can. Life, even with all these difficulties, deserves to be lived. And I like to look for nice things. Even the smile of a child, or flowers—I try to find something.

I'm not optimistic about the future for Palestinians. Israel is strong, and the Western powers give them their support. On the other hand, I don't think Israel can continue this forever. The world will not support Israel forever with all their behavior towards Palestinians. One day, changes will happen—history proves this. One day, sooner or later, the

Palestinians will have their rights. It's a matter of time and hard work for Palestinians and everyone who supports human rights.

When the world looks at Palestine I do not think they see the full situation. If people want to see the reality of the situation, they will see. If they want to hear the reality, they will hear. But if they don't want to know the reality of the situation, they won't, even if it's right there in front of them. Some people have open minds, some people have a blockage in their mind. They don't want to see, they don't want to hear, they don't want to act—they are blindly taking points of view without thinking.

ABEER AYYOUB IN JERUSALEM

ABEER AYYOUB

Journalist, 26
Born in Gaza City, Gaza &
interviewed in Gaza City, Gaza

In the spring of 2013, we manage to cross Gaza's tightly sealed border. Up to this point, all of our interviews have been in the West Bank or Jerusalem, and we have only a couple of weeks to gather stories from Gazans. Our guide and translator during this time is a young journalist named Abeer Ayyoub.

During our time with Abeer, she is constantly on her phone or tablet. Like many full-time journalists, she compulsively checks her e-mail, keeps track of social media, and plans meetings throughout the day. But her real weakness is Instagram. If she's not using her devices for work, she's taking pictures of what she's doing. Sitting at a café: picture. Walking down the street: picture. At the corner store: picture. Nothing is too banal to make her Instagram feed, but it makes for a thorough view of life for a young working woman in Gaza. Her goal, she says, is to show people outside Gaza that there is a complex and thriving culture in Gaza.

Abeer earned her B.A. in English literature from the Islamic University, which she says, was the only option she had (she dislikes Islamist control over universities in Gaza). She graduated in 2010 and immediately started working as a human rights researcher. After one year, she got her name in print and quickly figured out that making her own name was what she wanted to do, so she began focusing on writing.

As part of Gaza's relatively small middle class, Abeer has better access than other Gazans to resources that are hard to come by in the midst of the blockade that Israel has imposed since the rise of the political party Hamas.[1] She also has access to small comforts that make her the envy of her friends. "My friend from the American consulate was going to Jordan, and he asked me if I wanted him to bring me back anything," she tells us. "And I said, 'As many lip glosses as you can carry.' I'm usually out on the streets looking for stories for ten hours a day, and I need three things in my bag: a notebook, a pen, and lip gloss."

GAZA WAS LIKE A HOLLYWOOD MOVIE

Oh, well, of course it was just *lovely* growing up in Gaza. It was like a Hollywood movie. But not a romance or comedy—more like an action movie. I've witnessed two Intifadas, two military offensives, one Hamas coup.[2] Still, the more trouble I've witnessed, the more I've felt lucky to survive, and to be alive.

I was born in Gaza City the year the First Intifada started, in 1987. By the time I started school, I'd already become used to the sight of Israeli

---

[1] The political party Hamas and associated militias have been in power in Gaza since 2007. The party was originally formed in 1987, during the First Intifada, as an offshoot of the theocratic Muslim Brotherhood of Egypt. For more information on Hamas, see the Glossary, page 276.

[2] In 2006, Hamas won parliamentary elections in Gaza and largely took control of the government through democratic means. However, in June 2007, Hamas clashed with the Palestinian Authority and its leading party, Fatah, in a series of armed confrontations. Following the armed conflict, Fatah and the PA withdrew from Gaza. For more information, see Appendix I, page 267.

soldiers patrolling the streets every morning. I used to be really scared of them—my grandma used to warn me that I shouldn't talk to them. In school, we'd teach each other tips about dealing with the soldiers. For example—when you see an Israeli jeep, don't run, 'cause the soldiers will think you're doing something bad. But we were naïve as children, and I didn't think too much about who the soldiers were or why they were around. I only knew there were strange people with green uniforms every-where. And I wondered, *All of the soldiers have guns, but nobody else I see ever does. Who do they need to protect themselves against with guns if everyone else only has rocks as weapons?* But I didn't understand the occupation at all. It just wasn't something my family talked about when I was growing up.

I belong to the middle class, and I grew up feeling like a typical Gazan. I have four brothers and five sisters. I'm number eight out of ten kids. My dad had a good income when I was young—he ran a metal-working business. But because there were ten children, it cost him a lot to send us all to school. So even though my family was relatively well off, my childhood seemed typical. I got the things I needed, but not all the things I wanted. We'd get new clothes for school, but not whatever we asked for or anything like that. Like most people in the community, we'd go to shop when the school year started, and then shop around Eid Al-Fitr, the feast after Ramadan, and then Eid Al-Adha.[3]

We lived on a street that was made up entirely of my family. My dad had one house for his family, and he had four brothers with their own houses on the block. So between my siblings and my cousins, I spent my whole childhood playing with family. As boys and girls, we'd play soccer together in the street, go to school together, then come home together. We had a few neighbor kids nearby who would come play with us as well.

---

[3] Eid Al-Fitr and Eid Al-Adha are the two major feast days of Islam. Palestinian custom is to purchase new clothing for the feast days, when family members exchange visits.

My mother was a typical housewife in many ways. She worked very hard and tried to give all of us kids the attention we wanted. I remember when it was time to do homework, she'd try to help us all. Of course, she couldn't spend much time with any one of us! I still remember her teaching me how to write my first words, though, in Arabic and in English. She didn't know English herself, but she thought education was very important, so she'd memorize the English lessons and try to help me understand them. I remember her reciting the days of the week in English, so that I'd learn, even if that's all she knew.

The Second Intifada started in 2000, when I was twelve or thirteen. I saw a lot of shooting and violence—there were direct clashes around the Israeli settlements.[4] And I used to go to school some days and not other days, because there was sometimes too much happening out in the streets. Other young people from schools around the area, they used to come and get us out to go and participate in the clashes. It was violent all the time. Mostly, we just tried to stay safe. A lot of days, we'd leave school early because there were often clashes at the end of the school day. If we slipped out before the day ended, we might not have to walk home through tear gas.

During the time of the Second Intifada, I was a teenager, and back then I was the stereotypical stupid girl who wanted to get married at the age of sixteen. I'd never dream of having male friends I might just hang out with alone.

The separation of boys and girls was actually something that surprised me at first, but I got used to it quickly. Some of the neighbor boys I used to play soccer with every day suddenly stopped talking to me around the time I turned fifteen, and my brothers and cousins told me I should just pretend I didn't know them. This was the culture—these boys I'd played

---

[4] In 2000, there were twenty-one Israeli settlements in Gaza and a little over 6,200 settlers.

with for ten years every day were suddenly strangers to me, since they weren't related and I was a young woman. It was disappointing, but I got used to believing that wearing a hijab was something important, that I had to hide myself from men.[5]

My dad always told me that I was the most clever of his children, and I got great grades. But I never had any examples of women who went on to have impressive careers, and nobody ever encouraged me to think in those terms. But I studied very hard. Honestly, I didn't think I was very pretty, and I thought I'd have a hard time finding a husband. I thought I'd prove I was special instead by getting good grades and a very high grade on the college qualifying exams. And I did. My parents were so impressed by my score, they told me that they'd support me in going to any school and in any field I chose. I was studying for the exams in 2005, and that was a big year in Gaza as well. It was the year Israeli soldiers left Gaza. That felt like a real achievement.[6]

The next year, I started at Islamic University of Gaza here in Gaza City.[7] I wasn't happy about religious control of the university, but it had a curriculum in English Literature that I wanted to study, and it was impossible to attend a university at the time that wasn't under Islamist control if you lived in Gaza. I'd been studying English through school, and I wanted to keep that up. I thought it might be a good way to get a job doing something important after school.

So I spent my first year at university studying English Literature. Then, in 2006, Hamas captured Gilad Shalit, and Gaza became a different

---

[5] The *hijab* is a garment that covers the head and neck and is worn by many Muslim women throughout the world.

[6] In 2005, Israel announced a unilateral withdrawal plan from the Gaza Strip. For more information, see Appendix I, page 267.

[7] The Islamic University of Gaza is an independent university system in Gaza City. It serves just under 20,000 undergraduates.

place.[8] Israel began cracking down, and we had less money and less freedom. Gaza started to witness its worst days ever. We didn't have as much money coming into our household, and my dad wanted to pull us out of school. My mom is fond of gold and accessories, but she got all of her jewelry together and sold it all to pay for our college fees. So she's the reason I could continue my education. In many ways, it was my mom who made me what I am today.

I WOULD WAKE UP AND SCREAM, "I JUST NEED TO SLEEP!"

In my second year at university, I took a course where the teacher asked us to do a research project on people working with English-language skills. I hit on the topic of news editing. I don't remember the reason. I just wanted something to write about so I could hand in a paper. But when I started searching, I found so many books on the subject, and they were really interesting.

Then as part of the project I interviewed a journalist here in Gaza— his name was Saud Ramadan—who was a freelance journalist who wrote for newspapers all over the world. Our interview was really lovely, and he told me he'd be happy to mentor me as a journalist if I wanted. I accepted. Here in the media world, there are so many creeps who expect something from a girl. I've met so many men who will be like, "I'll teach you about journalism, but you have to do something for me." Bad stuff. But Saud wasn't like that, and through his office I also met a journalist named Fares Akrem, who was a journalist and also a research consultant for Human

---

[8] Gilad Shalit was an Israeli Defense Forces (IDF) soldier who was kidnapped in Israel in June 2006 by Gazan militias affiliated with Hamas that had built an extensive tunnel under Gaza's barrier wall. He was released as part of a prisoner swap in October 2011.

Rights Watch.[9] They were both professional, and I learned a lot working with them. I started training with them once a week until I figured out it was exactly what I wanted to do. I wanted to be a journalist.

I was still a student when Israel sent soldiers into Gaza in 2008.[10] Because of the bombing, I was shut in at home for twenty-two days with my extended family. There were more than thirty of us in a single apartment, and we'd have breakfast, lunch, and dinner together—being together made us all feel a little safer. There was no electricity at all during that time. It was very cold, and we spent many hours huddled up under blankets. We cooked our food on an open fire and we had a little tank of propane gas to cook with as well, but we were trying to conserve the gas as long as possible. Nobody was selling things out in the open in Gaza during that time. During the days, some of my brothers would sneak out and head to secret black markets they knew about for some basic supplies. I spent most days listening to a battery-powered radio. I tried to get as much news as I could, and I was trying to understand the situation as a journalist. *What is really happening? What's the real story? How are journalists trying to cover these stories?* As scared as I was, I felt like that time was a kind of training for me.

There were air strikes day and night. We were all especially scared at night, when we were trying to sleep. I remember falling asleep for a couple of minutes, then hearing the bombs start to fall. I would wake up and scream, "I just need to sleep!" By the final days of the campaign, we were all crying because we wanted to sleep so badly.

---

[9] Human Rights Watch is a non-profit organization based in the U.S. that investigates human rights abuses around the world. HRW conducts fact-finding missions with the help of journalists, lawyers, academics, and other experts.

[10] The strikes on Gaza in 2008 lasted around three weeks, from December 27, 2008, until a cease-fire on January 18, 2009. The invasion was named Operation Cast Lead by the Israeli military. For more information, see the Glossary, page 267.

We learned to distinguish two types of noise: the *zzzz* of drones passing overhead, and the *whoosh* of F-16s coming in for air strikes. The sound of drones was annoying, but hearing the *whoosh* of F-16s was frightening—it meant bombing was about to start. My nephews, who were just infants at the time, they learned to tell drones apart from planes. Nowadays, they don't even wake up for drones. We were never hit, though we did have windows broken on our building from nearby strikes. The windows on an apartment above ours came down. Nobody was injured, but I still remember the sound of the bomb falling—*schhhhh*.

I became paranoid after so many days of bombing. I used to think, *My house will never be targeted because we have no one engaged in military work*. But it could be for any reason—a militant passing by in a car. Maybe someone in one of the empty fields by our building—the bombers used to target empty fields because militants might use them for launching rockets.

Then, after three weeks, there was a cease-fire. I went back to the university the day after the cease-fire, even though it was still dangerous. When I saw the campus, I cried. It had been demolished. In many ways I hated that school—I didn't like the strict religious element—but the devastation made me cry. The school made many repairs over the next month—fixing broken windows and making sure standing buildings were safe enough. And then all of us students went back to classes, even in buildings where the roofs were still broken. I was in school another year before I graduated, in 2010.

Then, for the next year I worked as a fixer—someone who helped journalists make contacts in Gaza, set up interviews, that sort of thing. I was actively learning about journalism, meeting a lot of journalists. It was a good apprenticeship.

ABEER AYYOUB

I WAS NAÏVE AND ANSWERED ALL
THE QUESTIONS THEY WERE ASKING

I had my first big exposure to how the media world works in Gaza in January 2011. I was going to take part in a solidarity gathering with the Egyptian revolution.[11] I was also going to meet one of my mentors, Fares Akrem, who was going to cover the story. There were about twenty-six of us at the demonstration. But really, as soon as everyone showed up, the Hamas police force was already there preparing to shut it down. I think Hamas was afraid of protest movements in the Middle East spreading to Gaza and challenging their authority.

Just as I arrived at the scene, I got a call from Fares, who told me the demonstration was off, and he told me where to go to find his car so he could give me a ride home. I went and got into his car, and then a Hamas policeman walked up and said, "Your identity cards, please." Fares gave his identity card to them.

But while this was happening, some female police officers were attacking some of the female protesters. One of the protesters wasn't wearing a head scarf, and the female officer pulled her by the hair, slapped her, asked her why she wasn't a real Muslim. I was worried I might get in trouble—Hamas would check to see if men and women riding in cars together were married or related, and if not, there could be an arrest. The officer at our car was distracted, and so I just stepped out of the car and started walking. After a couple of minutes, I found the policeman following me on his motorcycle. And when I turned around and made eye contact, he pulled up and said, "Your cell phone and your identity card." I started crying like an idiot and gave him the phone and my ID.

---

[11] In January of 2011, millions of protesters throughout Egypt with diverse political, socio-economic, and ethnic backgrounds gathered to demand the ouster of Egypt's president, Hosni Mubarak, who had been in power for three decades.

Then he said, "You can come and retrieve them from the police station." I followed him to the station. And when I entered, I found four other women from the demonstration. They were acting strong and tough, but I was crying. My family didn't know where I was, and the police refused to give me a phone call. Then they began interrogating me, and I was naïve and answered all the questions they were asking.

I was interrogated by a female officer, and she kept asking me about Fares and what I was doing with him. I was like, "I don't know him. We just met. He's a journalist, but I don't know where he lives." The interrogator said, "He's the brother of so-and-so, we know." And I was like, "Eh, no, he's not." She was trying to outsmart me.

Then the officer started going through my bag, asking me what was in it. She found a prescription drug I was taking for an injured leg, and she wanted to know about that. Then finally she said, "Okay, call your family members to come." And that was the worst moment, because I thought, *What should I tell my mom and dad?* I called my brother—he has good relations with people from Hamas. And then I signed a paper saying I wouldn't participate in such events later.

I went back home to find the story all over the news in Gaza. Everyone was talking about it, because it was the first time that Hamas had arrested women for protesting. It was a big story to see women arrested for activism. They had my full name on the news. I felt like I had made it big!

Then the rumors started. The media had its own spin. Suddenly commentators on the news were like, "Maybe it wasn't a protest, maybe these girls were just immoral and showing off, not even covering their hair," and stuff like that. I cried for a couple of days, because it was a little overwhelming, the whole exposure.

The experience of getting arrested, and then the media spin that maybe we were just prostitutes or something, it was crazy, and I decided to write about it all on a personal blog. So I wrote about this online and then someone from Hamas's Ministry of Information e-mailed me and said, "It's insane what you wrote. It's biased." This guy with the ministry said he would go to the website and start leaving comments if I didn't take down the post—*Abeer's not a professional journalist, you shouldn't hire her*, and stuff like that. It was my first run-in with Hamas over my writing. It was a little intimidating, but since then I've learned better how to deal with the government.

MY ONLY FEAR WAS ABOUT MAKING DEADLINES

I chose journalism as a career, which is not a very acceptable job for a girl here in Gaza. After I started working, some of my own relatives started to say bad things about me—my uncles and cousins would talk. And they were always pushing on my parents, like, "This is not the way Abeer should be, and everyone's going to talk about her, that she goes around talking with guys alone." Some of my cousins, they'd say things like, "This is the bitch who goes with guys all the way." My parents could have reached a point where they'd say, "Enough. Just stay at home and don't do anything because everyone is talking about you, and we know you are not doing something bad, but it's our reputation at the end of the day." But my family didn't have that reaction. No.

Slowly, my parents began to trust me with travel, with my work. I was getting assignments for web stories for outlets like the *Egyptian Independent*. Basically, eyes-on-the-ground sorts of stories about what was happening in Gaza. At first, I might get an assignment that would mean I'd have to travel to Rafah crossing, and my parents would be like,

"Make sure you have a driver. We're worried."[12] And they didn't want me to leave Gaza City. But the more they saw that I could take care of myself, that nothing happened, the more they trusted me.

I also got some work as a researcher and fixer for Human Rights Watch. For my work with HRW, I got a chance to get out of Gaza and go to Jerusalem for the first time in early 2012. I got a pass from Israel to be in Jerusalem for eight days. When I went to Jerusalem, I was sure it was a dream. So I kept waiting for the moment I would wake up and find myself in bed. And then an hour passed, two hours, three hours, four hours, and I was slapping my cheek, like I should wake up. Then when the night came, and I slept, and then woke up again and I opened the window and it was Jerusalem—I was sure it wasn't a dream. I went to East Jerusalem, and I was seeing other parts of my homeland for the first time.

I had a friend from HRW in Jerusalem, and she took me for a ride. She wouldn't tell me where we were going, but we kept driving up and up. Suddenly, out my window I saw the Dome of the Rock.[13] I started screaming like an idiot. This was an image that I saw on posters or framed pictures in every house in Gaza when I was growing up, on all my school notebooks. And here it was, right in front of me.

But being in Jerusalem was a strange experience. One amazing thing was that other Palestinians in Jerusalem were seeing a Gazan for the first time. I remember going into a hotel in East Jerusalem. I wanted to tell everyone I met I was from Gaza, and I talked to the receptionist at the hotel—a Palestinian man. He was shocked. Then he made a dumb joke and asked me if I had any bombs in my pockets or something like that.

---

[12] The Rafah border crossing is the sole border crossing from Gaza into Egypt, and since Israel imposed a blockade on Gaza in 2007, the Rafah crossing is often Gazans' only accessible point of exit from the Gaza Strip. The crossing is often closed as well, however, and since 2007 it is very difficult for Gazans to leave the Gaza Strip.

[13] For more information on the Dome of the Rock, see the Glossary, page 276.

Then the next day I got to take a bus ride to Ramallah, and I made small talk with a man on the bus who was from Bethlehem. When I told him I was from Gaza, he was as surprised as the receptionist. He said something like, "No way you're from Gaza, you're cute and smart!" The trip out of Gaza was really eye-opening for me.

IT WAS GOOD THAT I STAYED HOME

In 2012, I got a scholarship to go to Sweden for six months. My father wasn't ready for me to travel that far yet. He was worried. So he wouldn't let me go, and I cried for days. But it was good that I stayed home, because it led to one of my first big breaks.

During the first Israeli strike on Gaza, I was still doing my training, so I was reading news all the time, but I was stuck at home. But in the second strike, in November 2012, I had become a professional journalist, so it was a bit different.[14] By this time I was only focusing on how to get news. My only fears were about making deadlines.

I used to go out into the street immediately after the air strike happened. I got used to seeing bodies: corpses lifted out from under the rubble. I would go into the hospital as well.[15] In the hospital, I was always watching the entrance. And cars would speed in so fast after a strike. Everyone outside would scream to back up, to give the arriving passengers more space. And I'd stay in my spot, watching women, and then men, and then children, and then old women—people of all ages and all different backgrounds—come in with all sorts of injuries from the air strikes.

---

[14] Operation Pillar of Defense was an eight-day assault by the IDF starting November 14, 2012, officially launched in response to rocket attacks from Gaza. The IDF struck about 1,500 locations within Gaza, and 133 Palestinians were killed, according to Gazan officials. For more information, see the Glossary, page 276.

[15] The Al-Shifa Hospital in Gaza City is the largest medical facility in Gaza.

And during the strikes I would be outside the home most of the day, and I even slept outside the home. The strike lasted eight days, and then afterward, I thought, *I was under the rockets and I didn't even cry*. It was the most important phase in my life, because I wrote for the biggest newspapers in the world, and I used to have my voice on international radio. I was turning in reporting for the *Guardian* in the UK and *Al Jazeera*. *Ha'aretz* in Israel hired me, because they weren't legally permitted to send journalists to Gaza to cover the strikes. I thought, *This is my real start*.

And after, I felt like I had all of these experiences to deal with, all of these feelings, but I didn't have time to even think about what I'd seen. It was insane. I felt like I needed a break just to process what happened, but there was no time. I got a lot of new opportunities to cover stories about the aftermath of the strikes, and there was just no chance to get away. I wanted to do something for the Palestinian cause itself, and I wanted to be a journalist, and I knew Gaza was the best place for me to be a journalist. But it was hard to keep working here without a break.

HEY, IT'S NOT ROCKETS ALL OVER GAZA

I'm studying again at the Islamic University of Gaza, where I got my B.A. in English Literature. I'm studying Hebrew because I want to learn a third language besides Arabic and English. There's nothing much I hope to do with Hebrew. I just want to speak the language and listen to Israeli news and Hebrew news, because some of what comes out of Israel is better news, when it comes to the Israeli-Palestinian conflict. Honestly, you're more likely to hear the truth from a few of the good Israeli sources than from Hamas sources. After my work for *Ha'aretz*, Hamas announced that Gazan journalists would no longer be allowed to work for Israeli media. I contacted them to ask why, and they told me I better just go along with the ban without complaining. I said, "I would understand if you stopped Israeli or American journalists who are totally pro-Israeli. I would understand if you banned *them* from working here. But I don't understand when you ban *me*, as a Palestinian who works for Israeli media—which I actually consider a kind of resistance." It was my pleasure just to sit down with a laptop and just write things to the Israeli audience. It was a kind of resistance, addressing the Israeli community and being credible at the same time. I would say exactly what's going on and convince the Israelis of how misled they are about Gaza by most of Israeli media.

But people around the world have the wrong idea about Gaza, not just Israelis. My mission in life is to destroy the stereotypical image about Palestinians in the media, so I keep taking photos of things that people don't think exist in Gaza. This is what I do in my news, and my reports, and my feature stories. In my Facebook and in my Instagram. So when I take photos, I try to take photos of girls without hijab, or young girls wearing shorts and stuff like that. And the beach. Hundreds, thousands, going to the beach just to swim, thinking of nothing. No fucking occupation, no fucking Hamas, nothing! They just want to have fun. I go to the market, take photos of mannequins with short dresses. And it's something normal to see a young girl with hijab, but I would try to avoid catching photos of her, because Western people in Europe and America, they already know about these people, and they are not my concern. I would rather focus on the type of people Western media never heard about. I also take photos all the time of fancy hotels and fancy restaurants—like hey, it's not rockets all over Gaza. We have cafés, restaurants, clubs, gyms, whatever you can think of. So this is my main mission.

I would love everyone—not only in the U.S.—to know that Gaza is not Afghanistan. We have everything here. We have educated people and people who have nothing to do with the ongoing clashes. They should give themselves the chance to see the picture from outside and stop having this preconception when it comes to Gaza, because we have everything here, and the Western media always intend to prove the preconceptions people have. They would see that for most of the people, they are harmed by what's going on rather than being a part of it.

The thing is that I'm an Arabic-speaking journalist who writes in English, not my mother tongue. If I write in my mother tongue, then I will be addressing Palestinians themselves. And why would I address Palestinians themselves? Palestinians know that they were occupied, and they know their rights, they know their duties, they know everything. I'm writing in a second language, so I need to use that, because one in one hundred international writers will come regularly to Gaza and go do their stories. Usually, these people come with a preconception, the preconception of what they hear. And they come to prove what they have in mind, not to rectify it.

Still, being a Gazan journalist is not always easy. Every time I write something sensitive, I keep my phone with me because I'm waiting for someone to call me from the government offices in Gaza. I'm strong enough to face it. Every time I write something sensitive, I read the story ten times because I attribute every controversial quote to someone who actually said it, not anonymous sources, so I won't be accused of making it up. So even though I like to cover daily life in some of my work, I also want to uncover what's really happening in Gaza. I don't think you are doing anything unless you are risking something. I'm not going to consider myself a real journalist if I'm just covering the openings of new shopping malls in Gaza City.

With time, my relationship with the government has become fine. I have good relations with the government members and ministers and everything. I think they decided, *Sure, that Abeer is a journalist who talks a lot, but she never makes up stories.* It's true that I write about the government, but it's true also that I write about the Israeli occupation. There is a big difference if you are focusing only on Hamas or on Israel or the Palestinian

Authority. I write everything. But it's not my fault if the Hamas government commits five human rights violations in a row and I write about the five violations.

I DO STUFF THAT
GIRLS HERE DON'T USUALLY DO

To help cope, I try to live a non-traditional Gaza life as much as that's possible. I wake up in the morning, go to the gym, hang out with friends, spend the night out. Now I'm applying for a swimming class. I do stuff that the girls here don't usually do. I'm learning a third language, just because I want to get my time as busy as possible. Also because I don't want to feel the occupation is limiting things I can do. I'm busy 24/7, but that doesn't mean that I'm working 24/7. I have some specific hours of work and specific hours of fun: sport, swimming, hanging out, sleeping. But I never had a time of thinking, *I can't do anything.*

I feel like my society does not accept me, but I always say, "It's their problem, not mine." I pray for them—that they will have enough awareness and education to understand what I'm trying to do. Society wants me to get married when I'm twenty years old and wake up at six a.m., cleaning, and serving my men. This is not the life I want to live.

There is a word that means "against the feminine." *Patriarchy.* I hate it, and I feel like I'm totally opposing this idea. So this is how I got my power and inspiration—just because I want to prove, you are a man, but you are not better. Never. I can do whatever I want and even be better than you. I see men looking at me, but I don't give a shit because me being a girl doesn't mean that if you look at me, I'm a bad girl. No. If you look at me, then it's your problem. You have a problem with controlling your desire. Then I go to do my work in places that are usually occupied with men, and when I enter, everyone's like, "You can't be here because you're the only girl." And I'm like, "So what? Does it mean that you will all rape me? Because I'm the only girl here?" You know, this is the main obstacle in my life. I'm here now just because I want to prove to myself I can go out at a late time and go back home, and no one will ever talk to me or do anything bad to me, because my brothers do it and they know no one will make trouble for them.

IF PALESTINE WASN'T OCCUPIED, EVERYONE WOULD WANT TO VISIT

I always say, if Palestine weren't occupied, then everyone would want to visit. I've been to the West Bank, and it's like a heaven. They have everything—mountains, hills, deserts, ancient cities. In Gaza we have the sea and a beautiful beach. But Palestine is this small besieged territory, and even the residents here can't move around freely. All of this powerlessness over movement leaves Palestinians feeling very dependent on other countries, as though we can't be independent.

I belong to this place for many reasons, because I was raised here. The apartment where I was born is my grandfather's family house. And my family is originally from Gaza, so I do belong to this place. And I love it. I love everything about it.

I'm a journalist, and I want to have my name get bigger and bigger. I will never have a better place than Palestine in general to achieve this dream. I would love to leave Gaza for a month a year, just to explore around. Just to meet new people, to make new relationships, and work on improving my writing. I would like to do assignments abroad. Like if I can be sent to Turkey or Egypt, I would love to do that. But I'll always return to Gaza. I'll never live outside this country. Never.

WEST BANK FARMER WITH
SETTLEMENT IN BACKGROUND

ABED AL-TA'AMARI

Farmer, day laborer, 32
Born in Bethlehem, West Bank &
interviewed in Jubbet Al-Dhib, West Bank

The first thing we notice as we drive to Abed Al-Ta'amari's home near Herodion
is the challenge presented by the roads.[1] Some roads are almost too steep to climb,
and others almost too muddy or rocky to navigate. The bottom of our car crunches
and scrapes as we slowly approach his village, Jubbet Al-Dhib.[2]

Eventually we reach the compound where Abed lives with his family. Abed's
house, the family's olive trees, and another house belonging to his extended family
are surrounded by a short rock wall topped with barbed wire outlining their
property. When we pull up in our car, a dozen or more kids come spilling out to

---

[1] Herodion is a huge, cone-shaped hill with a flattened top jutting upward from the desert.
It was the site of the fortress and palace built by Herod the Great, the king who ruled Judea
for the Roman Empire from 37 to 4 BCE. Today, it is a site of great interest to archaeolo-
gists, historians, and biblical scholars. It is three miles south of Bethlehem.

[2] Jubbet Al-Dhib is a village of 150 people near the base of Herodion that was established
in 1929. It lacks most modern resources—it has a single dirt road, no electricity, and the
nearest school is over a mile away.

greet us—Abed's children and nieces and nephews. Some wear cracked plastic shoes, some wear no shoes at all.

Abed a skinny thirty-two-year-old with a wife and four young kids. The six of them sleep in a twelve-foot by twelve-foot room that includes a wardrobe, a crib for the baby, and twin bunk beds piled with blankets. This is the main room of the family's living space. They also have a small kitchen and toilet, all of which is on the second floor, above a chicken coop.

After a tour of his house, we sit with Abed on plastic chairs outside, and he tells us about the ways his community has changed since 1996, when Israeli settlers first moved near his home. Abed is one of up to 200,000 Palestinians living in Area C—the roughly 60 percent of the West Bank that is still under full military and administrative control of Israel following the Oslo Peace Accords of 1993–1995.[3] Area C also contains many of the West Bank's Israeli settlements, a collection of villages established by Israeli citizens following the occupation of the region in 1967. Today, there are 400,000–500,000 Israeli settlers in the West Bank outside of Jerusalem.

The guard tower of a nearby settlement looms above Abed's property as we sit and talk. He tells us that although he wishes to remain on his property, pressure from the settlements may force him to someday relocate his family.

THE DAYS THAT HAVE PASSED ARE BETTER THAN THE DAYS THAT ARE NOW

I was born in Bethlehem in 1980, but I've lived in Jubbet Al-Dhib for twenty-five years, since I was a little boy. My grandfather brought his whole family here from Bethlehem—my father and my uncle and their

---

[3] For more on administrative Areas A, B, and C in the West Bank, see the Glossary, page 276.

wives and kids. My extended family had land here going far back, and my grandfather inherited a piece of it.

The days that have passed, they are better than the days that are now. I remember how much fun it was as a child, taking care of my family's farm and chasing animals in the wilderness nearby, and just living on the land. We went on picnics. It was nice. It was normal. We worked and moved easily with no restrictions. We were happy, with a simple life.

Then, when I was around fifteen years old, the settlers came onto our land. There had been settlements in the area since I was a boy, but none so close. First, we started seeing roads going in sometime around 1996. That same year, the first settlers showed up in trailer homes. There were maybe fifteen to twenty trailers that showed up near our village.[4] These first settlers were never without guns—AK-47s, big guns. The first thing they did was come to the village to see if they would have any trouble. They were pretty rough. There were some clashes at first over land. I remember one old man whom the settlers struck on the head—he almost died. They also started building a fence around the settlement and some of our farmland right away. We had a fence around most of our property, and that helped keep the settlers from building directly on our land, but they took the land where our sheep graze outside the fence, about a thousand square feet of grazing land. They also took some of my father's sheep. And they took other villagers' land and sheep when they could.

At one point in 1996, the villagers had a big protest. We set up tents around the village, and there were about a hundred of us protesting the settlers taking our land. There were human rights groups at the protest, and we explained things to them. But it didn't matter. The settlers just attacked us, struck us with their guns. After that protest and some early clashes with the settlers, the villagers here just gave up.

---

[4] Sde Bar was settled in 1997. Today it has around fifty residents.

THEY SAID A BULLDOZER WAS COMING

In the summer of 1997, the Israeli military came to my family's home and demolished our sheep barn. It was a Saturday evening, and sixty or seventy soldiers arrived in jeeps. They gathered up my family—I was with my parents, six brothers, and four sisters—and they told us to stay in a single room. We also saw them go to my uncle's house, which was on the same property. At first they were just securing the area, making sure nobody protested or made trouble.

They said a bulldozer was coming. My father tried to argue with them. He said that the sheep barn was the start of a new home that he was building for some of his kids—that he needed to build to house his growing family. But the soldiers told him to be quiet and stay in the room, and then they locked us in. We could see what was happening out the window, and we watched for an hour and a half while they drove the sheep out and knocked down the barn. We cried. We had just built the barn the year before, all by hand. It had taken months of work and it was a big investment.

We knew the soldiers might come. We'd gotten a demolition order the year before, while we were still building the barn. It was on our land, but the Israeli authorities said we didn't have a permit to build it. Many people in the village got similar notices that demolition was planned on houses or buildings they'd built without permission from Israel. But the Israeli military only demolished two buildings that day—our barn and one other home in the village, the home of some neighbors half a mile away. I'm not sure why they chose our barn. Afterward, we had to take turns sleeping outside with the sheep, to protect them. We live near a forest, and there were wolves and jackals to worry about.

I remember the feeling I had after that day, a suffocating feeling. Our family was large, it was growing, and we weren't allowed to build. My father wanted to grow the farm and build homes for his children, but he wasn't allowed to. His plan had been to build more floors on the sheep barn. The bottom would be for sheep, and then the upper floors would be a place for his children to live. After the barn was demolished, we built a fence for the sheep, but that was the most we could do.

My family tried again a couple of years later. Around 2000, we bought stone to build a new house on the property. We paid about 60,000 shekels.[5] Then we tried to get a permit to build. There was so much we had to do, so many requests of us—money, negotiating with lawyers, endless paperwork. My father tried three times, but we couldn't get a permit. The stones we bought to build a new house are still on the property today. They've been sitting there for twelve years.

Five years ago my father tried to build again without a permit, and he got another demolition order. He was going to build a small house for just himself. Instead, he had to stop construction and turn the building into a chicken coop. Eventually, we decided our only option was to build onto the house we already have. My father has paperwork that goes back to 1943 that proves ownership of the house we live in, and of my uncle's house. They won't demolish those. But anything else we try to build on the property, they'll demolish if we don't have a building permit. And we can't get a permit.

Many people in the village have gone elsewhere. Some of my uncle's family members who used to live on the property have gone to live in Morocco. The Israelis, the settlers, it seems like they want us to go away. If we didn't have this land, we'd go back to Bethlehem. It's a better place— it's easier to live there. But if we leave, we won't be able to protect the land, which has been in our family for generations.

---

[5] At the time, 60,000 shekels equaled approximately US$17,000.

WE ARE LIKE PRISONERS HERE

I got married a couple of years after the demolition on our sheep barn. I needed to find a job to make more money, since my wife and I wanted to start a family. So I found work at a marble company in Jerusalem, and worked there for years. During this time, my wife and I started having children. But I was entering Israel illegally to work, and around 2008 I got caught. They put me in jail for two months, and I couldn't apply for a permit to work legally in Jerusalem for years.[6]

Since then I've worked around the family home. My family has sheep and goats, but I just take care of chickens. I have about forty of them, and I get around ten eggs a day. The eggs we don't eat we sell in the market. We also grow most of our own vegetables—cucumbers, cabbage, beans. And we have about three hundred olive trees on the property. We make about thirty kilos of olive oil every year, and we sell what we don't use.

I also work in the settlements.

Most days during the week, I wake up at six-thirty in the morning and go to work by seven. Right now I'm working in the olive groves on the farm in Sde Bar.[7] It's the time of the season when we dry the olives. I actually don't like working in the sun—I get dizzy and I get headaches—so my job is to work inside where I help get the olives ready for packing. I usually work from seven to three, but sometimes I get overtime and stay until five. I've also done work in the nearby settlements preparing firewood, making bricks, doing other jobs. I talk to the boss, and he tells me where I should

---

[6] Palestinians in the West Bank need special permits to enter Jerusalem. Some permits are granted on a one time only basis for special reasons, and some are granted for access to work in Israel. The application process can be difficult and expensive, so many Palestinians risk imprisonment by entering the city illegally.

[7] Sde Bar was established partly as a work camp and rehabilitation center for troubled teens. It was shut down in 2010 by the courts after allegations of drug use and child abuse, though many of the former teenage residents of the work farm stayed in the small settlement.

go to find work. In general, I like working in the settlements because I can travel back and forth easily, see my kids more. But the work I get around here doesn't pay much. I get about 100 shekels a day, usually. My friends who go into Jerusalem, they get a little more—150 or 175 shekels.[8] I used to go with them sometimes, but you need a special permit, and I haven't been able to get one since I was arrested.

The settlement near my home has about forty or fifty settlers. Then there's a handful of soldiers or private security guards that patrol the area in four or five jeeps. They have a tower set up nearby so they can watch everything. We can't move off our property without them seeing us. There are maybe ten to twelve of us Palestinian men who work in the Sde Bar. Me personally, I'm not afraid of the settlers. They know me, I've worked in the settlements, so they go easy on me. But with my kids, some of my other family, some of my neighbors, the settlers can be rough. My family and many of my neighbors feel like they're trapped at home, trapped in the limits of our own land. The settlements are all around us, and they have private security. If you leave your land, security guards will see you and come hassle you. We are like prisoners here in this area.

Sometimes, tourists will come onto this land to have picnics, especially in the springtime. It's right near a national park, Herodion. Sometimes settlement soldiers will come and surround them and tell them the area's closed off. And for a long time, some settlers would come to our house maybe twice a month and shout at us, tell us to go away. They'd have guns with them, and they'd scare my children. They'd say things like, "If we see you in the street, we will shoot you. If we see you with the sheep over in those fields, we'll shoot you, we'll take you to jail. If you don't stay in the house, we'll shoot." They'd tell the children they couldn't go outside our fence. Now I don't really let my kids leave the property, except to go

---

[8] 100 shekels equals approximately US$28. 175 shekels equals approximately US$50.

to school. And my kids have nightmares—they dream of being shot.

But it's actually gotten better. When the settlers first arrived, they were much rougher. Some of those people left, and some of the new people are a lot less threatening. But I remember an episode a while back where some settlers caught a man near the settlement, and they stripped him naked. They took all of his clothes, and they made him walk home naked. Everyone in the village saw him, and he just kept his head down and walked all the way home. The settlers are nicer now, but they say the settlement is going to expand. It makes me feel like I'm choking. We already feel afraid all the time. I think it'll get worse when they get bigger.

THE BIGGEST PROBLEM IS WATER

We have electricity sometimes through our generator. But gas is expensive. We usually only turn it on around once a week to wash clothes in our washing machine. It's hot now, and we have no electricity for fans. In the winter, we have no heat to keep us warm. When it gets cold, we stay in bed all day under the blankets to stay warm.

The biggest problem for us is water. The pipes run through the settlement, and we're the last in line in the village. During parts of the summer, we hardly ever have water come through the pipes. We have to ask the soldiers at the nearby military base to turn on the water. We have to ask a lot, and then they might turn it on for a day or two.

We have to buy some water in tanks, and then we get some from a well on the property. The well doesn't have enough water in the summer, so we're buying a lot. Each tank is about 60 shekels and holds a few hundred gallons of water.[9] We also save water as much as we can. The water we bathe with, we'll save and use to flush our toilets. The children

---

[9] 60 shekels equals approximately US$17.

all wash using the same bucket of water. There's very little waste.

At the moment there are about thirty of us in the family living on the property, and about ten in the family who are temporarily living elsewhere for work. Then there are the animals and the olive trees. We have to make priorities. We make sure the children have enough water first, then the adults, then the animals. I don't think there will be enough water this year for our olive trees. We won't see any olives from them this year.

At the nearby settlements, not just Sde Bar but also Tekoa and Nokdim, there's no problem with water.[10] People living there don't have to have tanks on their roofs or anything, they get enough from the pipes. The settlements look like heaven to us. They even have swimming pools there.

WE LOVE THIS LIFE

Right now my wife is pregnant with our fifth child. We have one room where we all sleep, and then we have the kitchen. Still, it isn't enough, and we can't build. The kids, they need a place to run around and play. There's no electricity, so they can't even watch TV. They spend a lot of time fighting each other.

There are things I love about living here. It's not the city. It's not overcrowded. It's simple to make a life here—we raise animals, live off the land. We love this life. It's normal for me. We are coping with the situation, we are coping with the settlements. We have lived through hardships from the beginning. I'd like to move, but I can't leave my land here. We grow our food, we live by our agriculture. So if I go, what is the nature of my life? I work in the settlement, so it is very difficult for me to move

---

[10] Tekoa and Nokdim are larger settlements surrounding Herodion (3,000 and 15,000 residents, respectively). Nokdim is home to Avigdor Lieberman, the Foreign Affairs Minister and Deputy Prime Minister of Israel. The settlements are served by a newly constructed highway into Jerusalem, sometimes called "Lieberman's Road."

and find work. My land, my family, my father and mother are all here on this land. Even if I move, my parents will not go.

But still, we feel like we are suffocating. If the settlements keep growing and surround our property, our lives will be hell. Right now, we are depressed from being worried all the time. I can't describe my feelings. We feel inferior, and no one helps. The settlements will only grow, and so will my family. Right now I'm just trying to make money, so that we can have a better life. For my children, I hope they live in safety, that they are not hurt or attacked, that they study and are good at school. Knowledge is the last thing that remains for us to achieve, and I want them to study at university. People we know in Bethlehem, they have water, electricity, it's a much better life. A number of villagers have moved already—they've gone out looking for something better. Someday we might move. Here, there's no room to build and grow.

GUARD TOWER AT DAMUN PRISON, ISRAEL

ABDELRAHMAN
AL-AHMAR

Lawyer, 46
Born in Bethlehem, West Bank &
interviewed in Bethlehem, West Bank

Abdelrahman Al-Ahmar lives with his wife and four children in a small apart-
ment complex on the edge of the refugee camp where he grew up. The complex is
surrounded by trees and garden greenery and is also home to three of his brothers
and their families, as well as rabbits, birds, puppies, and even a horse. During the
course of several interviews, the house is full of the sounds of his children playing.
Sometimes they come to sit and listen to their father's story, interjecting parts of the
narrative they know by heart.

Abdelrahman's comfortable house is a retreat from the harsh conditions he has
faced his entire life. Abed was born in the Deheisheh refugee camp, where his family
struggled against extreme poverty and regular attacks from soldiers and settlers. He
later spent nearly twenty years in prison, most of it in administrative detention,
where he was interrogated using torture techniques that have now been outlawed by

the Israeli High Court.[1] In 1999, the court ruled that the Israeli Security Agency (Shin Bet) does not have legal authority to use physical means of interrogation. It found tactics must be "reasonable and fair" and not cause the detainee to suffer. According to the Supreme Court case, a common practice during questioning was shaking prisoners violently enough to lead to unconsciousness, brain damage, or even death (in at least one reported case).

That practice was outlawed, as well as a number of prolonged stress positions that in some cases led to unconsciousness and permanent mental and physical damage. Although testimonies from prisoners indicate torture is still in use, human rights organizations report a reduction in the severity of torture by Israeli intelligence and police forces after the 1999 decision. However, in a society where 40 percent of men have spent time in prison, thousands of people still bear the physical and psychological marks of these methods.

Abed seems reserved at first during our initial meeting—he speaks little and watches us carefully as we ask questions. But as he relaxes, his dark humor and natural gift for storytelling begin to emerge. He switches between English, Arabic, and Hebrew as he speaks, and the only time he becomes quiet again is when talking about the most extreme forms of torture he endured. However, he also tells us he also talks about how the most difficult moments in his life have inspired him to become a leader in his community.

WE DIDN'T EVEN HAVE COCA COLA

I'm the same age as the occupation. The war of '67 started in June, and my mother was pregnant with me at the time.[2] She and my father were living

---

[1] Administrative detention is a system of detention without official charges used by occupying military forces. For more information, see the Glossary, page 276.

[2] The war in 1967 is known as the Six-Day War. For more on the war and the subsequent occupation of the West Bank, see Appendix I, page 267.

in the Deheisheh refugee camp in Bethlehem.[3] They'd been pushed out of their homes in Ramla during the war in '48, and that's when they'd moved to the camp.[4] You know, a lot of people fled their homes during the war in '67, and a lot of those people ended up living in Jordan, especially in Amman.[5] But my father said, "We're not leaving again." He didn't want to lose his home again. They had lived in tents for over ten years, and he had finally been able to build a house. They didn't want to give it up. So he and my mother went up in the woods and hid for a few days and then came back. She gave birth to me a few months later in the camp, with the help of a midwife.[6]

I remember the camp of my childhood was a neighborhood of shacks made of cinder blocks and aluminum roofs. My father built our house— many people in the camp built their own houses. We all had leaky ceilings, no plumbing, no bathrooms. There were just a few public restrooms we would all share. We didn't even have a septic tank in camp, and the toilets would flush into the gutters in the streets. We didn't have showers. We'd heat up water in a basin and wash with that. We depended on UNRWA for clothes.[7] I remember getting clothes twice a year, and they were often

---

[3] The Deheisheh refugee camp was established for 3,000 refugees in 1949 and is one of three refugee camps in the Bethlehem metropolitan area. Deheisheh is located just south of the city. Current estimates of the camp's population range up to 16,000 persons living in an area that is roughly one square mile.

[4] Ramla is a city of 65,000 people in central Israel. Today the city is approximately 20 percent Arab/Muslim, since most Arabs fled the city during the Arab-Israeli War.

[5] Amman, the capital of neighboring Jordan, is a city of around 2 million residents. Amman grew rapidly with the influx of Palestinian refugees after 1967.

[6] In 1967, the Israelis seized the West Bank from Jordan, which had administered the region since 1948. For more information on the wars in 1948 and 1967, see Appendix I, page 267.

[7] The United Nations Relief and Works Agency (UNRWA) has provided services such as education and medical care to Palestinian refugees since 1949. For more information, see the Glossary, page 276.

the wrong size, and sometimes all that was available were girl clothes. We were so cold in the winter. For heat, we had fires in old oil barrels outside our homes, and families would gather around them to warm up. I remember the fires would get so high, we couldn't see the faces of the people on the other side of the barrel. But in the winters we were always cold. And there was so much disease—cholera, infections of all sorts.

Growing up, we could hear our next-door neighbors every day. We knew their fights, conversations, everything. And there were so many places that you couldn't get to by car because the spaces between buildings were too narrow. You had to walk between the houses.

As children from the camp, we'd feel different from other kids when we went out into Bethlehem, the city. We would see kids who had bicycles, but we didn't have any. They had good clothes, but we didn't have them. They even had Coca Cola! And it was hard for my parents, too. They weren't accustomed to the kind of poverty we were living in. They were born in villages with nice homes and big properties near Ramla.

When I was a kid, my father used to work in Israel. He was a stonecutter. But he wasn't making enough money for the family—he had four boys and two girls to support. There was no one in Deheisheh with money. So everybody was struggling financially, but at least it gave us this feeling of being equal.

OUR WINDOWS WERE ALWAYS OPEN, SO WE GOT USED TO THE SMELL OF TEAR GAS

I felt pressure from the Israeli army and settlers at an early age. The most difficult issue that we had to deal with was the settlers. I was only six years old when the settlers started coming through the camp in the early seventies, so I grew up seeing them. The main road from the settlements in the south runs through Bethlehem to Jerusalem, and it goes right through the camp. I think the settlers who passed through saw Deheisheh as something they needed to control.

The settlers were led by a man named Rabbi Moshe Levinger, who saw all of the West Bank as part of Israel.[8] They wanted Israel to claim the land around Rachel's Tomb especially, and that was just a little north of the Deheisheh camp on the main road.[9] They found ways to make life miserable for us. They would come in buses maybe once a week. They'd get off and start shooting randomly in the refugee camp with live bullets. They'd shout, throw stones, provoke fights. Whenever anyone tried to fight back, the settlers would alert Israeli soldiers who would chase us through the streets and fire tear-gas canisters. Our windows were always open, so we got used to the smell of tear gas.

I remember settlers entering my UNRWA school and smashing desks, doors, windows. The teachers couldn't protect us. There was always a sense of fear and insecurity. When I was younger, these things affected me tremendously. They affected my relationship with my teachers and the way I looked at them. You kind of lose respect for them because you've seen them degraded. And after some time, we stopped listening to them because we knew they were powerless.

Then in the early eighties, the military built a fence around the camp. It was twenty-six feet high, and the only way in and out was the Hebron

---

[8] Rabbi Moshe Levinger was born in Jerusalem in 1935 and helped lead the movement to settle the West Bank after the Six-Day War. He was especially active in asserting settler presence around Hebron, a large West Bank city fifteen miles south of the Deheisheh camp. The road that connects Hebron to Jerusalem runs through the Deheisheh camp.

[9] Rachel's Tomb is the supposed burial place of Rachel, mother of Joseph—figures who are revered in the scriptures of Judaism, Islam, and Christianity. The tomb, which is a holy site for Muslims and Jews, is less contentious than the Temple Mount/Al-Aqsa Mosque in Jerusalem, but it remains a flashpoint during periods of conflict between Palestinians and Israelis. The path of the current barrier wall positions the site within Israel's control.

Road, the one that settlers passed through. We had a curfew—you had to be in by seven p.m., or the soldiers guarding the entryway wouldn't let you back into the camp. I remember hearing that tourists who came to Bethlehem would see the fence and wonder if it was the wall of a city zoo!

Around the same time, settlers brought trailers to the site near Rachel's Tomb and tried to establish an outpost there. I remember being stuck in the camp after curfew and hearing the patriotic music of the settlers blaring through the night.

The soldiers worked so closely with the settlers most of the time. When I was fourteen, I got a backpack—the first time in my life. Before that, I would carry my books in plastic bags, like most kids in the camp. I was so happy I finally had a backpack. It was green. My dad bought it for me. I was going to school one morning, and a group of six soldiers and an armed man in civilian clothes—a settler—called me over. The settler kicked me and slapped me and then took my backpack and threw it into the sewer. I tried to get it out of the sewer, but they hit me again and threw it back into a gutter full of sewage. My books were wet and ruined, and they still didn't allow me to get the pack. I watched them do the same thing to some of my friends—they threw their books in the gutter, too.

At the UNRWA school, they would give us the books for free. I told them what the soldiers had done, and they gave me new books. But I had to put them back in plastic bags again. I couldn't forget these things. Of course, the soldiers knew the backpack was important to me because they could see how impoverished we all were and that we were deprived of everything. They knew this backpack was important to me, and they took the pleasure out of it for me.

Refugees in the camp would retaliate by throwing stones. Even as children, we'd think about what we could do against the soldiers and settlers. I started throwing stones at age ten. Kids a little older might be a little more organized. Different groups of kids would decide to do something—a group of five over here, a group of six over there. By the time I was thirteen, I was among them. We started to incite other children to put flags up. At that time, it was illegal to hang the Palestinian flag.[10] So, we would tell the kids to hang the flag and to write slogans on the walls. That was also illegal then. You could be arrested by the Israeli army and go to prison.

When they saw us throwing stones, the soldiers or settlers might shoot. When they shot at us, yes, we were afraid. But with time, with all the injustice and the frustration, we were just stuck, and we didn't care if we died. But we thought throwing stones made a difference. We saw the settlers as the occupiers, and they were the source of injustice and deprivation, so we had to fight back. This was before the First Intifada, but for us in the camp it was already Intifada, it was always Intifada.

"WHAT DID YOU DO? WHAT DID YOU DO? WHAT DID YOU DO?"

Eventually, my friends and I graduated from throwing stones to throwing Molotov cocktails. It wasn't hard to make a weapon out of a bottle of kerosene and a wick. We wanted to throw them at the outpost set up by Moshe Levinger and at the soldiers who were helping the settlers to come and wreck our neighborhood. By this point I was fifteen, almost sixteen. Some in our group were younger—one was fourteen. We made a couple and tested them out by smashing them against walls in the camp when nobody was looking.

December 11, 1984, was a cold, snowy night. I was in the home of

---

[10] After the Oslo Accords were put into effect in 1995, Bethlehem was administered by the Palestinian Authority. Between 1967 and 1995, however, Israel maintained full control of civil administration and security and outlawed symbols of Palestinian nationalism such as the Palestinian flag.

á boy in our group, there were five of us, and we were making cocktails. Suddenly, soldiers swarmed in. We were cuffed and found ourselves being taken away. We were driven to Al-Muskubiya.[11]

When we got to the interrogation center, it was very chaotic. There were maybe forty guys in all who had been arrested and brought to Al-Muskubiya that night. For the five of us, they took off all of our clothes, stripped us naked. Then they tightened our handcuffs, took us outside in an open area, and put bags on our heads. The snow was coming down, and we were naked out there. I couldn't see the others, but I could hear their teeth chattering, and the sound of the handcuffs shaking was so loud. The cold weather still bothers me now—it makes me remember that night. This is where we stayed for a week in between interrogations. Our bodies turned blue, we were out in the cold so long.

My interrogation and torture lasted two months. During the interrogations, they beat me, and there was loud music playing the whole time. We were allowed to go to the bathroom just once a day. They would tie our hands to the pipes. It was really painful for me. After some time, I stopped feeling my arms—sometimes I didn't know if I still had them or if they had been amputated. There was constant beating, all over my body, to the point where my skin would be as black as my jacket. If I lost consciousness, they would throw water on me so I'd wake up. Or they would slap me until I woke up.

This mark on my wrist is actually from the handcuffs during that time in prison. The handcuffs were so tight, they cut to the bone. I still have marks on my legs from the beatings. They wouldn't give us any medical treatment. And the interrogators wouldn't ask you direct, obvious

---

[11] Al-Muskubiya ("the Russian Compound") is a large compound in the Old City of Jerusalem that was built in the nineteenth century to house an influx of Russian Orthodox pilgrims into the city during the time of Ottoman rule. Today, the compound houses Israeli police headquarters, criminal courts, and a prison and interrogation center.

questions. They would just keep saying, "What did you do? What did you do? What did you do?" And that was it. And with all the beating, I couldn't focus anymore, even if I was conscious. And I couldn't remember anything that I did from the time before prison, even if I had anything to confess. Most of the other kids told the police what they'd done—make some Molotov cocktails and tested them out. I didn't tell them anything, not because I was being secretive, but because I was too confused and disoriented from the beatings. It was a very hostile environment.

Sometimes they would give me four hours of sleep in a week. Other times they would keep me awake for fourteen days straight before they gave me four hours of sleep. And with the pressure of sleep deprivation, I started hallucinating, and I didn't actually know what was happening around me. I would imagine I was in a kindergarten and there were a lot of crying kids causing all this chaos, but I couldn't do anything to calm them down. And I stopped knowing if what was happening was real or just my own imagination.

Eventually, a lawyer came to visit me. Her name was Lea Tsemel. She was an Israeli lawyer.[12] She came to meet me in the visiting room one day. She told me she was taking on my case. I was so confused. I just asked her if what was happening to me was real, or was I just trapped in my imagination. So many times I was convinced that the prison was full of snakes. I asked her about that, and she told me I was just hallucinating. She told me about my charges and let me know we'd be in court soon.

There was one guard who was nice. One morning, I asked to go to the bathroom, and the interrogators wouldn't let me go until midnight. When this guard saw me in pain because I had to go so badly, he said, "Godammit! What happened to these people? Why do they torture people? Godammit!" And he was so angry. And he sent me to the bathroom.

---

[12] Lea Tsemel is a prominent human rights lawyer in Israel.

Then he brought me tea and said, "Rest, rest." This was very risky for him, and I really appreciated it.

The whole interrogation was two months. I was afraid that they were going to kill us because we had heard all these terrible stories of torture. I had an uncle who had been arrested a while before, and I knew that he'd died in prison. He participated in a hunger strike, and when the prison guards force-fed him, he choked to death.

The main thing that consumed my thinking was that these people were crazy, and they wanted to torture me and mentally destroy me. And they would actually say it right to our faces. They would tell us, "We want to ruin you psychologically." In fact, many prisoners do become mentally ill. Some of them die. I didn't go crazy because of the fact that I was one of a huge population. I was not the only one suffering. And also, I think people who are really religious have a hard time with this kind of abuse sometimes. They pray to God for help, and when none comes, it breaks them mentally. But that wasn't me, and I was able to focus on the future and what I needed to do to get myself out of that situation.

After two months of interrogation, my friends and I were taken to trial and charged with terrorist activities. The judge sentenced us to four to six years each. My mother was in the courtroom, and she fainted when she heard the sentence.

WE WERE ALL STILL DREAMING OF GROWING A MUSTACHE

After my sentence, I was sent to Damun Prison.[13] I learned more in prison than I would have at a university. I met the leaders of the resistance.

---

[13] Damun Prison is in northern Israel, near Haifa. The facilities were once used as a tobacco warehouse during the British Mandate, but they were converted to a prison by Israel in 1953. It houses up to 500 prisoners.

I was so proud of myself. They were the big fighters. And the other boys I was arrested with, they were all so happy. We thought we were so grown up, even though we were all still dreaming of growing a mustache. We'd actually shave four times a day to try to get our beards to grow in stronger so we could look older. I acted angry about my sentence—not because I thought it was too long, but because I thought it was too short! They gave me four years, I wanted twelve years. I thought it was sort of an honor.

In Damun, I was in with a bunch of lowlifes—Israeli mafia guys, drug dealers, all sorts of criminals. I think the soldiers wanted to put young guys in the resistance in with real degenerates, sort of to corrupt us. But we all got along, and before long I was one of the leaders in prison. I became the representative of a group of young prisoners in dealing with the guards. I'd voice our demands and objections to the ways we were being treated.

In 1986, I led a hunger strike. We were actually protesting about not getting enough food. And besides that, it was winter, and there was no heat, and we only had one thin blanket each. And we weren't getting enough exercise time outside. So there were dozens of us not eating as a protest. I remember we used to dream of food at night. The Israeli soldiers, they would tease us. They'd have barbecues outside the walls of our cells, and the smell would come into our cells through the windows and give us physical pains, it made us so hungry.

We stuck at it for eighteen days, and on the eighteenth day I announced we were going on a water strike as well. The guards quickly brought in doctors from the Red Cross, and they told us that we'd be dead in two days if we tried that. So I said, "Okay, we won't do that." But it was enough to make the guards think we were crazy enough to try. The next day, the warden came and agreed to our demands—more food, two more blankets at night, and fifteen more minutes of exercise time a day. It felt like a big victory. For two weeks afterward, we had to relearn to eat, like we were babies all over again. All our stomachs could handle was milk, a little soft potato, that sort of thing.

So I had a reputation as a dangerous prisoner, not because I was violent, but because I was an instigator. The authorities decided to transfer me to Ashkelon, which was where they put the prisoners they considered the most dangerous.[14] Inside Ashkelon, there were a lot of leaders of Palestine's resistance movement. To Israel, this was where the worst of the worst went. But as a Palestinian, I felt much safer in Ashkelon than I had at Damun.

Those of us who were young and in prison for the first time started to study. We wanted to know everything. We would sit with the older men in Ashkelon, and they told us about their experience. The older prisoners would even organize more formal education—lectures and lessons every day. These were guys who had been in prison forever. Some of them had been in since 1967. I think a few of those guys had been around to hear Jesus lecture! So they had a lot of wisdom to pass on.

We learned about history, economics, philosophy. We had to wake up at six in the morning and start reading and studying. At ten there was a lecture until noon, and then there was a ninety-minute break. After that if we wanted to read again, we could. If we wanted to have a nap, we could do that as well. After the break, we had to write an article—it could be political, educational, whatever. But we had to write something. Every day one of the inmates had to lecture the others about what he had written and read earlier. And then we would go back to reading. They served us dinner at seven, and then between seven and ten we could read, and then we would go back to sleep. If we didn't finish our writing, we could

---

[14] Now called Shikma Prison, the facility is a maximum-security prison just outside Ashkelon, a city of 125,000 people just north of the Gaza Strip. Shikma was built following the Six-Day War in 1967 as a lockup for security prisoners in the newly occupied Palestinian territories.

stay up late and write. We didn't have enough time for all our activities. It became an addiction, and I was consumed with, *What am I going to read next? What am I going to write?*

Each of the inmates had his own specialty. Some of them were political, some of them philosophical. One specialized in economics, another in Marx. So I got to learn from all of them—about politics, about Vietnam, the Soviet Union, such places. I took a two-year course in Marxism. Some people taught chemistry and explosives inside the prison. We also learned languages. Some of the prisoners knew Greek, Russian, Turkish, so they would pass on their languages. Getting into Ashkelon for me was like getting accepted to Harvard or Oxford!

But the treatment in the prison was still very harsh. Solitary confinement at Ashkelon was the worst in all the prisons in Israel. Prisoners could be isolated from others for years.[15] One inmate I knew lost his mind because of all the pressure from solitary. He needed psychiatric help.

To protest this, we set all the cells on fire. Every prisoner was part of it—we all piled up clothes in the middle of our cells and lit them with smuggled matches. The smoke was terrible, and many of us suffocated. Forty-eight prisoners had to go to the hospital, but our protest got attention. They still used solitary confinement to torture people afterward, though.

The relationships you form inside the prison are very strong. There are a lot of people from different cities: Ramallah, Nablus, Hebron, so many places. So there's a lot to learn, and you become more knowledgeable about the situations in other cities. When you get out of prison, you're

---

[15] In 1986, the same year Abdelrahman was transferred to Shikma Prison, Israeli nuclear technician Mordechai Vanunu was captured by Israeli intelligence officers in Rome and sentenced by military tribunal to Shikma Prison for revealing details of Israel's secret nuclear weapons program to the international press. He spent eleven of his eighteen years in prison in solitary confinement.

going to stay friends with them. And they're really influential in their own societies. So many of the leaders of the First Intifada met in prison.

I got out of prison in 1988, during the First Intifada. I was still only twenty, but I was more influential in our society because people respect someone who's been in jail—we weren't seen as criminals, but leaders.

I WAS JUST LIKE THE POPE

I didn't stay out long after my release in 1988. I was only out for six months. I hadn't done anything this time, but because of my record and people I knew, and because it was the Intifada, I was rounded up.[16]

This time after my trial I was sent to Ofer Prison.[17] I was there six years, from around 1988 to 1994. In Ofer, I learned Hebrew. Ofer was like a big open-air prison with lots of tents, and one of the tents was the "Hebrew tent," where only Hebrew was spoken. I would visit there a lot, and that's where I picked up the language.

I had a lot of experience and I knew a lot, so the new inmates would ask me how to do things. I was just like the Pope. They would respect me and ask me for things. In prison culture, if you're an alumnus of prison, you get special treatment from both the inmates and the wardens and guards. I would get the best bed in the tent, you know, the one in the corner. The guards also gave me special treatment because I was an asset to the prison. They knew that I could influence everyone else, and if I said something, everyone was going to listen to me. It was a give and take.

I was out of prison by 1994, but of course, the Israeli authorities kept an eye on me. The authorities have this obsession, that once someone

---

[16] Abdelrahman was arrested under suspicion of being a member of the Popular Front for the Liberation of Palestine.

[17] Ofer Prison is a large detention facility outside of Ramallah.

like me has been to prison, then we're a terrorist for life. I got picked up a few times, and sometimes I'd be held for a day, sometimes for two weeks. Then, in 1996, I was arrested, and this time they took me to Al-Muskubiya. They didn't have charges, they just wanted to interrogate me about people I knew. During the interrogation, I was tortured.

After a week of not being allowed to sleep, not getting enough to eat, that's when the interrogators started shaking me. There are two kinds of shaking they'd do—one of the head and neck only, and one for the whole body. Of course when they start after a week of no food or no sleep, you can't really physically resist at all. You're too weak, and your neck starts to flop around, you don't get oxygen, and you pass out. They'd bring us prisoners close to death.

I remember waking up in the hospital. I'd been taken to Hadassah.[18] After I was better, I was taken back to Al-Muskubiya and interrogated some more. They'd use other methods, too. One thing the interrogators liked to do was to make the handcuffs really tight and bind you to a chair that slants downward. They would leave you like that all day, and the handcuffs would slowly cut into your wrists. Sometimes they'd only ask me a few questions, for just fifteen minutes a day. And then I'd be bound up in the chair for the rest of the day. Sometimes they'd say they were going to give me "stomach exercises," and then two interrogators would twist my body in opposite directions while my hands were cuffed. They would put me in these stress positions until I threw up or fainted.

This time, they held me for over two years without charges. They didn't have anything to accuse me of, but they didn't want me out on the streets. Also, they wouldn't let my lawyer, Lea Tsemel, see me. They wouldn't let Israeli citizens visit security prisoners at the time. So instead, Lea sent a lawyer from the U.S. whom she was mentoring to visit me at

---

[18] Hadassah Medical Center is a health care complex in Jerusalem.

Al-Muskubiya. Her name was Allegra Pacheco. I think as a prisoner, I had developed a keen sense of who was dangerous, who was safe, and who I could trust. I knew I could trust Allegra right away.

They sent me to Ofer Prison again. They never charged me; they just gave me a six-month sentence of administrative detention. By this time, I was a real expert at life in prison. And I'd learned Hebrew so well during my first stay at Ofer, I didn't even have an accent anymore. When I was first put in again, I convinced some of the guards that I was a Jew, and they would believe me because my accent was perfect. They used to ask me, "You're among Arabs. How can we help you?" I asked them for a mobile phone, because at that time you couldn't have one inside prison. They gave me the mobile.

I got away with other tricks because of my good Hebrew. We had newspapers inside, and there were ads in the back. One was for a pizza place. I used my mobile and called the pizza place, and I acted as if I was the warden in charge of the prison. I ordered seventy-five pizzas, enough for all the inmates. And the pizza guy told me they'd deliver in two hours. In three hours, the warden came to my tent and gave me a long look. "Do you still want pizza?" he asked. So I answered him, "If you're going to give it to us, why not?" He was pretty mad. He said, "I know that you're the one who asked for the pizza, because you have really good Hebrew. Now you're going to solitary." So I had to spend two weeks in solitary. There was another ad in the newspaper for belly dancers. I wanted to call and ask for dancers as well, but because I got busted for the pizzas I didn't have the nerve to do it.

THE JUDGES HAD NO MERCY

During the time I was in prison, I kept seeing my lawyer, Allegra. She helped me appeal every six months during my administrative detention hearings, and she kept me thinking about the future. I must have proposed to her twenty times while I was at Ofer. She told me I was crazy.

Finally, I got out of administrative detention in 1998, and I started working for human rights groups, like the Palestinian Human Rights Monitoring Group. We'd investigate cases of human rights abuses against Palestinians. And I stayed in touch with Lea and Allegra and other lawyers as well, who were fighting in courts to end the torture of prisoners. In 1999, they took some cases to the high court in Israel, and they won a huge victory that made certain kinds of torture, like shaking, illegal.

It was also around this time that I got Allegra to agree to marry me. I think I just had to ask her enough times. As a prisoner, I'd learned to be persistent in speaking out for what I wanted, and I used the same tactics to win over Allegra. We just sort of agreed we might get married someday soon, and then she went to the U.S. on a fellowship. She was working on a book about how a Second Intifada might be right around the corner. But she didn't finish it, because the Second Intifada started in 2000 while she was still writing and that spoiled the concept of her whole book!

During the Second Intifada, I was still working for the Palestinian Human Rights Monitoring Group, and sometimes I'd sneak into Jerusalem to talk to Palestinians for reports on human rights abuses. I also worked with a reporter with *Ha'aretz*, which is Israel's major newspaper. I'd show him around the refugee camps and help with stories. When I went to Jerusalem, I'd always bring a really nice leather briefcase, so I'd look like a businessman. But in May 2001, I was stopped by a police officer in Jerusalem and arrested for not having a proper permit to travel into Jerusalem. So once again I was headed to prison.

I was taken back to Al-Muskubiya. Already, interrogation had changed, but not much. They still put me on a chair that was angled downward with tight cuffs. And now, instead of hitting, shaking, that sort of thing, they tried to mess with my mind more. They would do things like show me a photo of my house in ruins and tell me it had been demolished. But it was all Photoshop work.

At the time, Allegra was in the United States, and she was supposed to be done with her fellowship and come back to Israel in June. She was in Boston trying on a wedding dress when she heard I'd been picked up. She got back just in time to represent me during my administrative detention hearing. She showed up along with Lea, her mentor and my first lawyer. They had a photographer from *Ha'aretz* with them, and they brought a lot of snacks—bourekas and cola.[19] We got to have a reunion in the lawyer's meeting room, and that's where we got formally engaged. We had a little party with the bourekas and cola, and then Lea took some bourekas to the judges to tell them we were getting engaged and asked if we could have a little more time in the meeting room. Meanwhile, the *Ha'aretz* photographer took pictures of us exchanging rings. It was beautiful!

But the judges had no mercy. The lawyers for Israel kept bringing up how I was mean to my interrogators, cursed at them, called them sons of bitches, and how I wouldn't cooperate. That was their big case for me being a security risk to Israel, just that I wasn't nice enough in the interrogation room. Allegra was wonderful—she demanded that the judges look at the deep grooves in my wrists from my recent interrogation. But they refused. And so I ended up spending another year in administrative detention in Ofer.

When I got out in May 2002, Allegra and I were married, and she got pregnant a little before I was arrested again in November. This was right in the middle of the Second Intifada still, and a lot of former prisoners were being arrested. The night they picked me up, they were looking for my brother. But because I had a record, they decided they'd pick me up as well. I was sentenced to six months administrative detention and sent

---

[19] A boureka is a pastry stuffed with cheese, potatoes, or other fillings.

back to Ofer.[20] And then our son Quds was born in April 2003. When June came around, I was up for another renewal of detention. This would have been the seventeenth six-month detention I'd been given during my lifetime. My lawyer Lea tried to bring a little photo book with pictures of Quds into court near Ofer to show me. It would have been the first time I'd seen my son, but the judge refused to let me see the book. He gave me another sentence of six months, and then I got two more after that. So I didn't get to go home and see my son until he was almost two. By that time I had spent almost seventeen years in prison all together, with ten of those years being in administrative detention without charges.

THIS IS LIFE FOR THOUSANDS OF PEOPLE

I've been out of prison since 2005. When I got out the last time, I started studying law, and now I'm a lawyer, like Allegra. In January, I'll be in military court to help my friend. I'll be arguing his case in front of a judge who has sentenced me to administrative detention many times before. I'm going to rub it in his face. I've been waiting a long time to be a lawyer, and I studied so hard. I'm not nervous.

I also defend prisoners who have been arrested by the Palestinian Authority.[21] The conflict with the Palestinian Authority is even more complicated than the occupation. I make visits to the prisoners in the PA prisons, and in some cases they get tortured and humiliated there even more than with the Israelis. Also, most of these prisoners have already

---

[20] At the time of Abdelrahman's arrest in 2003, there were approximately 1,000 Palestinian men and women serving administrative detention sentences.

[21] The Palestinian Authority was chartered to administer parts of the West Bank and Gaza following the Oslo Accords in 1993–1995. As part of the Oslo agreement, the PA is responsible for security control in parts of the West Bank such as Bethlehem. For more on the Palestinian Authority, see the Glossary, page 276.

been in prison on the Israeli side. I visit my clients in prison every day. And I sit down and talk to them and listen to them. The conditions are extremely harsh. In the important cases, the investigation is shared among the Americans, Israelis, and the Palestinians, together. These prisoners are usually fundamentalists from Hamas and the Islamic Jihad parties.[22]

I still see many of the people from my time in prison, including other prisoners and my first lawyer, Lea Tsemel. She's like a mother to my wife and me. She still visits me now. She's a good person. She's seventy years old. But if you're going to write that down, say it was sixty, because she'll be upset if we say she's seventy. Or maybe you should put thirty!

Now we have two girls and two boys. It's even. The boys are ten and seven, and then the girls, five and two. To raise a baby girl is much easier than raising a boy. They're much calmer, and they're nicer, easier to deal with. Boys just want to rebel all the time. But they're not aggressive. The kids just want to play. They're very sweet.

Of course, I worry about my kids and the situation they're growing up in. I want my kids to grow up in a good atmosphere, with justice and liberty and freedom, and a life with no problems. We've been deprived of so many things, and that, of course, always takes its toll on you. So whatever my kids ask from me I get for them. I buy them expensive bicycles and that sort of thing. Allegra says no, but I spoil them because I didn't ever have things, and I was deprived of so many things when I was a child. I admit, I have a psychological problem with shoes! I buy them for my kids all the time. Every one of my four children has dozens of pairs of shoes. Every time Allegra asks me, "Why did you buy that?" I say, "You can't possibly understand." One of my daughters also has five backpacks.

My family would like to go to the U.S. to be with my wife's parents.

[22] For more on Hamas, see the Glossary, page 276. The Islamic Jihad movement is not a political party, but a movement or coalition of militias that, like Hamas, formed from the Egyptian Muslim Brotherhood.

My wife is an American, but they rejected our visa application.[23] I've been trying to get a visa for a long time. The lawyer for the visa asked for $120,000. We've stopped trying.

From a physical aspect, I do still have effects from the torture. I still can't feel my left hand completely due to the nerve damage I got from being handcuffed. And it's not easy to live with the fact that I went through such a horrible experience. It has impacted me.

I would have been different if I hadn't gone to prison. Probably I would've gone to med school instead of law school. But I've never really thought about the question of how my life would be different if I hadn't gone to prison because this is life for thousands, millions even, of people in refugee camps here, in Lebanon, or in Syria. It's not a personal problem, it's a broader thing. I want to solve it because it affects everybody else, not just me. If the situation doesn't change, my son Quds may soon have the same experience. This is a problem for generation after generation; we've been fighting for sixty-five years. It's going to be the same thing until we break the cycle.

---

[23] It is very difficult for any Palestinians who have spent time in prison to travel, and especially to get visas to the United States, even if they were held under administrative detention and never charged with a crime.

INTERSECTION IN RAMALLAH, WEST BANK

RIYAM KAFRI

Chemistry professor, blogger, 34
Born in Amman, Jordan &
interviewed in Ramallah, West Bank

Riyam Kafri was born in Amman, Jordan. Her father was one of thousands of Palestinians displaced to Syria, Jordan, or Lebanon during the Six-Day War of 1967—marking a second wave of Palestinian refugees after the massive displacement of 1948. Riyam's parents waited for the opportunity to return to the West Bank instead of leaving to pursue lucrative jobs elsewhere. They finally returned to the West Bank in the early 1980s, after years of legal wrangling. On returning to Palestine, they settled in Ramallah.

We interview Riyam in her spacious kitchen in Ramallah. As she talks, she stirs pots, washes dishes, and checks the oven, effortlessly putting together a dinner for six as she tells her life story. As we get to know Riyam, we learn that this kind of multi-tasking is normal for her. She is the mother of twin toddlers at the same time that she teaches organic chemistry at Al-Quds University and helps to run the university's liberal arts program (designed in conjunction with Bard University of New York state). She also writes a blog with a fellow professor, and her essays,

*whether funny or brimming with frustration, are sharply observed explorations of
daily life in Palestine.*

*Writing is Riyam's passion, but she came to it later in her career. She received
her Ph.D. in chemistry from the University of Tennessee in the United States and
had the opportunity to live a comfortable life abroad. She chose to return to the West
Bank where she started teaching, and she found her voice as a writer in describing
life as a resident of the West Bank. She writes that Palestine is "like a distant land
that inhabits the warmest chambers of one's heart, so close yet so unattainable."[1]*

A DESIRE TO LIVE JUST LIKE ANY OTHER TEENAGER IN THE WORLD

When the war broke out in 1967, my father was an electrical engineering
student in Germany. After the war, Israel gave ID cards to Palestinian citizens. The cards were required for citizens to be able to remain in Palestine,
but since my father was abroad at the time they were distributed, he
wasn't able to get one. My mom, who hadn't yet met my father, was in
the West Bank at the time and was able to get an ID card. A little after
the war, my dad moved to Jordan. He met my mother through a family
relative. They got married in the late seventies, and then they started
working to return to Palestine. At first they thought that since my dad
was marrying someone with an ID card, it would be easier for him to apply
for one as well. But the Israeli government said that they needed to have
a child to prove that the marriage was real. So they got pregnant really
quickly—and I was born nine months later, in Amman, Jordan, in 1980.[2]

After I was born, my parents applied again to get my father an ID

---

[1] For more of Riyam's writing, see Appendix VI, page 312.

[2] Amman, the capital of Jordan, is a city of nearly 3 million residents. The population of
the city greatly expanded after 1948 and 1967, with waves of Palestinian refugees fleeing
the West Bank, which was administered by Jordan until 1967.

card. This time, the Israeli authorities told my mom that she needed to have a boy, because a girl didn't count. Who knows what their reasoning was. My mom had to make the choice to get pregnant as soon as possible again, so that she could try to have a boy and reapply for an ID for my father. Two years later, my brother was born, and that's when they applied for an ID again and were successful. And so our family finally moved to Palestine at the end of 1982, to Ramallah.[3] I was about two and half, and my brother about six months.

In Ramallah, my father was an electrical engineering professor at Birzeit University.[4] My mother was a teacher, and later a principal. I grew up in a politically active family. I also grew up with a father who thought that his children had to leave a mark on society. We were raised to think that we *had* to do something that had a purpose. And the main purpose, the underlying goal, is to serve Palestine in one way or another.

I was sheltered from some of the problems many Palestinians have, but I can't say I grew up completely sheltered, because I was educated about the struggle. You know, I grew up during the beginning of the First Intifada, so the entire atmosphere was different. Everyone, from teenagers to adults, was more aware of Palestine, of the political situation, of the prisoners and arrests.[5]

When I was a child, the Intifada actually seemed fun. I remember the

---

[3] Ramallah is a town of over 30,000 people. It has experienced rapid growth since it was adopted as a de facto administrative capital by the Palestinian Authority following the Oslo Accords. Numerous nongovernmental organizations (NGOs) and diplomatic outreach offices are also based in the town. Ramallah is located about ten miles northeast of Jerusalem, the city many Palestinians consider Palestine's true capital.

[4] Birzeit University is a renowned public university located just outside Ramallah. It hosts approximately 8,500 undergraduates.

[5] Israel carried out the mass arrest of Palestinian citizens during the First Intifada. More than 120,000 Palestinians were arrested or spent time in prison from 1987 to the signing of the Oslo Accords in 1993.

demonstrations that brought the neighborhood together. I also remember learning how to knit. At that time, women would knit navy-blue v-necked shirts that they could send to prisoners. So that's how I learned knitting. The prison would only accept that color, and it had to be v-necked, and it had to be a plain v-neck—we couldn't even use any stitches but the most basic ones. And my mom was part of a women's group that would go into refugee camps to help distribute aid, and they would also collect these knitted shirts and send them to prisons.

I don't remember much about my first couple of years at school. Actually, the Israeli military shut down most schools in the area during the First Intifada. Schools might operate for only a few hours a week. So we did distance learning. I was enrolled at the Friends School, and I'd go once every two weeks to drop off my assignments and pick up new ones.[6] The first day of the year, we'd go to pick up our books, get our first assignments, and then immediately go home to start working on them.

We were really responsible for our own education in many ways. My mother, a teacher, taught lessons to all the kids in the neighborhood. It wasn't just the kids in the same building we were living in—kids from all around would come to our home, and my mother would teach them. Finally, when I was around twelve, the school reopened. But even then it was only open for half days.

Around the time I became a teenager, the Intifada took on a different emotional quality for me. I wasn't just knitting sweaters anymore—I was watching my friends get arrested. I remember the powerful desire to live just like any other teenager around the world, to spend my time listening to music and not having to care about politics. It was suffocating. I say this with a lot of humility, because I didn't even see what it was like to live

---

[6] The Friends School of Ramallah is a Quaker-run institution that was opened in 1889, during the time of Ottoman rule.

in a refugee camp. So if *I* was suffocating in the middle of a city, with a home that had all the amenities that anyone could ask for, I can't imagine what it was like for anyone in the refugee camps.

And then I saw this complete switch, with Oslo, around 1993.[7] Things started to open up more. We could get to places we couldn't get to before, including Jerusalem, and Haifa, and Jaffa.[8] By the time I graduated from high school in '96, even the topics of conversation with my friends were completely different—more the day-to-day concerns with living and work. We didn't need to talk about fighting just to live and struggling just to exist.

I WAS *IN LOVE* WITH THE
CONCEPT OF A ROAD TRIP

I lived in Ramallah until I was seventeen. Then I graduated from the Friends School, and I received a full-tuition scholarship to Earlham College in the States.[9] The Friends School had an arrangement where they'd send one or two graduating students to Earlham on full scholarship every year. I'd applied to a few other liberal arts colleges in the States, but I really wanted to get into Earlham, and when I got the scholarship, my

---

[7] The first Oslo Accords negotiations took place in Norway, the U.S., and France during the summer of 1993. The Accords outlined a plan for the Israeli military to withdraw from Gaza and the West Bank in stages while further negotiations would be carried out regarding Palestinian statehood, security, borders, and Israeli settlements. For more information, see Appendix I, page 267.

[8] Access to Jerusalem was significantly restricted to Palestinians from the West Bank before the Oslo Accords in 1993. Haifa is a city of 300,000 people in northern Israel. Jaffa, now part of Tel Aviv in Israel, was home to many Muslim Arabs before the Arab-Israeli War in 1948.

[9] Earlham College is a Quaker-affiliated liberal arts college in Richmond, Indiana. It has an enrollment of 1,200 students, and has regularly accepted a large cohort of Palestinian students since the signing of the Oslo Accords.

family discussed it. It was a little bit of a conflict. It was very tough for my dad, particularly. My mother is a very realistic woman, and she felt like her children leave home was inevitable. But I think for my father it was harder. He viewed the United States as a country that helped Israel. So it was a political struggle for him. It was a matter of principle that his daughter was leaving this country to study in the U.S. Coming to terms with that was a huge adjustment.

In the end, we decided that I'd go with the idea to become a physician, and that I would return to Palestine after my education. Those were the conditions of my parents. They announced, "We'll allow you, our first daughter, to go to the United States on her own, at seventeen, only under the following terms: you will not return with a bachelor's in biology or chemistry, because you could always do that at Birzeit, and you will try to get into medical school." I agreed that I wouldn't leave for good. I would finish my education, no matter how long it took, and then I would come back and work here in Palestine.

All I knew about Earlham was that it was a small school, that I wouldn't have more than thirty or forty students in my classes, which was true. Except for introductory classes, I think most of my classes were like that. I think at seventeen you don't know what to expect out of college, and I soon learned that the school was extremely challenging. I worked really hard. But the social life was far better than I expected. The kindness of people on campus made me feel really cared for in a small setting. And Earlham was very pro-Palestinian. As a Quaker institution, they were very interested in educating Palestinians—they'd been giving scholarships to Palestinian students since 1948.

I took biology in the first year, under the assumption that I would be a pre-med student. But I was broken by the anatomy and physiology course. I just couldn't do it—the smell, the formaldehyde. I worked so hard, and I could barely break a C in the course.

And in the meantime, I was taking organic chemistry, and I was practically sleeping through the course and I was getting an A, you know? And that's when things kind of shifted. I had a great organic chemistry professor, who's still my friend and colleague, and I decided to become a chemist. And I thought, "Well, I'll get a Ph.D. instead of an M.D." And I wanted to work in the pharmaceutical industry. That part really enticed me—the idea of *creating* things.

By the end of my undergrad experience, I felt very much at home at Earlham, and I do think those were the best four years of my entire time in the United States. You know, the one thing that fascinated me the most in living in the United States was the ability to *drive anywhere*. I was *in love* with the concept of a road trip. I learned driving just to be able to drive out for endless hours, because it was mind-boggling to me that I could cross state lines and be in Tennessee for a couple of hours, and on the same day drive back to Indiana, no problem! That was new to me, and I loved traveling, even after starting my Ph.D. program.

I did my Ph.D. in medicinal organic chemistry at the University of Tennessee, and I learned to do computer-based drug design and discovery, which was the latest form of medicinal chemistry. I learned to design compounds by modeling enzymes on a computer. I worked with a team that researched anti-HIV compounds.

I considered staying in the U.S. When you're in graduate school and doing research, all you see as important is the science that you're doing. And you don't have a concept or understanding of what life really is, right? Because for a scientist, life exists within the walls of the lab, and the library, and on your computer. And so for a while I really thought that I should stay for a post-doc there. But my parents weren't willing to live through another year of not having their children around. They were really adamant that we should all finish and return as soon as we were done. So an opportunity arose in Ramallah at a research company called Pharmacare, and it sounded interesting enough. Also, I thought, *If I'm willing to try living in the United States and adjust to its cultural values—the way it works, its social structure, everything—then why not give this chance to Palestine itself?*

So after my Ph.D. program I returned to Palestine around 2008 and began researching the antioxidant activity of Palestinian plants with Pharmacare. It was part of a project where we were looking for anti-cancer compounds. I looked into traditional Palestinian medicines for new compounds. I worked with herbalists throughout the West Bank. We started the lab from scratch. But I was more interested in the antioxidant activity of potential cosmetic products. I've always been interested in skin care, and during this time I started to think about starting my own company.

THERE'S A RHYTHM IN PALESTINE THAT REALLY GETS UNDER YOUR SKIN

Once you go to graduate school abroad, it's an entirely different experience living in Palestine. Believe it or not, the culture shock was easier to get over going to Earlham from Palestine than the culture shock that I faced coming back after almost eleven years of being away.

I can't exactly pinpoint what the reasons are for the difficulty. I think one of them is that I spent eleven years on my own, in a country that's fairly free and accepts anything and everything. And I learned to think for myself, learned to accept people for what they are and who they are, and not judge them for what they think or what they look like or what they believe. And I came back to a country that's fairly systematic. There's a specific, almost rigid, structure in society here that you have to fit into.

Beyond that, there was a huge shift in society that I didn't know about. Palestine was a different place when I returned. I had missed the entire Second Intifada. I was gone eleven years. My Ph.D. took six and a half, so for around seven years I didn't come back. I *couldn't*. Because I wasn't able to travel home and leave a chemistry experiment running and come back to it a month later—that just sets you behind. I was in the lab all day and all night most of the week.

And then I came back here to Palestine, and I had social obligations and family obligations, and I was no longer able to read in my free time. Even the way I dressed had to change. So it was very difficult at the beginning.

But even in those early days back, I felt like Ramallah had a way of making me feel comfortable. And it's not just the city—it's the people. There's a rhythm in Palestine. Every country has its own rhythm, but there's a rhythm in Palestine that really gets under your skin, even with all the difficulty of travel, with all the difficulty of being stuck on the road in traffic. There's something that just gets under your skin, and it's very difficult to leave, once you start to get settled in here.

I also finally found old friends, and a lot of my friends were going through the same difficulties. They'd been gone for a while, they were educated outside, whether in France or England or the U.S., and had returned. So we had something in common, and a common language, and that's kind of what's got me slowly coming back into living here.

OUR FIRST CLASS

I worked for Pharmacare for two years, until around 2010. But there were several reasons why I thought it was not the right place. I was spending my entire time in a lab with only one other person, and I realized more and more that I was a people person, and I wanted to work with people. And what does a Ph.D. do with people, other than teach, right? When I was nineteen years old, my undergraduate adviser—the organic chemistry professor I had—told me that I would end up in teaching, and I thought he just didn't know me. He said that I had it in me.

So in 2010, I applied to Al-Quds University and Birzeit University for teaching positions.[10] Al-Quds had recently developed a relationship with Bard College in the U.S., where Bard would establish a liberal arts teacher-training study program within Al-Quds.[11] And Bard thought I was the perfect candidate to teach for them—I was a liberal arts college graduate. I would understand the concepts and the teaching methods of liberal arts education.

Originally, it was a part-time position for a semester, so I only taught one class. After that first semester, Al-Quds and Bard immediately offered me a full-time position. They kind of took me in. They didn't care that I didn't have an extensive publication history or anything like that. It wasn't an old boys' club like Birzeit University.

I became a core faculty member and one of the founding faculty members. We had no program—only thirty students—and I remember running these internal transfer campaigns, where we encouraged students from Al-Quds University to give it a try for one semester. We basically opened it up for *everybody,* so good students and bad students were applying, and we accepted all of them just to be able to run a program. Then I started building the science program, and now we have the largest and most successful division in the entire college. Now I have sixty students who are hoping to complete their degree in either biology or chemistry right now. This year, at the end of June 2014, we were able to graduate our first class.

---

[10] Al-Quds is a university system with three campuses—one in Jerusalem, one in Abu Dis just outside of Jerusalem, and one in Al-Bireh, adjacent to Ramallah. The system currently serves over 13,000 undergraduates.

[11] Bard College is a liberal arts college in Dutchess County, New York, on the Hudson River. It serves just over 2,000 undergraduate students. Bard formed an alliance with Al-Quds University in 2009, with the idea of bringing training in liberal arts education to Palestine.

I WORE A HEADPIECE THAT'S 200 YEARS
OLD AND MADE OF GOLD LIRAS

In the spring of 2008, I met a man named Ahmad through a friend of mine who works with him in the municipal government. We saw each other occasionally for a year and a half, but I wouldn't say we were dating, really. I saw him once or twice, and I think we were both busy with our careers, and so it kind of just took its time.

We would send each other messages every now and then, check on each other. Then it took a more serious turn in the fall of 2010, in September. We started seeing each other among groups of friends so that we could keep it on the down-low, so no one would really catch who was dating whom.

Then in the end of December, we decided that we wanted to be together. He invited me to dinner on December 30 at his family's home. He said that after dinner he'd love to go to my parents' home—he wanted to meet them. From there, things developed really quickly. On Friday morning, New Year's Eve, he called me and he said that his older brother would like to talk to my father and that he'd like to make this official, which is the culturally correct way of doing things. And so they set a date to talk to my parents officially and ask for my hand in marriage.

The night of New Year's Eve, Ahmad surprised me by proposing in front of 360 guests at the Mövenpick Hotel New Year's Eve party.[12] So, by the next morning, the entire city knew that we were engaged!

It was right at the beginning of the second semester for me, so it was a little bit hard to think about getting married during the semester, but semesters at Al-Quds University are never properly planned, because

---

[12] The Mövenpick Hotel in Ramallah is part of a Swiss chain of international luxury hotels. The hotel in Ramallah was opened in the fall of 2010.

there are strikes, and there are closures and political reasons not to go to school. So we thought about April for a wedding date, and then it didn't work with one of his brothers, whose daughter was expecting a child, and they wanted to be with her when she had the child. We decided that it would have to pushed till June, but his mother was not willing to see that happen. She felt like she was old, and you never know what happens, and she wanted to be there for the wedding. And so we actually ended up getting married in March 2011, on a very cold, rainy day.

We had a full-on traditional Palestinian wedding. I wore a traditional dress, and I also wore a headpiece that's 200 years old and made of gold liras—*Ottoman* liras. The wedding party was a huge, there were over 700 guests. I should have known that my life would be loud after that. After the big wedding, we had a smaller wedding reception for the family and close friends.

Within less than a year, I went from being single and career-oriented to a wife, a pregnant woman, then a mother of two. I had my twins on November 10, 2011. I came from a small, nuclear family where everybody's educated, and we had a very quiet breakfast every Friday morning, and suddenly I shifted from *that* into this huge, clan-like family, with fifty brothers and sisters who are all married with children, whose children were having children. Life with my husband's family was loud and lively, and I learned how to cook for forty people—while pregnant. And I found myself completely entrenched in Palestinian life in a way I hadn't been before.

I DISCOVERED THE WRITER IN ME

My husband worked as the mayor of Ramallah's right-hand man. When we married, in a way, I thought I was marrying Ramallah. My friends actually nicknamed me "Lady Ramallah," because I was everywhere, I would go to all the cultural events, always out in the city.

When I finally got to know my husband's family well, I realized that I didn't marry the city, I married Abu Shusha and Zakariyya, which were the two villages that his parents had left in 1948. I suddenly found myself completely entrenched in Palestinian culture that I've only read about—the diaspora refugee culture. Now, my kids are descendants of refugees. It's been a total switch, for me. And it was more eye-opening to me—there's *real* suffering in Palestine, there's *real* heartbreak. And it's a lot more than what people think it is. When I began to see these things, that's when the writing happened.

In July 2010, Bard sent me to do this writing workshop called "Language and Thinking," which is part of our core program for all of our students, and all faculty from all fields are encouraged to teach the course. And that's where I discovered the writer in me. At the Bard workshop, I discovered how much I love human beings and that I like to learn from them. That is when I started to write in earnest. Before long I had started a blog about Palestine called *The Big Olive.*

I started it with a woman I met at a wedding named Tala. I met Tala exactly two weeks before I went to that writing workshop, so all these things started to come together at the same time. Initially, the blog was supposed to be about Ramallah and about my return to the city, and how the city helped me really adjust. But it became more about growing close to this big Palestinian family of my husband's as well.

Another reason I felt I needed to write about the real Palestine was that I was traveling a lot through the West Bank doing school recruitment. I spent a lot of time traveling to the campus Abu Dis near Jerusalem, visiting Bethlehem, going from checkpoint to checkpoint. The blog became a place where I could examine what it was like to live in this growing, cosmopolitan city—Ramallah—and then going out and observing a culture that you don't see within the city.

Back when I was living in the U.S., I used to get asked about life in Palestine quite a lot by my friends there. I would tell them to imagine that you are commuting from New York City to a small town in New Jersey, which should be an hour drive. But in order to get there, you can't take the regular highway, you have to take all these back roads. And even the back roads aren't all open, and at any point in time, any of the state police might stop you and ask you questions for an hour or more without giving any reason. Suddenly most of your day, most of your work, has been commuting home. It's exhausting. That's what living in Palestine is like, and that's what I wanted to capture in my blog.

I'd always tell my American friends, "You take your freedom to move too much for granted." Not that it's always easy in the States either. I remember being stuck in traffic going to JFK, on a visit I made to the States in 2010. I was trying to get to the airport to go back to Palestine, and I was really getting antsy. I was with my friend, and I said something like, "Oh my God, I'm going to miss my plane, and I can't understand this traffic." And my friend looked at me and said, "What do you *mean* you can't understand this traffic? You're the one who lives it *every day* in Palestine." But that's the thing—we take gridlock for granted in Palestine. It's possible to be surprised by terrible traffic in the United States. And so I think that's the difference between traveling here and there.

As Palestinians, we can't take any of our day-to-day plans for granted. I may plan to start my class at eleven o'clock, and on any day I could easily be fifteen minutes late, an hour late, no matter how early I left—for no reason other than a random pop-up checkpoint somewhere between home and school. There may not even be a tense situation or security reason for the pop-up checkpoint. It could be just because.

The stress of getting to work and then back home rules our lives. And now that I have children, I feel it's even further compounded. I *have* to get to daycare to get my children, and to bring them home so that I can have an hour with them during the week, so then I can put them to bed on time. And that's such a basic human want. That's something that working mothers all over the world have to worry about. But I have to worry about it several times over. Every day I have to figure out how I might improvise if I can't get to daycare to pick up my children on time.

This stress makes you age faster, I think. In certain areas of Palestine, you can cut the tension and serve it up on a platter. And it's because people are not able to be regular human beings, because they're completely controlled by these random blocks that will stop life from happening.

When I was pregnant, I constantly feared that my water would break in Qalandia and I'd be stuck.[13] I had twins who were breach, so there was no room for natural birth. They were breach sideways, and so there was no room for them to come out. I knew that. And so, the last time I drove, I was in week 32, about a week from giving birth. I went as far as making arrangements with a doctor in Bethlehem so that, should my water break, it would be easier to go to Bethlehem and give birth there than drive the few miles to my hospital. So I had a friend, and he agreed that he would have an ambulance on standby starting my week 32 in Bethlehem, which would come and pick me up at the drop of a hat and would take me right away to the French women's hospital in Bethlehem that's really, really good. He would also make sure that he was in contact with my OB/GYN, who could explain to him on the phone the details of my pregnancy. Every time That's an extreme example, but the truth is that every time I leave the house, I have to have contingency plans. I never know how long it might take to run simple errands.

If you're in much of the U.S., you're pregnant with twins, and you work an a few miles away from home and the hospital, you can get to any hospital at any time, no matter when your water breaks, no matter if your

---

[13] Qalandia is a town of over 25,000 people located between Ramallah and Jerusalem.

twins are breach, or both pointing downward with their heads and ready to be delivered naturally. You have that access. Here, you don't.

The only access from one city to the other is roads, and when those roads are blocked, then life stops. And that's how women end up giving birth at checkpoints. I wrote about giving birth at a checkpoint on my blog, and I was writing about my own fears. It was something that kept coming at me. And even when I was driving, I kept thinking, "What if I get stuck in this crazy traffic, and someone hits me, rear-ends me, and then I lose one of the babies because of the shock?"

For anyone who doesn't know the road Wadi Nar—actually, it's a little better now that the roads are a little bigger—but it's this winding, uphill road between Ramallah and the cities southeast of Jerusalem where trucks of all kinds and sizes and cars of all kinds and sizes are traveling two ways. There are no clear two lanes, and literally, when you are going up, if you look to your right, you're practically on the edge of a cliff. If your car gets hit, there's nowhere to go except down the valley.

I tell my friends that it's only by the grace of God that I make it from sunrise to sunset every day, and I go to Abu Dis, and I still have the energy to take care of two kids every day.

The only way for me to deal with this stress is to write. I've gotten such positive responses to the blog from everyone who reads it, but I'm not sure if I'm actually a good writer, or if people just want to be nice to me. And this is where one of my fears exists. It's not a fear, it's maybe that I'm not willing to believe that I'm good at something else other than science.

On the other hand, I found this open-armed place with this community where anything you write is up for discussion, and it's up for editing and up for improvement, and people are willing to read what you write. Because every time you write, you're putting yourself on that paper. And I'm always submitting pieces to a magazine called *This Week in Palestine*, or just putting work up on the blog, and thinking, *Dear God, please have mercy on me. There's a piece of me within those words. So don't let them batter it because it would break my heart.* And so I'm in between, as a writer, I'm still searching for the voice. I don't know what narrative I'm going to take, I don't know what I am trying, I don't even know what story I'm telling.

So I'm somewhere in between, and I'm still trying to find my voice. I'm not ready to give up science completely and become a writer, and just do writing. And at the same time, I can't just let the science take over, because I'm so extremely happy to finally have that part of me alive again.

ELI SETTLEMENT, WEST BANK

ASA EILAND

Security officer, 32

Born in Kfar Etzion, West Bank &

interviewed in Eli Settlement, West Bank

We first meet Asa Eiland, head of security of an Israeli settlement, in 2012 while on a United Nations–sponsored tour of freshwater springs in the West Bank. Much of the West Bank outside the valley of the Jordan River is arid, and the struggle for control over water resources is a major flashpoint in the tensions between Palestinians and Israeli settlers. At Ein Al-Arik, which is located halfway between the West Bank cities of Ramallah and Nablus, the springs have been developed into natural bathing pools and park by the nearby Eli settlement.[1]

As part of a group of journalists and NGO workers, we walk among olive trees on a sloping, rocky hillside while our guide tells us of the Palestinian villages cut off from the spring by its recent development by the settlement into a park. Soon an Israeli security truck pulls up, and Asa and one of his deputies get out to see what's going on. Before long, Asa and the head of a local Palestinian village are

---

[1] Today, Eli is a cooperatively-run settlement of nearly 4,000 people about thirty miles north of Jerusalem.

engaged in heated argument—the Palestinian man claims the lands where the springs reside belong to his family. After things calm down, we approach Asa and explain our work.

Later we meet Asa in his office, where he oversees security for Eli, a settlement laid out over eight hilltops twenty minutes north of Ramallah. His office is modest, without much more than a computer and some security monitoring equipment. He's not there very often. His real office is his truck, which he drives from neighborhood to neighborhood in the settlement. Asa takes us on a tour of Eli in his truck, showing us mountain views, soldier memorials, and Bnei David, a pre-army school that Eli is known for.[2] He also invites us to his home, a trailer he shares with his wife and two young children. The floor of his small living room is strewn with plastic toys, and one wall of the room is packed with books. During our conversation, Asa tells us of his family's history as some of the earliest settlers in the West Bank after the Six-Day War, his military service in Gaza, and his frustrations with the legal ambiguities of the small town he calls home.

"WE'RE ZIONISTS, WE'RE GOING TO ISRAEL"

I was born on a kibbutz in Kfar Etzion, south of Jerusalem in the West Bank, in 1982.[3] I have five siblings—two younger brothers and three older sisters. I'm the oldest boy. The kibbutz where I grew up was part of the only Jewish settlement that was demolished in the '48 war. The Jordanians and other Arabs conquered it in '48 and killed almost everyone.

---

[2] *Mechinot* are schools that prepare Israeli youth for military service. Instruction usually lasts for one year and focuses on religious study or secular citizenship issues, depending on the school. Bnei David was the first religious mechina and a model for others in the occupied territories.

[3] Kfar Etzion is a settlement of under 1,000 people located four miles south of Israel. A kibbutz (Israeli collective farming community) was built on the current location in 1927.

Then in 1967, a man who had been a child there and one of the few survivors of the '48 war came back and established a new settlement.[4]

My parents both grew up on the kibbutz. They weren't born on a kibbutz, though. All my family is originally from New York City and Long Island. My grandfather, my father's father, fought for the U.S. in World War II. He married my grandmother in 1950 and told her, "We're Zionists, we're going to Israel."[5] First they moved to Haifa.[6] My grandfather wanted to go into the army and build settlements, so that's what he did. My mother was from a very blue-collar family that lived in Haifa.

I was born in Kfar Etzion, but in 1986, when I was three and a half, my family moved to South Africa—to Mossel Bay.[7] We lived there in the apartheid days, and we had five helpers living in the house. I played soccer and learned about computers. I was a good student, a good kid. And then we returned to the kibbutz in 1989, when I was seven.

I remember being a kid on the kibbutz, and it was frightening. I couldn't go out of the house because of security problems.[8] Where we were, I could be kidnapped, I could be killed. So I'd go to school on an

---

[4] The kibbutz at Kfar Etzion was completely destroyed after a two-day battle during the Arab-Israeli War in 1948. The destruction of the village by Arab forces (in retaliation for the destruction of an Arab village), is memorialized throughout Israel. After the 1967 Six-Day War, a newly established Kfar Etzion was one of the first planned Israeli settlements in the occupied West Bank. The new community was led by Hanan Porat (1943–2011), a prominent settlement activist who, as a child, was one of four survivors of the original Kfar Etzion's destruction. For more on the wars of 1948 and 1967, see Appendix I, page 267.

[5] Zionism is the movement to create a Jewish homeland that led to the formation of Israel in 1948. For more information, see Appendix I, page 267.

[6] Haifa is the third largest city in Israel, with a population of over 1 million across the entire metropolitan area. The city is located on the northern coast about 100 miles northwest of Jerusalem.

[7] Mossel Bay is a coastal city of over 60,000 people located 250 miles east of Cape Town.

[8] During the First Intifada, the collection of settlements south of Jerusalem known as the Gush Etzion region (including Kfar Etzion) was a frequent target for Palestinian militias.

armored school bus, and then I'd head straight back home after school. To go visit friends in another settlement, we needed to make an appointment two weeks ahead for an armored escort—it was crazy.

But we had a nice home, a big home with a pool. My father is very intelligent, and he got into the computer business sometime in the early nineties, right around the time the Internet became popular. I learned about computers early, and as a thirteen-year-old, I wrote HTML—and that was when it had just been invented. As a teenager, I also taught computers to adults. I taught Excel, PowerPoint, Word.

I left school a year before graduating from high school, in eleventh grade, because I was bored. I felt like I was wasting my best years and I thought, *What am I doing now?* I have a problem with not doing anything. I like to be busy. So I dropped out. Then I came to Bnei David, the pre-army yeshiva here in Eli, studied here for a year, and then I joined the army.

ELI IS STILL NOT
LEGALLY RECOGNIZED BY ISRAEL

The settlement I came to for school, Eli, was established in 1986. Eli comprises eight separate hills. We're on top of a hill in the original part of the settlement that was established by twenty, thirty families.

Plans were made to settle the area in the late sixties, after the '67 war, and settlers started coming here in '76, something like that. Originally, the Israeli government planned a town of 100,000 people, and the first residents came from Shilo, just south of here.[9] Building Eli was all part of

---

[9] Shilo is a settlement a few miles east of Eli. Shilo was established in 1978 and has a population of nearly 2,500. It is located on a site of significant historical significance within Judaism. It was one of the first settlements constructed by the Gush Eminum movement to claim all of Judea and Samaria (the West Bank) for Israel. For more on Gush Eminum, see the Glossary, page 276.

the dream of many of us settlers to bring as many Jews as possible to this part of the West Bank—a million Jews to the West Bank. In the 1980s, the government of Israel tried to encourage people to move to this region by paying for homes, roads, everything.[10] And then in the mid-nineties the government stopped promoting settlement.[11] So Eli didn't grow as fast as its planners had originally hoped.

Bnei David was established in 1989 by a rabbi who wanted to make a new kind of school that would be a pre-army yeshiva.[12] The goal was that students would study the Torah to build themselves into better soldiers, better civilians, better people.

Bnei David was the first school like that. And now it's a revolution in the Zionist community. There are twenty mechinot that are religious like the one here in Eli, and there are twenty secular pre-army academies. I teach here at Bnei David, and I teach in Tel Aviv in a secular one. It's a revolution, definitely. And it started here in Eli. Most of the population of Eli today graduated from this yeshiva, and now we have high-ranked officers in the army who live here. Generals, major generals, we have lived and taught here. Plenty of them—ten, fifteen generals in a small town of almost 4,000 people, because of Bnei David.

But the problem we have in Eli is that the town is still not legally recognized yet by Israel. Or I should say, Eli was recognized by the state of Israel, but they didn't finish the process. They encouraged the settlement

---

[10] The number of Israeli settlers in the West Bank quadrupled between 1980 and 1983, from 8,000 to approximately 32,000. Expanded construction of settlements in the West Bank and Gaza was promoted by the government of Prime Minister Menachem Begin following the Camp David Accords and the peace agreements with Egypt, Israel's most powerful neighbor.

[11] The first Oslo Accord was signed in 1993 and slowed the building of settlements in the West Bank throughout the 1990s. For more on the Oslo Accords, see Appendix I, page 267.

[12] A *yeshiva* is a Jewish religious school dedicated to the study of the Talmud and Torah.

back in the eighties but haven't officially recognized the settlement following the agreements in the mid-nineties. The secretary of defense needs to sign an order to recognize us, but most of the secretaries of defense in the past twenty-five years have been too far left politically to acknowledge settlements like Eli.[13] That's one problem. The second problem—we live in a place that is in between two administrative areas. There are Areas A and B, which are supposed to be governed by the Palestinians, and Area C, which is for Israel and the settlers.[14] We're exactly in between. That means that land ownership and enforcement of the law in this area are very unsettled. That's an understatement.

For the Arabs here, there's no bookkeeping about who owns what land, and so a lot of Arabs make claims on land as personal property without having any records. No one knows the facts. They conquered this area, the Palestinians. But there are no books, we can't prove anything about land ownership, and they cannot prove anything, so it's starting to be problematic all over the area.

WHEN IT'S WAR, IT'S WAR. WHEN YOU'RE MORAL, YOU'RE MORAL.

After graduating from Bnei David, I joined the army. In 2001, when I started, the mandatory conscription was for three years.[15] I was in the

---

[13] The Israeli government officially recognizes over 120 settlements in the West Bank, and over 100 more have been established without formal recognition (and contravening Israeli law), but with support for infrastructure and security.

[14] For more on administrative Areas A, B, and C, see the Glossary, page 276.

[15] Israeli citizens (with some notable exceptions) are required to serve in the military, usually starting at age eighteen. For more information on the Israeli Defense Force, see the Glossary, page 276.

Golani Brigade.[16] And in Golani they have special units, and I was in a special unit that has expertise is demolition. I worked with explosives—RDX-10, C-4.[17] Our job was to demolish Palestinian bunkers and weapons caches throughout the Gaza Strip, in the West Bank, in Lebanon. Our unit could do crazy stuff with explosives. We could go into a building and blow up only one room without hurting the building, for instance. There were situations where we might find Palestinian explosives in a room and need to detonate them, but we didn't want to destroy the whole building. We'd have to make a hole in the wall and set up our explosives a certain way so the explosion was directed out of the building. It was very difficult. Sometimes it didn't go as planned, and the whole building would crash down. We tried to do our best so that nobody was hurt or killed.

The most difficult period of my service was fighting in the Gaza Strip in 2004 through 2005.[18] It was very extreme, very frightening there. Plenty of friends were injured, plenty of my fellow soldiers. In Gaza we were fighting mostly Hamas. But we couldn't always distinguish who was Hamas and who was not, and my soldiers and I had plenty of talks about how to be moral about war. Questions that you don't hear plenty of people ask. When it's war, it's war. When you're moral, you're moral. The two don't always go together. But we tried to ask the questions, *How do you do it? How do you act morally in this situation? If a child gets caught up in our operations, what would we do?*

---

[16] The Golani Brigade (also called the 1st Brigade) was responsible for major combat operations throughout the West Bank and Gaza during the Second Intifada and against Hezbollah during the Second Lebanon War. For more on the Intifadas, see the Glossary, page 267.

[17] RDX-10 and C-4 are both explosive compounds used commonly in warfare.

[18] Fighting throughout the Gaza Strip during the Second Intifada lasted until the unilateral withdrawal of Israeli security forces and settlements between August and September of 2005.

And it was so dangerous, too. I was shot at by Palestinians when I was a soldier, hitchhiking to the base. I was in a civilian car, driving to a base, and Palestinians ambushed us and shot at our car. I stopped the driver, and I ran after the two gunmen. We ended up capturing them, and they were sent to Damun Prison.[19]

When you join with a military force, you divide the world into the good guys and the bad guys. I've been there. That's how you educate soldiers. A soldier needs to know that he's good and the enemy's bad. If he thinks that he's maybe a little bad and the enemy's maybe a little good, then he's not a good soldier. That's the army world. But now I live in the civil world, a much more complicated world.

I'M MARRIED TO MY WIFE AND MY M-16

After the war, I came back to Eli and started teaching at Bnei David. Then I met my wife through a friend in 2007, and I knew right away I wanted to marry her. When my students ask me how you choose your wife, I tell them, "First of all, you need to have chemistry. And then you have to have the same ideas about what you want in life. Then you need to earn her— not *win* her—you need to change to be better to earn her."

When we met, my wife worked with handicapped adults. And when I saw how she treated them, I knew she was a good person, that she had a big heart. And I wanted a big-hearted wife. I told her, "You'll be my wife, now you just need to decide that I'll be your husband." And it happened. We were engaged half a year after we met and married in eight months. Our first child was born in 2009 and the second in 2011. Around the time my wife was pregnant with our second child I also started working as head of security in Eli.

---

[19] Damun Prison is a maximum-security prison camp near Haifa, in northern Israel.

I drive my truck a lot on the job. I have a knife, a Motorola, and my automatic M-16. I'm married to my wife and my M-16. It goes everywhere I go, 24/7.

As head of security of Eli, I have not had to shoot my rifle. And I don't want to. I know when to hide it and when to show it. The people of Eli all own a lot of weapons, mostly pistols. It's common. It's for their own security. But people are threatened here, you can't hide from the truth. It's not that people in Eli are feeling threatened, people *are* threatened. But many settlers don't know how to use their guns, which is dangerous.

There are areas where it's much more dangerous, and areas where there's less danger. Now, it's quiet. From 2001 till 2005, shootings in the roads in this part of the West Bank were common.[20] But in the past three years that I've had my job, there have been three shootings in the roads here. Still, we're surrounded by neighboring Palestinian villages, and each one has about 5,000 people. So we're surrounded by 12,000 or 15,000 Palestinians, and there's only 4,000 of us here in Eli.

Palestinians don't like us. The Islamic Palestinians are educated to kill us. I can show you television, children's television, educating children to kill as many Jews as they can. And when I see a Palestinian youth, I know that this kind of thinking is going through his mind.

When I have security situations, I'm very stressed. But I run and I swim. That's how I calm down. We live a regular life here in Eli, but we always carry something inside—fear. Because every night when I get a telephone call from my subordinates saying the radar system we use sees something weird, I jump. Because I can't stand the sight of a murdered family. You go from your town, the town next to you, and you're afraid that your wife and your kids will get hit by stones. It happens every day.

---

[20] This was the period of the Second Intifada. For more information on the Intifadas, see the Glossary, page 276.

And the Molotov cocktails thrown at cars—that happens once a week, every two weeks.

In the summer of 2010, I got a call that there was a fire just east of Eli. So I got my deputy and a couple of other guys, we called the army for security, and we went to put out the fire.

Palestinians from the village just east of here, Karyut, they had burned out one of my security cameras on the edge of Eli's jurisdiction.[21] I knew it was set on purpose, because it was started with a burning tire. Setting fire to tires and putting them by something else is a good way to burn something down, and something I've seen villagers do before. The wind was from west to east, the fire spread to an olive grove, and olive trees were burning. I had the phone number of the head of security of Karyut, and I speak a bit of Arabic. So I called him, and I told him there was a fire burning down Palestinian olive trees.

I decided to extinguish the fire in the olive grove myself. I don't like olive trees burning. We believe that the trees have a place in the world, that they're important. I don't like trees burning.

So the head of security in Karyut came, and he brought cameramen. I came with fire-extinguishing equipment, and he brought photographers. While we extinguished the fire in the olive grove, they photographed us. I took pictures of them taking pictures of me. It was crazy. He told me, "I am taking pictures to show how you are burning down our trees!" I put out the fire anyway, despite the Palestinians' accusations against me, because it was the right thing to do.

What I feel isn't anger. It's frustration. Yes, we all know there is a conflict. I'm not trying to hide the conflict. But there is a way to solve the conflict—that's through negotiation. You want to come and negotiate, come. You don't, pay the price.

---

[21] Karyut is a village of under 5,000 people located a mile east of Eli.

TO ME, "SETTLER" IS A GOOD WORD

We stay here despite the threat because of ideology. Zionist slash Jewish slash God—different sides of the same thing.

They kicked us out of Europe—thank you very much for kicking us out of Europe. We don't care who wants us and who doesn't. We decided, *We're here and you don't play around with people like us. We're here, and we're able to fight to stay here.* Last night I had a conflict with a Palestinian. And he told me, "Now you're strong, so you can kill us or whatever you want. But when we are strong, we'll kill you." I said, "Yeah, okay, so when you think you're strong enough, call me. In the meantime, I'm strong." That's an answer for people who understand power.

I feel powerful now. In the larger world, "settler" is not a good word when talking about the West Bank. But to me, the word "settler" is a very good word. I see a settler as a person who is trying to live with the land, to combine people and the land together in a positive way. We're trying to build, to grow here in Eli. We want to bring as many people as we can here. Plenty of the wives here work only part-time jobs, because the main goal is building a new generation. Now my wife is a social worker, working with kids, broken families, divorced parents, parents in prison. But it's only a part-time job. We want to grow our family.

I don't hate Arabs. I don't want to kill them, I don't want them dead. I'm not against them. The Jewish nation's place is here. I don't want a conflict with you. You can live here. You're invited. Meanwhile, there is a Palestinian state. In Jordan. We need to put everything in place. I don't want Egypt, I don't want Syria, I don't want to conquer Europe. We want our place. Mine. This small border, this is mine. Give me my place. I don't want your place.

I'M VERY OPTIMISTIC ABOUT LIFE

I hope that my kids will be much better than I am. I don't believe that I'm so good, but I pray that my kids will be much better than I am. Because the world is going forward. It's not going backwards. It's getting better and better every day. And I'm very optimistic about the future.

Today, I know how to control myself and my anger. I've worked on it the last few years by studying the Torah. Now I think of how to choose every minute of my life. I have responsibility for my feelings. I choose my feelings, I know how to control them. Because everything you feel, everything you do, you choose.

There is a national conflict, and I believe that is a moral conflict. I need to ask myself in what ways we are we acting immorally towards the Palestinians and try to fix that. And I know what apartheid is in South Africa—I lived there. The basics are very different. The English, French, and Dutch came to South Africa as conquerors, as imperialists, and conquered Africa—that's very different from what's happening here. To say that we are treating Palestinians like the South Africans—it's wrong, it's not happening here. In Israel, Israeli Arabs, they have full rights to do everything.

I don't believe that, as a whole, Arabs in Israel want to push all Jews into the sea. It's much more complicated than that. Whoever holds Islamic ideology definitely wants to kill all the Jews. They say it, loudly. You just have to listen. Read their books, their newspapers. Whoever embraces the Palestinian national identity, they want to kill us in a war. They say it. When they draw the map, they don't draw the '67 borders, they claim all of Israel.[22] They want everything. Haifa, Jerusalem, Tel Aviv, Jaffa.[23]

---

[22] The '67 borders are the borders demarcated by the Armistice Agreement of 1949, otherwise known as the Green Line.

[23] Haifa, Jerusalem, Tel Aviv, and Jaffa are Israel's major metropolitan areas.

I do not think that everything Israel does is moral. Definitely not. There are plenty of problems. There are plenty of moral problems, we are not as good as we want to be. We are far away from that. We have plenty of problems. My explanation for the problems is that we don't know yet who we are and what our goals are. We have problems with human rights with the Palestinians. And the extreme left wing wants to keep these problems in place, actually, so they can show we are not moral people, and the Jews are not as they say, as they want to be. So I try to fight that perception.

To build our identity as Jews in Israel, who we are, we have to start by asking questions. And we have to have problems to force us to ask questions. So, thank God we have the Palestinians. Thank God we have that problem, so we can ask ourselves who we are. It's more than useful. It's an integral part of who we are.

What is immoral about settlement buildings? The world expects the Jews to be more moral than others. When I educate, I explain that criticism comes out of a belief. When you criticize something or someone, you believe they can change. If you don't care about someone, you don't criticize them. The world is looking up to the Jewish nation and the Jewish community and the Jewish country because they believe there is something different here.

KUFR MALEK, WEST BANK

EBTIHAJ BE'ERAT

Homemaker, 52
Born in Kufr Malek, West Bank &
interviewed in Kufr Malek, West Bank

*We first visit Ebtihaj Be'erat at her house in the hilltop village of Kufr Malek in
2010. Her house is easy to find: a giant banner in honor of her son, Abdul Aziz,
hangs against a whitewashed wall above red geraniums. Two years before, just up
the road from the house, Abdul Aziz was shot and killed by Israeli soldiers. Inside
the house, there is a room devoted to him, with pictures and plaques on the walls
and more pictures piled on the floor.*

*Ebtihaj is a warm woman with deep dimples that appear when she smiles.
Her name, in fact, means* joy. *Yet, the death of her son is clearly still part of her
everyday life. As we ask her about her childhood in Kufr Malek, her experiences
during the First Intifada, and her family tree, her answers circle back again and
again to the loss of her son and the day he was shot. Still, evidence of her five other
children also covers the walls: photos of them dancing in a well-known dance troupe,
framed university degrees, and various awards. Throughout our interview, her house
is bustling with family members and neighbors coming and going. And although she*

downplays her skill as a host, she offers us an impressive spread of food, including homemade bread, jam, pickles, as well as local eggs and herbs.

When we come back to the house two years later, the banner honoring Abdul Aziz has been moved further up the street to the place where he died. Ebtihaj is now able to tell the story of his death without being completely overcome with grief, and she's more willing to talk about the life that continues in his absence. Besides telling us of her son, Ebtihaj shares stories about the changes she remembers in her home village since the Six-Day War in 1967, a conflict that led to Israel's occupation of the West Bank, which continues to the present day. Though Ebtihaj and her family had the opportunity to join the hundreds of thousands of Palestinians who emigrated from the West Bank following the Six-Day War, she decided to stay in Kufr Malek and raise her children in a Palestinian community.

OUR WEDDING PARTIES
ARE THE MOST BEAUTIFUL

My name is Ebtihaj, and I'm from Kufr Malek, which is a very social village where everyone knows everyone else.[1] I was born in the spring of 1962.

All my family is from the village. My grandfather and my great-grandfather were born here. The people of this village have always been known for their hospitality, and anyone who comes to Kufr Malek loves it here. It's beautiful. We receive visitors with hospitality, male or female. We're more moderate than some nearby villages. We're more civilized. We're not like the other villages where a man can't enter a woman's house when she's alone. Our wedding parties are the most beautiful in the area because all of us wear traditional dresses, even the small girls.[2] Also,

---

[1] Kufr Malek is a village of about 3,000 people located nine miles northeast of Ramallah.

[2] Traditional Palestinian wedding dresses can be elaborate and costly to produce, and are often paid for by the groom's family as a show of status.

many people in our village have lived in Latin America, so they can speak Spanish. I don't know the exact numbers, but approximately 20 to 40 percent of the people born in this village are living at the moment in Colombia and Brazil. A number of families emigrated during the First Intifada, but they come back for visits.

I was the sixth of seven children. I have four sisters and two brothers. My father worked for the post office in the village. It was his job to go to Ramallah and pick up the mail, and then to deliver it to everyone in the village. He also had a second job as a butcher in the market. When I was a young child, Kufr Malek was surrounded by farms. Many villagers had farms on top of Fasur Hill behind the village, and many farmers grew grapes.

Then in 1967, Israeli soldiers invaded the town.[3] I remember fleeing with all the other villagers to a grove of almond trees. Some villagers fled to their fields. My family lived under almond trees for two weeks while the war was going on, and I remember we each had a ration of food to last us—just enough food and water to last two weeks.

Later that year, the Israeli military moved in and built a base on top of the hill. They cleared a lot of the farms on the hill and demolished the homes of some farmers as well. Fasur Hill, where our village is located, is the highest hill in the West Bank, and the Israeli military usually build their bases at the highest places so they can survey the land below.

We got used to seeing soldiers in the village. There weren't any Jordanian policeman anymore, just Israeli soldiers. We got used to hearing about homes being raided as well. Soldiers would take men and boys in the middle of the night, from young children to the oldest men. Sometimes they'd arrest someone every month or two, sometimes it seemed like every

---

[3] 1967 was the year of the Six-Day War that culminated in Israel seizing all of the West Bank from Jordan. For more on the Six-Day War, see Appendix I, page 267.

night. Checkpoints were set up, so we couldn't travel to the top of the hill anymore, where the base was, and there was only one entrance into and out of the village. Sometimes, depending on what was happening in Palestine, they would set up a checkpoint at the main entrance of the village, and they wouldn't allow anyone to enter or leave except to go to neighboring villages. Even when someone was sick, or even if a pregnant woman was having a baby, they'd go to Taybeh, the next village, instead of to the hospital in Ramallah because when the soldiers set up the checkpoint, they wouldn't allow even the sick people to leave.[4]

I met my husband when I was very young, when I was fifteen years old and he was twenty. He fell in love with me. He's my cousin, a relative from my mother's side.[5] We were engaged that same year, and we married when I was seventeen. Nowadays, it doesn't happen like that. Mostly now, women wait until they finish school and then they get married. I was sad because I wanted to finish my studies. But my father told me, "No, you have to get married." I didn't even finish high school.

I moved into my in-laws' home right after our marriage in 1979. Before the war in 1967, my husband's family had farmed at the top of Fasur Hill. After the war, soldiers ordered his family out of their home and blew it up, so they came to live in the village. When I married my husband, he was still a farmer and also worked as a stone cutter.

In 1980 we had our first child, my daughter Maysa, when I was eighteen. By then I'd settled into my husband's home as a housewife. I did the housework along with my mother- and sisters-in-law, I cooked, and if any visitors came, I welcomed them. Over the next few years I had two more daughters and a son—Haifa, Rafa, and Fadi. Every day I would cook

---

[4] Taybeh is a neighboring Christian village of 1,500 people about one mile away from Kufr Malek. It's locally famous for a brewery that makes Palestine's only beer.

[5] Marriage between cousins was once considered an ideal match in Palestine, especially in rural areas.

lunch for my children and for my husband. I'd buy my own groceries. And I'd tend to the garden—we planted mint, fruit. During Eid, I'd make cookies, you know, *ma'amoul.*[6] Everyone would ask for them.

During this time, in the early eighties, many villagers were leaving to live abroad. I had two older brothers and an older sister get visas to work in the United States, and my brothers encouraged our family to fill out the paperwork to do the same. There was more opportunity to work there, and more freedom. In the U.S. we wouldn't have to worry about soldiers coming to our house. So we filled out the paperwork and applied, and when we didn't get a visa the first year, we kept reapplying every year. Finally, in 1986, my family was granted visas to live in the United States. But by this time, I had three daughters, and I wasn't sure I wanted to raise them in America. My sister had brought two daughters to the U.S., and they had ended up marrying foreigners. I wanted my daughters to grow up and marry Palestinians—hopefully, young men from the village. So we reconsidered it and decided to stay. My husband found work as a taxi driver in Ramallah, so he was able to support our family.

THE SOLDIERS FORBADE
US TO LIGHT CANDLES

I gave birth to my middle son, Abdul Aziz, on December 7, 1987, in Ramallah, when the First Intifada had just broken out.[7] He was born nine pounds, blond, and with green eyes. The nurse who was on shift, she

---

[6] *Ma'amoul* are shortbread pastries filled with dates or nuts and pressed in a wooden mold with an intricate design, and are commonly made during Eid Al-Fitr and Eid Al-Adha, the major Muslim holidays. Palestinian Christians also make them for Easter.

[7] The protests, clashes with Israeli military, boycotts, and other acts of civil disobedience that marked the beginning of the First Intifada started in December 1987. Most of the organized action began on December 9, two days after Abdul Aziz's birth. For more information, see Appendix I, page 267.

held him and said to everyone, "Come and see the child from Kufr Malek. He is so beautiful." I named him Abdul Aziz after his grandfather—his father's father.

When I got out of the hospital, Israeli soldiers were closing the shops because they said that the Intifada was moving from Gaza to the West Bank. I couldn't even find a pharmacy to buy vitamins or a bottle, the basic things we needed with a new baby in the house.

The soldiers imposed a curfew, and it was forbidden for anyone to be outside, even in our own yards, for over a month. We had to stay inside our houses, and we couldn't even open a window to look outside. The soldiers even forbade us to light candles. If they saw the light of a candle in a house, they would come and break the windows. During this time we ate mostly bread, olive oil, and *za'atar*.[8] When we were able to find other kinds of food, my mother-in-law would have to hide it well in the house, because if soldiers searched our home, they would know we had broken curfew if we had fresh food.

All the men in town had left the houses, because if the soldiers came in and saw a man in the house, they would beat him so badly. So all the men stayed in the fields, and sometimes they would go to Ramallah to look for food. During the night, they'd sneak home with food and basic supplies like sugar, and then go back to the fields.

My house is in the center of the city, so the soldiers would come often. Once, when my Abdul Aziz was two months old, I was sitting outside with him because I was cleaning the bread oven. My mother-in-law was at a neighbor's house and my husband was in the fields. A few soldiers saw me from the street, and they chased me into my house. I ran into the kitchen where the rest of my children were at the time—I was holding

---

[8] *Za'atar is* the name of both a spice similar to thyme that grows wild in Palestine and a blend of spices. Za'atar is a staple of local cooking in Palestine and much of the Middle East.

Abdul Aziz in my arms. The soldiers had these batons, and one soldier tried to hit me with one. I moved my head just in time to avoid the blow, and he struck the refrigerator instead. But he was aiming for my head. Abdul Aziz started to cry, and I think that made the soldiers back off. My son protected me.

Then the soldiers closed the kitchen door on me and locked me inside with my children. They left the key on the outside of the door, and we were locked in the kitchen for around two hours until my mother-in-law came back. At that time, there weren't any mobile phones like today. If my mother-in-law hadn't been at the neighbor's house, she would have been with me inside, and who knows how long it would have been before someone unlocked the door. When she returned and let me out of the kitchen, I just collapsed. I was so scared, I fainted. She didn't know what to do, and there wasn't any way to call a doctor or nurse. So she got the idea of throwing open all the windows and turning on a lamp in the window. It attracted the attention of the soldiers, and when more came to see what was going on, she begged them to get me a nurse or doctor. That was the only way she had to get me medical attention.

I believe Abdul Aziz always remembered that day. He had an image of it burned in his mind. At two months, he was too young to form memories. But the memory was like an inspiration from God, at least that's what I think.

WHAT HE FELT THROUGH THE STONE

As a child, Abdul Aziz was unique. There wasn't anyone like him. He was kind and beautiful. Abdul Aziz had a lot of friends, and he was a leader among them from a young age. Part of it was that he was just so affectionate and generous. I remember he used to come up to me when I was washing dishes or something and give me a big hug. He was the same way with his friends. If one of his friends mentioned that he saw a shirt in the market that he wanted, Abdul Aziz would save his money until he could buy the shirt for his friend. I had another child, Muhammed, in 1990, and Muhammed always looked up to Abdul Aziz.

Abdul Aziz was thirteen at the start of the Second Intifada in 2000. During the Second Intifada, the Israeli military closed the village for a month, and there was a curfew, so you couldn't go outside your own house. They even cut the electricity and water for a month. When the soldiers came, we'd close everything, all the windows, and we'd stay inside. I can remember two occasions when we forgot to close a window, and tear gas got inside the home. We felt like we were suffocating.

Abdul Aziz was born when the First Intifada started, so it was in his blood to be active.[9] But Abdul Aziz wasn't political. He wore one bracelet that said "Fatah," another one that said "PFLP," and another one that said "Hamas," all together on one hand.[10] I used to ask him, "Which one are you?" He'd say, "I'm Palestinian." That's another reason why everyone loved him.

Ever since he was a kid, he always talked about how much he wanted to throw stones at the jeeps and tanks when they passed our house, to drive them away. The kids don't have any weapons to defend their country, they only have stones—a stone versus a tank.

I knew my son loved to throw stones at soldiers when they came at night, and I knew that he was in danger. The soldiers arrested so many teenagers and they injured others. My cousin is now spending twenty-five years in jail for throwing stones, and another one was put in jail for fifteen

---

[9] Saying someone is "active" is shorthand for saying the person is involved in resisting the Israeli occupation. It can mean anything from organizing, to going to protests, to throwing stones, to more militant activity.

[10] Fatah, PFLP, and Hamas are political parties within Palestine. For more information, see the Glossary, page 276.

years. One of my neighbors has been in jail for eighteen years now, just for throwing stones at the soldiers.

The soldiers usually come into the village at two or three a.m. That is their normal time. Every time they enter the village, the youth have an agreement to start whistling to let everyone know. It's a signal for others when they are on the streets to go back home so the soldiers don't catch them and beat them. I'm always so afraid whenever I start to hear whistling.

There were many nights when I would hear whistling, wake up, and put on my clothes to go out and search for Abdul Aziz. I would go to his friends and ask them where he was. When Abdul Aziz came home in the early morning, I'd go hug him as soon as I saw him on the stairs outside of the house and tell him, "Thank God, you're okay and nothing has happened to you." I would make him sit and talk to me because he wouldn't listen. I used to tell him, "When the soldiers come, they have armor, they have weapons, and they are much stronger than us." I asked him if throwing stones would make them leave the village. He always said, "This is our village. Why did they come to our village?" I would ask him, "Can you forbid the soldiers or the tanks from coming into the village?" I would tell him that if they killed him, I would go crazy. He would say that if a patrol came into the village and he didn't throw a stone at it, it would hurt his conscience. He wanted to protect his country. He wanted to express what he felt through the stone, that this is our country not theirs. I was angry with him because I knew that something bad would happen to him.

Once, I left the house and all my neighbors were asking me, "Where are you going? The patrol is near." And I told them, "Let them shoot me. I want to go find Abdul Aziz." He was at the neighbor's house. I stood in the street and called to him, and I told him, "If you don't come to the house now, I will go to the patrol and make them shoot me." If they saw anyone at night in the village, there was a chance they would shoot. It didn't matter whether it was a woman or a man. He told me, "I'm coming, I'm coming," and he came back with me. We snuck home safely. He came back with me, but when I went to sleep, he snuck out again.

WHY DO YOU THINK
EVERYONE WANTS PALESTINE?

It was difficult living in Kufr Malek during the Second Intifada. I was so worried about my children. But still, I wasn't tempted to move.

In the summer of 2002, I visited my older brothers, who were still in the United States. They'd been there since the early 1980s and were living in Chicago. I loved America, I loved the people there. I liked how organized everything was in the city. In general, the people were welcoming to me. My brothers' neighbors were very nice. And people are free there. You don't have soldiers coming into your house at two a.m. and ordering you out into the streets. But Palestine is so beautiful—why do you think everyone wants Palestine? When I was in Chicago, I remember telling my brother, "I like America, but I haven't seen anything in the U.S. that I like as much as sitting on the front steps of my own home when there's a breeze, or being able to go into the yard and pick fresh grapes and figs." So my brother went out and bought me some grapes and figs, all the things I had named. But they didn't taste the same to me. I didn't like the grapes at all! Everything was imported, nothing fresh. I was supposed to stay in Chicago for four months, but I could only make it for a month and a half. I was homesick, and also, it was so hot!

A few years later, in 2006, my husband ended up going to the States to work with some family and neighbors who had a store in Miami. My husband would ask a lot about Abdul Aziz when he called home. He didn't ask about the other sons as much as he asked about Abdul

Aziz. He was worried. When he talked to Abdul Aziz on the phone, my husband would preach to him, "Calm down, don't throw stones."

It was hard to be alone with my children, but by that time my sons were all grown-ups and they were working. Only Abdul Aziz and Muhammed, the youngest, were still at school, and my three daughters were already married. Abdul Aziz finished high school in 2007, did the *tawjihi* exams,[11] and wanted to apply for Al Quds Open University.[12] He didn't like school so much, but he liked everything else: soccer, *dabka*,[13] and all his other after-school activities. After the *tawjihi*, he spent one year not studying, but he wanted to eventually study business—I have a cousin who runs a supermarket, and Abdul Aziz spent a lot of afternoons helping him out there, learning about how to run a small business.

I FELT I WOULD LOSE HIM SOMEDAY

Abdul Aziz was a soccer player, and he was the goalkeeper for the Ramallah team. He was also a coach in Kufr Malek for younger boys. In early October 2008, he was twenty years old and getting his passport ready, because his team had an opportunity to go play in Europe.

During that time, Abdul Aziz was still going out every night to be with his friends. On the night of October 16, I went to sleep at around eleven-thirty. Abdul Aziz called at one a.m. He had a habit of asking me when I answered the phone, "How are you, Ma?"

I told him, "I'm going to sleep now. Do you need anything?" He told

---

[11] The *tawjihi* is an exit exam for high school.

[12] Al-Quds Open University is a distance-learning university system with campuses in the West Bank, Gaza, Saudi Arabia, and the United Arab Emirates. There is also a separate university system in the West Bank called Al-Quds University, which isn't affiliated with the Open University.

[13] *Dabka* is a traditional Palestinian dance.

me, "I'm coming with friends, so please make us some dinner to eat." I told him, "I don't sleep very well because of you, and you want me to prepare dinner for you now?" So he asked me to speak with Muhammed, and he told his younger brother to prepare dinner for him, all his favorite things. My room is just beside the kitchen, so when Abdul Aziz came back with his friends, he'd close the door so they wouldn't bother me, and they'd sit outside to eat dinner.

Still, that night I heard him come in with his friends, so I got up and put on my dress. I looked at him through the door eating dinner with his friends outside. I looked at my watch, and it was around three a.m. I thought, *It's late. Abdul Aziz won't go out again. His friends will leave, and he'll go to sleep in his room.* And because I was comfortable that Abdul Aziz was at home, I went back to bed.

Not long afterward, I woke up again and opened the window. Although it was October, it was still hot. When I opened the window, I realized my son Muhammed was outside, crying and calling for a car. He told me that there had been a shooting. I went to Abdul Aziz's room and saw that he wasn't there. I put on my clothes and started screaming that Abdul Aziz had died. I knew then. I felt it immediately that he was dead. My heart dropped.

I went to our neighbors' house. I told Abu Adel, our neighbor, that Abdul Aziz died. He told me no, but I insisted that he was the one that had been shot. I told his son to take me to the hospital because he had a car, but he reassured me that it wasn't Abdul Aziz who was injured. But I insisted. I asked for a car to take me to the hospital where my son was. I wanted to be with my son. That was that. My son Fadi showed up at the house, and he and Muhammed tried to comfort me and told me it wasn't Abdul Aziz. I told them, "No, it is your brother. It is Abdul Aziz." They told me that Abdul Aziz was with his friends, and I told them that if that was so, to bring him to me. Then some of Abdul Aziz's friends came and told me that he'd run away with some of the others. I asked if there were any more soldiers in the village, and they told me there was a patrol nearby. And so I asked them, "Why did Abdul Aziz run away? Abdul Aziz doesn't run away if there's a soldier in the village, so I don't believe you."

When my three daughters heard that someone had been killed, they came running to my house with their husbands, asking, "Where is he?" They too felt that it was Abdul Aziz who had been killed. The women from our neighborhood came to my house for an hour and tried to calm me down, to tell me that it wasn't Abdul Aziz, or that he was just injured. I told them, "No, it is Abdul Aziz. I know that he is dead." Then finally someone else from the village came to the house and told me, "The thing that you've suspected is true." She had witnessed the scene.

In a few moments, a huge crowd showed up at the house, and they were all crying because they loved Abdul Aziz, and he was not there anymore. No one would take me to see him at the hospital because they felt it would be a shock for me. Finally, at around ten a.m., the Red Crescent ambulance brought his body back to the house.[14]

I learned the story from Abdul Aziz's friends who had been with him that night. They said that after I went to sleep, Abdul Aziz got a phone call from a friend who told him that a patrol of soldiers was coming. Abdul Aziz used to stand on a particular roof and throw stones from there, so that's where they both went to wait for the soldiers. But on this night, the soldiers were down below in the garden hiding between the trees, waiting for him. He was with his friend on the roof, and when they threw the first stone, the soldiers opened fire on them. His friend was shot in the shoulder, and Abdul Aziz was shot in the leg.

Abdul Aziz's friend told him, "We're being ambushed! Let's hand ourselves over to the soldiers." Abdul Aziz's reply was, "I would rather

[14] For more on the Red Cross and Red Crescent, see the Glossary, page 276.

die than hand myself over." Because Abdul Aziz was injured in his leg, he couldn't run, but his friend was able to run away. He wanted to help Abdul Aziz, but he couldn't. So Abdul Aziz told him, "Go, as far as you can. It's okay for me to stay." According to his friends, when the soldiers came up to the roof and saw that it was Abdul Aziz, they kept him there.

The bullet had entered the back of his left leg and come out the front. They left him to bleed, and they wouldn't allow a doctor to see him. They surrounded the area, and only after he died did they let the Red Crescent ambulance come and take him. The neighbors all came outside to check on him, to help him, but the soldiers told them, "If you come near us, we will shoot you, too."

He didn't die among his family or his friends. That's what hurts me the most. That's the most painful thing. The soldiers handed him over to the ambulance with the cuffs on his hands.

The day after Abdul Aziz died, my husband was in a café in Miami, playing cards. A relative had gone there to tell him the news, but before he even said anything, my husband saw the look in his eyes and told him, "Stop. I know Abdul Aziz just died." He came back to Palestine as soon as he could—he was home within two weeks. For two days after he returned, I couldn't speak to my husband. He did all the talking. And then he decided to stay in Kufr Malek.

The boy who was with Abdul Aziz survived. He's married now, and his wife is pregnant. That night he ran away, he was treated for his injury, and he was arrested and put in jail for two years. Many of his other friends have been arrested since. They were brought to trial on some made-up charges and all sentenced to five and a half years. I wish they had arrested Abdul Aziz and not killed him.

It was what God wanted. I always advised my son to stay at home, not to endanger himself. I would tell him that I felt I would lose him someday. Two weeks before his death, Abdul Aziz was with his friends in a car and he was hanging out the window. It was the night of Eid. And the guys told him, "Come inside, you don't want to get killed on a holy night." He told them, "I won't be killed. I won't die like this. I will die a martyr." He knew.

I'VE DECIDED TO LIVE

If you ask anyone in the village, they can tell you about Abdul Aziz. The day he died, seven satellite channels came to the village here to document what was going on. When they brought him in the hearse, there were hundreds of cars following behind. His funeral was so big. I didn't expect so many people.

After a death, we have three days for people to come and pay their respects. Three days after Abdul Aziz died, his friends from all over came to the house and called me to go outside. We have a tradition where you kiss a person's hand and hold it to your own forehead as a sign of respect. One by one, they all kissed my hand, held it to their foreheads, and told me they were my sons now instead of Abdul Aziz. Even now, they always come visit me, and I go visit them. There was also a bus of girls who were friends of Abdul Aziz from the *dabka* team, and they came crying and searching for Abdul Aziz's mother.

They even put a tent near the hall in the village center, and thousands of people came. The student senate at Birzeit University suspended classes because of Abul Aziz's death.[15] Usually they don't suspend classes if someone dies, not even a student at the university. But everyone knew Abdul Aziz, even the teachers, and they put up posters with his photo inside the university. One year after his death, one of his friends had to

---

[15] Birzeit University is one of the most prestigious universities in Palestine. It's located just outside Ramallah, not far from Kufr Malek.

present his graduation thesis, and he invited me to come. I went to the university and everyone, all the students were saying, "That's Abdul Aziz's mother. That's Abdul Aziz's mother." I didn't know what to do—to cry, or to feel proud, or to smile.

Even now, when I walk through the village, I feel so proud that my son was Abdul Aziz. Even the small children know that I'm Abdul Aziz's mother, and they always point me out. Two of my daughters have sons named Abdul Aziz now. All my children, when they have a boy, they want to call him Abdul Aziz after their brother.

When someone loses a son, what do you expect? I raised him for twenty-one years, and I used to look at him when he went out and think to myself, *Is it possible that this is my son?* And I lost him overnight. And he was so beautiful, my son. He is now with his God in heaven. He was beautiful. Whenever I go outside now, there's a banner with his photo on it hanging in the place where he died. Whenever I see it, I feel guilty because I couldn't hold him and hug him during the last minutes before he died.

After he died, life was complicated. For one whole year, I didn't sleep at night. For three years after my son's death, I was always sick and nervous, and the doctor used to give me sedatives. I drove everyone crazy after his death, especially at two or three a.m. It's the time when Abdul Aziz died, and I would always be awake then. I'd wake up and feel like I needed to leave the house. I either went to one of my daughters' houses or even my cousins, and I drove everyone around me crazy. I was so tired, and my daughters were so worried about me. I used to go to them so tired, and they'd take me to the doctor to give me shots.

Because I was grieving, my blood pressure got high. Once, I went to the doctor, and he found my blood pressure to be at very dangerous levels. He told me, "You will have a heart attack if you stay like this." It was so scary. For three whole years, they gave me sedative shots, sometimes every day and sometimes twice a week. I thank God because even the doctors told me to thank God that I was still alive.

Since Abdul Aziz died, I stopped doing embroidery. I used to make traditional dresses, but now I've stopped. I've cried a lot, and my vision has deteriorated from the tears. I cry every day for Abdul Aziz. I wear glasses now. I don't see 100 percent, and I need good vision to embroider. I used to sell the dresses to help my husband, as our financial situation now is very hard. My younger son, Mohammad, studies journalism at Birzeit University. He wants to continue and get his master's, and Birzeit University is more expensive than the other universities. My husband only works as a taxi driver. Even the taxi that he drives belongs to someone else. He only covers the university tuition and Muhammed's daily expenses. I can't ask my other son for help because he wants to build his future. My oldest son is twenty-nine years old and a teacher. Now he should start building a new house, but there are no good jobs.[16] He wants to get married, but it all depends on the money.

My second daughter once came and told me that Abdul Aziz is alive. In Islam, in our religion, we consider martyrs to be alive in heaven. She told me, "You are crying every day for Abdul Aziz, and he's only one person, and he's alive with God." She told me that there are fifteen people in our family, including the cousins and the grandchildren. She asked, "Do you want to die and leave us all too?" Since then, I've decided to live my life for my daughters and sons who are still alive, and my grief is only in my heart now.

Nothing is more precious than a child and a son. But I have two other sons, and I want to live for them. Every day, I suffer, I cry, but I don't let anyone know about it. Sometimes, one of my daughters comes and sees

---

[16] In Palestine, it's customary for men to build or own their own houses before proposing marriage.

my eyes are red and asks me if I was crying, and I deny it and say, "No, why would I cry?" I do it to make them feel stronger because they were affected by the death of their brother also. It's been four years now, and I feel every day that it was like yesterday, and I always see him and always remember him. In Palestine, we often say that a problem starts so heavy and then starts to be dismantled and disappear. But this stays. It's not fading. I am honored that my son is a hero who defended his land. He defended his country and his village. But Abdul Aziz is enough. Abdul Aziz is enough. I don't want my other sons to get killed.

JAMAL BAKER AT THE GAZA CITY SEAPORT

JAMAL BAKER

Fisherman, 50
Born in Battir, Gaza City, Gaza &
interviewed in Gaza City, Gaza

During our 2013 trip to Gaza, we meet Jamal Baker twice at the marina where the fishermen dock their boats. On each occasion Jamal was not fishing; instead, he was watching other boats with expensive nets, and the extensive manpower required to use them, as they brought in their hauls of sardines. Jamal has short-cropped grey hair and a trimmed salt and pepper beard. He has a small frame, and he wears black shoes and slacks even though he spends his days amid the water and muck of the marina.

Approximately 4,000 Gazan fishermen rely on access to the open waters of the Mediterranean to make a living, but the range in which they can travel by boat has been significantly restricted since Israel imposed a naval blockade on Gaza in 2007. Following the Oslo Accords in 1993, Gazans were permitted to travel up to twenty nautical miles in pursuit of large schools of fish. By the time of the Second Intifada in 2000, that range was reduced to twelve nautical miles, and in 2007, after the imposition of the blockade, the range was further limited to six nautical miles (and sometimes three nautical miles).

In 1999, Gazan fishermen harvested 4,000 tons of fish, and their sale repre-sented 4 percent of the total economy of both Gaza and the West Bank. Today, the fishing economy has collapsed, as Gazan fishermen have depleted schools of sardines and other fish in their limited range. Over 90 percent of Gazan fishermen are living in poverty and dependent on international aid for survival. To pursue fish beyond the permitted range means to risk arrest, the confiscation of fishing boats, or even shooting by the Israeli navy. Some fisherman report being harassed or attacked by the navy even within the permitted fishing zone. According to Oxfam International, an anti-poverty non-profit organization that works in over ninety countries, in 2013 there were 300 reported incidents of border or naval fire against Gazans, and over half of those were targeting fisherman at sea.

When we meet, Jamal tells us that he comes from a very long line of fish-erman, but that he now relies on international aid to support his family. Since the imposition of the blockade, he can't rely on catching enough fish to provide meals for his family, let alone catching enough to sell at market. He also shares with us the dangers of the Gazan fishing trade—a profession he has no plans to abandon.

MY CHILDREN ARE THE MOST
IMPORTANT PEOPLE IN MY LIFE

I was born here in Gaza in May 1964, and I've always lived off of the sea and what it provides. My family takes its job from our ancestors—we've been fishermen since long, long ago. I first went out on a fishing boat with a brother-in-law when I was twelve. I loved it immediately and knew that was what I wanted to do with my life. My father taught me to fish when I was thirteen. I got my own boat when I was sixteen, and I fixed it up until it was in good enough shape to sail in the sea. I've fished now for thirty-five years. I've never done anything else.

I'm very close to the other fishermen. I've worked alongside them for decades, and we see each other more than we see our own families! But my children are the most important people in my life. It used to be that my parents were most important, and now it's my children. I've been married to my wife Waseela for twenty-eight years—we are cousins, and our parents arranged for us to be married. I have eight daughters and one son. We fishermen love to make more and more children because we want sons to help us on the boats. I think of having more children, God knows, but I have to convince my wife! My son Khadeer is eighteen, and he's a fisherman already. He left school after the sixth grade because he wanted to work with me. He's been a full-time fisherman ever since, but he's not old enough yet to be very reliable. I love my daughters, but it's against tradition for women to be fishermen.

Before the blockade, my family used to go far out into the sea and get amazing amounts of fish.[1] We'd find mostly sardines, but also plenty of mackerel. I could make $500 in a single day sometimes. Fishing around Gaza City was actually better when Gaza was still occupied, since we had more freedom on the sea then.[2] But things have been especially difficult with the blockade, actually ever since Gilad Shalit was captured.[3] Before his capture, we used to have access to twelve nautical miles around Gaza City for our fishing boats. But since then, the restrictions have been much tighter. It might change a little, but whether it's three miles or six miles doesn't make much of a difference. We can't find much in those

---

[1] Israel's blockade of the Gazan ports began in 2007, partly in response to Hamas taking power in the Gaza Strip. Egypt also formally closed its borders with Gaza at the time. For more information, see Appendix I, page 267.

[2] Gaza was fully administered by Israel from the end of the 1967 war until the signing of the Oslo Accords in 1994. Israeli settlers and the Israeli military continued to occupy parts of Gaza until September 2005, when Israel evacuated all settlers from the strip and withdrew military forces. For more information, see Appendix I, page 267.

[3] Israeli Defense Forces soldier Gilad Shalit was captured in 2006. He was released as part of a prisoner exchange in 2011. For more information, see Appendix I, page 267.

waters—only a few sardines. There are no rocks for bigger schools of fish to live around, since it's mostly only mud in the zone where we're permitted to fish.

When we go out on the sea, we're often in crews of at least three or four. Our boats may be about twenty feet long, with roofs and a closed compartment in the center that we fill with ice and use as a cooler for our catch. We have lights mounted to the roofs of our boats to spot schools of fish in the early morning and late evening, and we use GPS devices so we can return to the best available spots and also make sure we're not crossing the boundaries of the blockade. When we find fish, we have nets we use to bring them in. But these days, it's not so easy to find fish.

Since the blockade, most months I don't make a single penny. It's not only that I don't make money, I even owe the gas station money because it costs a lot to fuel up the boat. Then I don't make anything, so I can't pay. So at the end of the day, most days, I'm losing money. When I do catch fish, I take them to the market behind the marina. But most days there's nothing to sell, so I just sit at the marina with other fishermen. The Gaza seaport—the marina—is pretty much a mile-long strip of concrete where fishermen tie up their boats. There's a gate separating the marina from the rest of the city's shoreline, but not much else there besides a strip of concrete. Recently, a Qatari–Turkish-funded project added some tables and chairs where families can congregate on Thursdays and Fridays. When we get together at the marina, we mostly talk about the fish we found or didn't find out at sea.

But even when there's not enough fish to sell in the market, I feed my family sometimes with the fish I can catch. We eat a lot of sardines when I can catch them. Mostly for dinner, but sometimes for lunch as well if we've caught enough. We'll grill them or fry them, and always eat them with rice. The best kind of fish I catch sometimes is the *denees*.[4] That is a delicious fish.

EVERY SINGLE DAY
I EXPECT TO BE KILLED

When I'm out on the water, I'm nervous about being shot. Shootings happen all the time on the water. I have a cousin who got killed a year ago, when he was just going out on the water for fun. He was nineteen, and he'd just gotten engaged. He went out on a Friday with his uncle, and, at the time, the fishing zone was limited to three nautical miles. They might have gone too far out. My cousin didn't do anything wrong, he was just a little out of the restricted area. There was no good reason why he was shot.

I probably see around three Israeli gunboats every day I go out. Usually, they are off in the distance, but sometimes they get quite close. They are about forty feet long, with a crew of twelve or so. Sometimes they'll pull close to a Gazan fishing boat like mine and simply shout curses through a megaphone. When this happens to me, I just pretend like they aren't there. They couldn't hear me if I tried to say anything back, anyway. They have water cannons that they sometimes fire on boats, as well as rockets and machine guns.

Every single day, I hear that someone got shot at. Every single day, I expect to be killed. Whenever I leave my home in the morning, I'm not sure I will go back alive. That is what it's like to be a fisherman in Gaza. I don't know how to keep myself safe, because we don't have time to think of how to protect ourselves when the shooting starts. When the navy starts shooting, a fisherman doesn't even have enough time to put on a life jacket.

---

[4] *Denees* is the gilt-headed bream, often called *dorade* in U.S. markets.

The soldiers often shoot for no reason at all. It doesn't have to be because someone went out of the restricted area, like my cousin. It could be because of something else that was happening in Palestine, or the mood of a soldier. Sometimes, if the soldier's girlfriend broke up with him, he comes and—just because he's angry—he shoots up the fisherman. They keep you guessing. I don't think soldiers who shoot always have a reason, really; they can just do whatever they want without fearing anyone.

In October 2012, I didn't work at all during the week of bombing.[5] After the cease-fire in November, I started going out again, and so did my son Khadeer. As part of the cease-fire, we fishermen were supposed to be able to go out up to six miles, so we were all eager to see what we would be able to find in the waters we could now get to.

At that time I had two boats—my old boat that I got at sixteen, and a newer, nicer one with a new motor that I had saved up to buy. Three days after we started fishing again, on November 28, Khadeer went out early in the morning to fish with three of his cousins. They took my new boat out on the water. Later that morning, his cousins showed up at my house. When I saw them, I thought right away that my son had been killed.

My nephews told me that they were fishing out in the sea, about two miles from the marina. There were maybe twenty other boats around fishing in the same area. Suddenly an Israeli gunboat appeared a few hundred feet away. Without warning, the boat fired a missile at my boat's engine and completely disabled it. It caught fire. Nobody was injured, they just destroyed the engine. That was their introduction. Then an Israeli navy guy called to Khadeer and his cousins through a megaphone and told them to strip to their underwear and to jump into the sea, because they were going to blow up the boat. My son jumped in the water, and

---

[5] Israel targeted Gaza with bombings during eight days starting in October of 2012, during Operation Pillar of Defense. For more information, see Appendix I, page 267.

they hit the boat with another missile and it exploded. After the boat was destroyed, the navy guys began shooting in the water all around where my son and his friends were swimming. They were all really scared. Then the Israeli boat pulled up and grabbed Khadeer out of the sea. His cousins watched him get handcuffed to the mast of the boat. He was in his underwear, and it was one of the coldest days of the year and very windy on the sea. Khadeer's cousins then swam to another fishing boat, got a lift back to shore, and came to see me.

That morning, I stayed home waiting for news of my son. I thought the police might call with news that he'd been arrested by the Israelis. At some point that morning, friends called to tell me that they'd talked to fishermen who had stayed for a while near the attack on my son. They said he was still okay, that he was aboard the Israeli boat. But I wasn't even focusing on what my friends were saying, because my heart was about to stop. Then, a few hours later, around three in the afternoon, Khadeer came back. When I saw him, I felt that I got my soul back. The first thing he said was, "We lost the boat." I told him, "You shouldn't have to worry about the money and the boat. It's fine. As long as I didn't lose you." It became a big huge gathering of friends and family, and everyone was crying.

Later, Khadeer told me that he was handcuffed to the mast of the Israeli gunboat for three hours. Then soldiers refused to take him to shore, because they didn't want their bosses to know what they'd done to him. They didn't have a reason or excuse for it. While he was handcuffed, they fired on another boat. Eventually, they threw him in the sea and told him to get the nearest fishing boat to take him back to shore. Imagine if something bad happened to him—how could you throw him again into the sea without checking to see if he was close to freezing to death? I think if something bad had happened to him, none of them would have ever cared. Maybe they would have said, "It was by mistake."

I felt really lucky because when I lost the $10,000—the value of the boat—I felt like I'd lost money, but then I got compensated with millions of dollars by getting my son back. I told Khadeer, "Don't think of it. Don't worry about it. This just happens." I didn't want to let him feel too scared by the experience. He started fishing again after one week.

By now, my family is used to the nature of this work. When we go to the sea, they know: my son and I are either going to be back home in the evening or we'll be killed. So we all live with this fact.

I feel really disappointed because my life is always in danger, and it's not even for any good reason. It's not for a good thing at the end of the day. Before the blockade, I used to face many hardships, but it was for something good, because I used to make a good income. But now I'm sacrificing my life for nothing. Now I have a dead heart. I don't care about shooting, or anything that comes to me. If anyone starts to feel a bit weepy about their lives, they shouldn't go out on the water.

The important thing is that I have Khadeer back, but the attack has totally affected my life, because the boat that we lost was the new one, and it had a good motor. Now I have only the older boat. Now I'm using my friend's motor because I don't have enough funds for my own.

Even this old boat is at risk. Another worry that fisherman have is boat seizures. The Israelis find all sorts of reasons to seize boats. Then they'll tell the fisherman that his boat will be returned, and it never is. Sometimes I think that Israel is financially fighting Palestinians in Gaza. Because they seize boats for reasons that have nothing to do with security issues, reasons that have more to do with fighting people and their source of income. Sometimes I think if they see a fisherman trying to haul in a huge amount of fish, they keep shooting until he leaves everything behind and runs. So the main target is to control what financial benefits people can get out of the sea.

It's really hard now to support my family through fishing. It's really bad. Before, I used to donate money to charity. But now I'm living on international aid. It's only because of this that I can survive. We get some support from CHF, but it's not money; it's just flour and oil.[6] I could make $500 a day before, and now I haven't made anything for a month. If I could make like $30 in a day, that would be an incredible day of fishing. But I never feel discouraged. I'm always hoping for the best.

I owe a lot of money to a lot of people. I've borrowed from family and friends. People don't hassle me about it yet, but I feel the pressure whenever I see them. Since the incident of the boat, I don't sleep much, only two hours a day. I didn't sleep at all last night. How would I sleep knowing everyone wants money from me? And, more than this, I wake up in the morning and I'm not sure I'll be able to feed my children. So it's becoming complicated, and it's affecting me and my state of mind because I'm not feeling fine. Still, I never thought of getting any other job because I feel like I'm a fish. If I leave the sea, then I will die.

---

[6] Cooperative Housing Foundation (CHF) is an international aid non-profit now known as Global Communities. Following the air strikes of 2012, Global Communities began distributing food to 22,000 Gazans in partnership with the United Nations.

MAN PRUNING OLIVE TREE

FADI SHIHAB

Computer technician, 34
Born in Kuwait City, Kuwait &
interviewed in Gaza City, Gaza

In 2012, Fadi Shihab made an unusual decision: he chose to move his family from Nashville, Tennessee, to Gaza City, despite heightened tensions between Israel and Hamas at the time. Up to that point, he had only visited Gaza once, for six weeks.

Fadi emigrated to the United States from Kuwait when he was thirteen years old, but his parents were originally from Gaza City. After marrying in the early sixties, his parents had moved to Syria, where his father pursued teaching work. They were there during the Six-Day War—when Israel began its military occupation of Gaza—and because they were not registered as living within Gaza at the time of Israel's initial census of the region, they were barred from returning and claiming any residency rights. They were left stateless, with no permission to even visit their extended families. The Shihabs' exile lasted decades, during which time they lived in Egypt, Syria, Kuwait, and the United States. But ties of family and culture were strong enough to pull Fadi's parents back to Gaza when they finally had the opportunity to return in the late 2000s.

We meet Fadi multiple times in 2013, mostly at the property he inherited from his father in the Zeitoun neighborhood of Gaza City. He has a small house and a vegetable garden with olive and lemon trees covering more than an acre. As we sit in the shade, Fadi explains the reasons why he left a lucrative job and comfortable home in Tennessee to move his family to a city where electricity is only available for a few hours most days and the threat of war is always present. He's tall, and speaks English with a truly interesting accent—Arabic inflections mixed with a Nashville drawl.

WE WERE STATELESS

My parents are from Gaza. My dad was born in 1941, and both his family and my mother's family have been here forever. After the war in '48, refugees from all over Palestine came to Gaza, and it was administered by Egypt.[1] Even in the early sixties it was hard to find work in Gaza, so after my parents were married, they moved to Egypt and then to Syria. My dad was a math teacher.

After the war in '67 when Israel occupied Palestine, they took a census, and any Palestinians who weren't living in Palestine at the time weren't allowed back in. Without the ID cards Israel issued after the war, my parents were no longer considered by Israel to be legal occupants of Gaza. So they were stateless, and they moved from country to country on visas—from Syria to Saudi Arabia to Kuwait. During this time, they started having kids. I'm the youngest. My oldest brother was born in 1965, and then they had four girls, a boy, and then I was born in Kuwait

---

[1] Approximately 750,000 Palestinians were displaced during the Arab-Israeli War, and many of them came to Gaza, which was administered by Egypt following armistice agreements in 1949. The migration of refugees dramatically altered the demographics of the Gaza Strip. Today, more than 80 percent of the 1.75 million people living in Gaza are refugees or descendants of refugees. For more information, see Appendix I, page 267.

City in December 1979.[2]

A couple of years after I was born, my oldest brother, Alim, got a student visa to study in the U.S. Meanwhile, my father taught in schools in Kuwait City, and I grew up playing with my siblings, making a lot of friends, and going to school.

Then in 1990, when I was ten years old, Saddam Hussein decided to take over Kuwait.[3] A couple of months later, the U.S. came in and kicked him out. I remember the war as being kind of an exciting time, as scary as it was. We were living in an apartment building with four floors, four apartments per floor. I'd go to the roof with my friend across the hall, and we'd watch the lights of missiles in the distance. We thought it was so cool, and we thought the U.S. soldiers looked cool—they even wore sunglasses! They were especially cool compared to the Iraqi soldiers, who were dressed in torn-up rags for uniforms. From the roof we'd watch the fighting on the border in the distance, and we called the U.S. *Al-hakim*, "the ruler." We had a lot of respect for the U.S. during the war. The whole neighborhood would sleep together in shelters every night, which, as kids, we thought of as a lot of fun.

Of course, it was a scary time. My dad had to find food for us during the days, and some days he'd have to drive out of the city to do that. One day he went out looking for food, and he didn't come home. We were terrified and thought he'd been captured or killed. But he came home after three weeks, and it turns out he'd been stopped by the Iraqi army, and they'd forced him to transport the corpse of an Iraqi soldier back to the soldier's family. The story of how he got back to Kuwait City is a long one—he had quite an adventure.

---

[2] Kuwait City is the capital of Kuwait. With a population of over 2.4 million in the greater metropolitan area, it is the largest city in Kuwait and is considered a global financial hub.

[3] Iraq invaded Kuwait City in August 1990. Coalition forces led by the U.S. military drove the Iraqi military from Kuwait in February 1991 during Operation Desert Storm.

For our family, life in Kuwait became hard after the war. Yasser Arafat supported Saddam, and so Kuwaitis sort of thought of Palestinians as traitors.[4] In fact, a lot of Palestinians living in Kuwait fled to Iraq after the war. We tried to stay, but my dad couldn't get our visas renewed because there was so much hostility. He'd had no trouble for fifteen years in Kuwait, but now we had to find somewhere else to live. And that's when we emigrated to the U.S.

AFTER SIX MONTHS I FELT LIKE
I FIT IN PRETTY WELL

I first came to the States on July 11, 1992. I was twelve, and I came with my parents, one older brother, and my sister who is a year older than me. Three of my sisters had already married or were studying, and one lived in Iraq, one in Sudan, and one in Libya. We moved to Nashville, Tennessee. My brother Alim, who had gone to school in Kansas, had since moved to Nashville for grad school. We moved in with Alim when we first arrived, and then we found a place of our own. My dad used his life savings, about $50,000, to buy a house straight-up in cash. He didn't believe in getting a mortgage, since he wasn't sure he'd get a job. But he found a gig at Wendy's flipping burgers. It was a little embarrassing for me, since I was used to him being this respected math teacher, but he'd say, "As long as I'm working, there's nothing to be ashamed of." My second oldest brother, Fawzi, who was nineteen, he got a job at Wendy's too and eventually became my dad's boss. That was a little strange. But

---

[4] Yasser Arafat was the leader of the Palestine Liberation Organization, the coalition of militias and political parties that would become the Palestinian Authority after the signing of the Oslo Accords. He supported Iraq during the invasion of Kuwait despite some strong disagreement within the PLO and opposition to the invasion from many other Arab states such as Egypt and Saudi Arabia.

my father wasn't committed to staying in the U.S., and he didn't pick up the language very well.

I don't remember much from the first months in the States, other than that they were really bad. Just the language barrier—I spoke no English. And people were different than what I was used to. Even their jokes were different. In the fall I started going to Cameron Middle School. The administration made me stay back a year—they placed me in the seventh grade, just because of the language barrier. It was difficult in school at first. One middle school teacher, his name was Mr. Jones, I remember him telling me, "You're very good in math." And I didn't even know enough English to really know what he was saying to me, if he was complimenting me or what. But math is like a universal language, right? It was the only subject I was good at.

I'd say it took maybe three to six months before my siblings and I started grasping the basics of the language. The good thing in the U.S. is that they had these English as a second language classes, so over time we just kind of picked it up, and English just started to flow. After six months, we were making new friends. My teachers saw me progressing so well within the first year that they moved me to eighth grade, where I belonged based on my age.

My sister Adiba and I, we were much better than my other brothers and sisters at speaking English. Adiba's just a year older than me, and the two of us don't even have much of an accent when we speak English. My older brother Fawzi, he was nineteen when we moved. So for him, his Arabic tongue is still heavy, since he didn't go to high school in the States. I'd say definitely, the younger you are, the easier it is.

After that first six months, I began to feel like I fit in pretty well, and I made some friends. I had an Iranian friend, Ali, who had the same story as me. He came to the U.S. when he was about ten or eleven years old. He speaks Persian, and I can't speak that, so we'd only communicate in

English, of course. Then there were a couple of Russian guys and a couple of Romanian guys. We just kind of clicked, because all of us were immigrants. We didn't dress the right way to fit in—we all dressed like we were just off the boat. We spoke broken English, so in a way we all understood each other. I also got to meet the Americans around my neighborhood. I think the Americans I made friends with saw me as kind of weird—they hadn't known anybody with a background like mine. Nashville isn't like Chicago, or New York, or San Francisco—some cities in the U.S. have had Arabs since the 1800s, 1900s. But Nashville is a pretty new city, and the Arab community hasn't been there long. But I got to know some of the kids who were from Nashville, and I watched some of my friends running around with the American kids, doing good things or bad things. But I just kind of moved with the groove. My friends and I went to Hillsboro High School—that's also in Nashville—and then I was done with that and I went to Tennessee State University.[5]

At the same time, my parents were working on getting U.S. citizenship. What they really wanted more than anything was to go back to Gaza, to see the family they'd been away from for thirty years. My dad passed the citizenship exam first, and once he got a U.S. passport, he was finally able to get back into Gaza. So in 1997 he moved back there. He built a house on some property he inherited from his father—a couple of acres with some olive, lemon, and fig trees—and he got it ready for my mom to move there too. It was weird to us kids, and we wanted him to stay. But it was his life's dream to go back to his home, to sit under the olive trees in the breeze. Or sit around a fire at night with his brothers and drink coffee. That's what he always talked about. He always said he didn't want to die outside Gaza. My mom failed the citizenship test a few times, so she stayed back in the

---

[5] Tennessee State University is a historically African-American university located in Nashville. It hosts approximately 7,000 students.

U.S. for a couple more years. We'd see my dad only when he came back to the States to visit us for three or four months every year.

I ALWAYS HAD A RED LINE IN MY HEAD
THAT I WOULDN'T CROSS

At Tennessee State I studied business information systems. I was interested in computers because during my junior and my senior year in high school, I was working at Intermedia, an internet provider. So I was already into solving internet problems and whatnot. My two older brothers studied computer science and computer languages, and they told me, "Try to do something different than us." I took some computer language courses, but also I got into IT hardware.

During this time I was still hanging out with my friend Ali a lot, along with my other friends I'd gone to high school with. But Ali and I, when we hung out—sometimes we'd hang out with some American friends, sometimes we'd hang out with each other. Sometimes we'd do the same things Americans did and go to bars and stuff like that. And then at the end of the day, sometimes we just liked to talk to each other, listen to some Arabic music or Persian music.

Sometimes we'd be with our friends from other countries, like Simeon, the guy from Romania who we went to high school with. We always asked each other, "Do you guys feel like Americans, do you feel *American?*" Ali, he'd say, "Well, basically we're Americans, but we have an advantage because we come from a different culture, so we can enjoy that culture and we can enjoy this culture." So it's hard to explain, but being both Palestinian and American felt like an advantage. Politically, I'm American, but in terms of culture, heritage, I'm Palestinian.

When I left school I was about twenty-one. I graduated on May 12, 2001. My friends and I wanted to celebrate, so we were like, "Where do we want to go? Somewhere special!" We drove to a casino in Paducah, Kentucky.[6] It's like an hour and a half, two hours away from Nashville. We had a blast. So that May, June, and July we'd go back to Paducah almost every two weeks. Growing up, I always had a red line in my head that I wouldn't cross. Like, *I'm gonna do some things that are bad—I'm gonna drink, I'm gonna go to casinos and gamble, do this and that, but there are some things I'm not gonna do, like drugs.* I don't know why I'm like that, how I developed those boundaries, but I figured it had to be because I was raised partly in Kuwait and not in the U.S. for my whole childhood.

I WAS LOOKING FOR
A SWEETNESS INSIDE

In July of 2001, I started working for a temp company, and then I got hired at Dell in November. While I started working at Dell, I was also working toward citizenship. I was twenty-three when I became a U.S. citizen. Of course, I had to take the citizenship tests and everything, but it wasn't that bad. The questions were like, "How many states are there?" I think they wanted me to name the thirteen colonies and the governor of my state and the two senators from our state, that sort of thing.

Then I got my passport, and that was really nice. In 2004 I left America, I took a leave of absence from work. By this time, all my siblings and I had grown up and left the house, and my mother had U.S. citizenship too, so she was ready to move back to Gaza and be with my dad. I was considering it too, actually. I was interested to find out what Gaza was all about. I'd heard so many stories growing up.

I traveled with my parents, and we first went to visit one of my older sisters who was living in Saudi Arabia at the time. Then we went to

---

[6] Paducah is a city of nearly 30,000 at the confluence of the Ohio and Tennessee Rivers.

Kuwait, to see my old neighborhood. I still had a special feeling in my heart for it. I saw the guys I used to know there, and the situation was so bad. People had graduated from college, but they had nothing to do—like, no jobs. I was just like, *Man, I'm glad I went to America.* And I had other advantages from being a U.S. citizen. Maybe most Americans don't think about using a U.S. passport to travel, but for me it was like a way to go to wherever I wanted. 'Cause as an American, you know that you tell the American embassy that you're going to Gaza or Saudi Arabia or wherever, and you just go. If I'd been a Kuwaiti citizen, I would have had a lot of trouble getting across some borders. So it was nice, just the freedom of traveling with a U.S. passport.

Then I was in Gaza for about six weeks. I got to see my dad's family, got to know them a little and stay in his house. I met some of his friends, too. My dad had a friend who was a teacher with him in Kuwait. After Kuwait, the friend moved to Yemen for a few years and then moved to Gaza. My dad ran into this friend one day while we were visiting Gaza, and the friend invited us to his house.

So we got to his house, and I met his daughter, Houda. I'd actually known her from Kuwait, but I didn't remember much—she was a few years younger than me. After we left their house, my dad was like, "You saw Houda, what do you think?" I just said, "I'm not sure." At that time, the idea of getting married was in my head. I was twenty-three, I had my own house in the States, I was somewhat stable financially, I had paid off my student loans and all that. But I wasn't sure I wanted to find a girl from Gaza, someone who thinks differently about life, someone who listens to different music, has different values—just everything could be different and it could be a bad fit. I really thought of myself as Palestinian, but maybe a little more American than Palestinian.

Then a week passed by and I said, "Okay, let's give them a call." The reason I kind of tilted toward seeing her again was that she already had three brothers in the U.S., and she'd already lived in Kuwait, so she wasn't completely unaware of the world outside Gaza. Plus I thought that her experience with Arab life could be a good thing for kids we might have— she could really teach them some of our Arabic culture when I might not be able to, just because I had lived so much in a Western country.

My dad told his friend that I was interested in meeting his daughter, and so we went back to visit a week later. At Houda's house, the two of us went into kind of like a private room, but with the door open of course. We chatted. It was weird, because I never really—she was nothing like the American girls I knew. All my life, I've talked to boys and girls, no problem. But it was weird being in a room with a girl like Houda. I didn't know what to talk about. She asked me some questions, I asked her some questions. Just small talk. I think we both left smiling.

Then soon after our talk, I asked her brother to come with us on a kind of date to the sea. Her brother was there as a chaperone. Even though our conversation was kind of limited because her brother was there, we felt a connection. We ended up going to the beach together every day, and even went swimming together, which made her mom go crazy. That was scandalous to her mom. She thought that was so inappropriate. Houda and I were really starting to feel comfortable together, though.

During that time that we were courting, one of the things I was trying to understand was her sensibility, and I was looking for something genuine. I wanted to know if she was one of those girls who maybe just wanted to leave Gaza. Some girls might just be thinking, *Hey, this guy's a U.S. citizen!* I was looking for a sweetness inside, like a smile that's too sweet to be fake. And I saw that, I saw something genuine in her. And she was pretty smart, too. She was getting a computer science degree, so we had that in common.

So before I left Gaza, I proposed. She said yes, and her parents agreed. She was still in college, and they wanted her to finish that first. We had the engagement party in Gaza before I left. It was on the beach, and we had all of our families there and we ate and danced. And then a year and three months later, in September 2005, she came to the U.S. and we were married in Nashville.

YOU DON'T ENTER HEAVEN UNLESS YOU ARE UNDER YOUR MOM'S FEET

For my wife, I think it was really easier for her to adjust to life in the U.S. than it is for many people, because she had somebody from here to help her out. She didn't have to deal with feeling like an outsider, a weirdo, as much as I did when I came as a kid. And she loved the U.S. right away. She fell in love with the way people were just friendly to her. Even strangers would smile and say, "Good morning!" She said it was so different from Gaza, where everyone was unhappy and people you'd run into on the street were just rude. America seemed like a happy island to her—a bubble where people weren't affected by any bad things happening in the world. Plus we had a nice house in Nashville, and I got my job back at Dell so we had a good income and didn't have too many worries.

We traveled some after we were married, and then we had our first child, our son Azhar, in January 2007. Later that same year, she got pregnant again, and it was going to be a boy. I called my dad, and told him I was going to name my second son after him. But before my second son Iyad was born, in January 2008, my father passed away.

I wasn't even able to go to the funeral—I flew to Israel, but the Erez crossing was closed at the time because of the war with Hamas, and I couldn't get in.[7] I was glad I got to tell him about my son, at least. Then

[7] The Gaza War, or Operation Cast Lead, was fought between December 2007 and January 2008. For more information, see the Glossary, page 276.

we had one more child, my daughter Nada in 2009.

Houda got a master's degree from Tennessee State—a teaching certificate. And we were so busy, way too busy for me to go back and visit my mother right away after my father's death. I really wanted to, though, especially to help settle his estate. But still, we were becoming more and more involved in the Palestinian community in Nashville, even though it was small. You just end up meeting these other families, and there were about twenty-eight families in the city that would get together sometimes. We'd talk about what was happening in Gaza and the West Bank, share food, talk. I started to become a better Muslim, too. I stopped drinking after I got married, and I read the Quran. And I started to want my kids to have a closer connection to the Arabic world. I wanted to pass along Arabic language and culture to them. And frankly, I was worried about them growing up in the States and getting pulled into some of the stuff I saw as a teenager—drugs and gangs, that sort of thing. I thought having a closer connection to Arabic culture could help keep them away from that stuff. I think my time in Kuwait helped me develop some boundaries, even though I drank and did other things as a kid.

Finally, in 2010, I flew to Gaza to stay for a week and a half. I was shocked to see how my mom was living—she was so alone. She had a couple of cousins, but nobody to really look after her, and she was seventy-two. I was like, *Man, it isn't right for her to live by herself like this for so many years.* But she didn't want to come back to the U.S. She said, "I will have nothing to do there. I want to die here, just like him." And she wanted me to stay. She wanted her family around her. It really bothered me. In Islam, there's a saying that you don't enter heaven unless you're under your mom's feet. It's a weird saying, but it basically means that your mom really has to be pleased with you when she dies for you to get into heaven.

And so I went back home, and I told my wife, "Listen, you know I've been at Dell almost ten years, and I don't want to let it go. Nobody does this, but I really feel like the right decision is to return to Gaza for a while. I have to do it for my mom. I can't live with myself if my mom dies and I'm not there." And Houda said, "You have two older brothers, let them help her out." My oldest brother, he was in Houston, he had kids who were about to go into college. He couldn't just leave his job. And my other brother, in Florida, he was a citizen, but his wife wasn't, and he was applying for her citizenship—he couldn't just throw all that away. And Houda was like, "Okay, fine, fine. I'm not sure this is the right decision, but I understand." I said, "It's probably not the right decision! I don't know if I'm gonna find a job there. I don't know how people think there, what their attitude will be." There's another saying in Arabic—you have to leave your destiny up to God sometimes, and just whatever happens, happens. And however bad it was going to get in Gaza, I couldn't imagine being fifty, sixty years old one day and thinking, *I wish I had gone to Gaza and helped out my mom.*

I also thought, *This is good for my kids. My kids are gonna learn Arabic, they're gonna be able to read the Quran.* Because if I stayed in the States another twenty years, yeah, I'm gonna be well off, my house paid off, everything fine, but it's not worth anything to me if my kids can't speak to me in Arabic, you know. So after considering my kids, I thought, *Screw it. I wanna do this for two, three years—what's the worst that can happen?*

GAZANS ACT LIKE BOMBINGS ARE A NORMAL PART OF LIFE

We came here in April 2012. My sons, Azhar and Iyad, were five and six, and my daughter, Nada, was three. It was a big adjustment for our family. But in some ways it was a bigger change for Houda than for me. You have to understand, she came from a family of Palestinian refugees in Gaza. Her family lived in Ashkelon before 1948, so they didn't really consider Gaza home.[8] For my wife, she felt like she'd finally found a home in the States, and she wasn't crazy about being back in Gaza. But we settled into the house that my dad had bought and my mom was still living in, which was in the Zeitoun neighborhood in the south of Gaza City.[9] My mom lived on the first floor, then there was a family renting on the second, and we moved in on the third floor, and there's another family on the fourth floor.

We moved to Gaza at a really interesting time. It was calm when we arrived, but it still felt like a dangerous place. The second month after I came here, my cousin had an injury, and he had to go to Egypt for an operation. He came back dead because they botched the operation. But there aren't any good hospitals in Gaza at all, so he had to make the trip. There's one hospital in Gaza City called Shifa, which means "get well" in Arabic. But its nickname is *Maut*—"death." It's terrible. You know a hospital's bad when there are feral cats running around inside, and that's what Shifa looks like.

Then in November of that year, Ahmed Al-Jabari, the guy in charge of the Qassam rockets, got assassinated.[10] I started hearing things like, "Hamas is gonna really have to retaliate for this." Everyone knew something

---

[8] Ashkelon is a coastal city of approximately 120,000 people and is located in Israel, around twelve miles north of Gaza.

[9] Zeitoun was a suburb of Gaza City built in the 1930s, but it became a densely populated urban zone after thousands of refugees settled the area following the Arab-Israeli War in 1948. It is known as the former home of Sheikh Ahmed Yassin, the founder of Hamas, who was killed in an air strike in 2004. Yassin's assassination is widely credited for the rise in the popularity of Hamas in Gaza, leading to its 2006 electoral wins in Gaza.

[10] Ahmed Al-Jabari was a leader of the military wing of Hamas, the Al-Aqsa Martyrs' Brigades. He had led military operations during Hamas's assertion of power in Gaza in 2007 and may have helped plan the capture of Israeli soldier Gilad Shalit. He was also credited with acquiring Qassam rockets, which were launched from Gaza into Israel throughout the 2000s. He was killed by an Israeli air strike on November 14, 2012.

was gonna happen. So after that we saw eight days of bombing.[11] At first it was kind of further away, but then they started hitting areas in the Zeitoun neighborhood, inside where I live, and east of my neighborhood, where there are a lot of militia bases and spots where militias launch rockets. You don't see the militias, but they're around you. Even right around where we live, they come and set up rockets and shoot from here. I wouldn't be surprised if there were missiles buried under these olive trees on our land. Seriously. The militias look for any open spaces they can shoot rockets from.

It was a scary time, and I remember my daughter Nada running back and forth in the apartment when she heard bombs. She couldn't understand what was going on. I'd look at her and I'd think, *Man, I really hope this doesn't affect her psychologically as she grows up.* Because you hear so many horror stories about kids losing their hearing, and you hear stories about how kids get their legs cut off, or kids that become mentally ill.

On the seventh day or eighth day, the F-16s mowed down a building about a quarter mile from here. They shot it up with machine gun fire, and my building and every other building in the neighborhood shook with the impact. An Israeli missile put a giant crater in the ground not far from our home, and that really scared us too. So during the seven or eight days, there were moments where I would be thinking, *Man, did I make the right decision here?* And I would be with my mom downstairs, and she would be scared too. And then we started hearing the news about how if you're a U.S. citizen and you want to leave, give a call to a certain number. I didn't. I thought, *I'm gonna hang on, I'm gonna hang around.*

I would be so scared during these times. I remember once or twice after a bombing, an hour or two after it calmed down, I would go outside

<hr>

[11] This was the series of Israeli air strikes on Gaza in November 2012, called Operation Pillar of Defense. For more information, see the Glossary, page 276.

and I would see my cousins at the corner, just chilling, you know. I was like "Hey, what are you guys doing out here?" And one of my cousins would be like, "Hey, this is nothing, man—just don't walk too far east right now and you'll be okay." So to them it wasn't a big deal, but I sensed that's just the attitude—*Hey, I'm not scared*—but at heart you cannot *not* be scared when you hear these bombs and the building you live in starts shaking. This was like Hollywood action—it was just crazy.

But a lot of Gazans just act like it's a normal part of life. There's a lot of pressure on men here to be strong. Like the kids in the street, when you're driving the car, say, you honk the horn to get them to move out of the street, and they're like, "No, you move!" Little kids have the mentality that they're grown men, and that can't be healthy.

I FEEL MY DAD'S PRESENCE

I admit my decision to move my family to Gaza is kind of strange. I mean, anybody here who's well educated, when I tell them my story, they're like, "Man, what are you doing here? Really. What are you *doing* here?"

I've had trouble finding work. I figured if I had some type of 9-to-5 job, no matter how much it paid, at least I'd feeling like I'm being productive. But I still haven't found one. I'm not gonna lie, coming to this situation after so many years having a solid job, it brings on depression sometimes. Sometimes the stress is so much that I'll smoke a pack of cigarettes in a day.

I'm responsible for Houda and the children. Anything happens to them, it's my fault. It's a lot of pressure. I've got gray hair. My brothers see my pictures and they're like, "What happened to you?!" I say, "Man, a year in Gaza is like five years in the U.S.!" I had some gray hair when I arrived in Gaza, but in the last year it just started going completely gray. It's a tough life here.

But I think the kids are comfortable. That's why I think that I really did the best thing for them at that age—they don't know any better. They go visit their cousins and stuff, but they're still—I don't even remember when I was four or five years old, maybe I remember seven and eight. So that's why I figured if I bring them here now, it's gonna be easier. Harder on me, but easier for them. If I bring them here when they're eight or nine, they're gonna want breakfast cereal; they're gonna want everything U.S. style. I hope we can stay here two, three years and then get out. Then, rather than taking them back to Nashville, I'm actually thinking of Austin, Texas, because the headquarters for Dell is in Austin and my manager—a lot of the managers I know—they moved up and they usually go back to the headquarters.

I also think that coming here has made me feel closer to my Palestinian identity. Just 'cause when I sit with my cousins, they tell me these stories about my grandfather, about my dad while he was here. They also tell me stories about Hamas, about Fatah, what happened with them. All the crazy things that have happened in the city.

I wasn't with my dad when he died. But when I'm fixing these olive trees and the garden, I feel I'm near him. I'll just feel his presence, and I'll sit down under the trees in the cool air. The breeze comes in from the sea, and it's real nice. I can kind of sense what he wanted to get back to by returning here.

MY WIFE WANTS TO LEAVE FOR GOOD

Things are still so hard here. Recently, the electricity schedule changed, so we'd have about six hours of power, twelve hours without in a cycle. It was like that for about a month and a half. Propane gas got really scarce. We use it for cooking, heating, but people were buying it up to run their cars, because gasoline shipments from Egypt got cut off. So it was a rough couple of months, but what are you gonna do? Then there was all the rain and the flood—we were fine because we're on high ground, but so many people we know who live more in the middle of the city were completely flooded, with raw sewage in their houses. Life in Gaza, it's full of surprises.

And Houda, she doesn't have anyone keeping her here. Her father is in the States now. He's actually ill and being treated in Cleveland. He had a stroke, and he's seventy-five. My wife wants desperately to go back and visit her father, but we can't get her out of Gaza at the moment. The border crossing situation is horrible. We went to the U.S. embassy to get them to help us go through the Erez crossing, but they wouldn't do it. Their attitude was, "We warned U.S. citizens not to come into Gaza, so this is pretty much your fault."

It's rare for people to get out through Erez, but the Rafah crossing into Egypt is shut down now, too. It's been opened and closed off and on, but it's been closed the last thirty-six days. To go through, you have to apply first. To apply, you have to go to an office that's basically like the DMV, but you have to get there at four in the morning and wait in a line that's got hundreds of people. Then after five hours in line, you register to cross on a specific day. But when that day comes and you go to the Rafah crossing, they might just say, "Sorry, border's closed today. Try again later!" And then you have to start the whole application process over again.

When you go to the Rafah crossing, it's amazing. There are hundreds of people waiting for the crossing to open again. Many of them are sick, and they need to get out for medical treatment. Some people have died waiting at the crossing. And then I worry about my wife's safety, even when we do get her across. Egypt isn't very stable right now, and that four- or five-hour trip from Rafah to Cairo is dangerous. We've heard of hijackings, kidnappings of people on that road.

But my wife really wants to leave for good. Her brother left the capital a few months ago, so she doesn't really have any family in Gaza. I always tell her, "I feel for you. Just be patient. Just a couple of more years, let the kids get some Arabic in them." But I don't know, sometimes it gets just really frustrating for her. One day, she told me, "You see your cousins every day, you laugh with them. You have a social life, but me, I'm just here, at the house with nothing." I said, "It's okay to sacrifice a couple of years of your life. Look at the benefits. Your kids knowing Arabic, reading and writing—God will give you rewards for that." I mean, I don't consider myself a really conservative Muslim, but I'm a Muslim, you know, and I believe in the Quran. I believe in the message of Muhammad. And she told me, "Yeah, but even the kids, they're not learning the best habits here in Gaza." I thought about that, and I remembered something that had happened a few days before. I said, "You know, a little while ago I was telling Azhar that it was the anniversary of the day my dad died. And he was like, 'Oh, God forgives all the dead people.' He said it in Arabic, and it made me cry." I would never imagine him saying that in the U.S., in English. I told her, "Let's spend a little more time here, then we can call it quits. At least they will have a base of culture to build on."

I don't know what the future holds, really. I've been to Austin, where Dell has offices, and I like the way the city is small but big at the same time. So we might move to Austin. We'd be about three and a half hours away from Houston, from my older brother, so I'd be closer to him. On the other hand, I might go to Dubai to see if I can find a job there. Because I think for the kids it'd be better in Dubai than in the States—they'd be speaking Arabic. And I'd still be close to my mom.

MAN BRINGING LIVESTOCK THROUGH TUNNELS INTO GAZA

WAFA AL-UDAINI

NGO worker, 26
Born in Deir Al-Balah, Gaza &
interviewed in Gaza City, Gaza

Movement of people and goods between Israel and Gaza has been somewhat restricted since at least the First Intifada. However, Gaza in the 1990s maintained strong economic and administrative ties to both Israel and the West Bank. Thousands of workers passed through the Erez border crossing from northern Gaza into Israel every day. Travel between Gaza and the West Bank was possible for many Palestinians, even if a bit of a bureaucratic hassle. All of that changed in 2000 at the start of the Second Intifada. Israel began closing the borders to Gaza in response to rocket attacks and suicide bombings, and it also destroyed Gaza's only airport. In 2001, Israel set up a military buffer zone around Gaza and began the construction of a massive barrier wall around the entire Gaza Strip. It also significantly restricted movement between the strip and the West Bank for most Palestinians. The border closures devastated the Gazan economy.

In 2005, toward the end of the Second Intifada, Israel unilaterally withdrew its military from Gaza and evacuated all Israeli settlements in the Gaza

*Strip, effectively handing administrative and security control to the Palestinian
Authority while opening up some of the closed border crossings to Gaza. However,
after the political party Hamas won control of Gaza in 2007, Israel again closed
the borders and imposed a blockade of goods into Gaza by land, air, and sea.*

*For Gazans such as Wafa Al-Udaini, the border closings would have made
life nearly impossible if not for smuggler's tunnels that allowed goods to pass from
Egypt into Gaza. Though seen as a military threat by Israel (a means of weapons
smuggling to Hamas), the network of over 1,200 tunnels provided Gazans with
food, construction material, medicine, and occasional luxury goods that wouldn't
otherwise be available to them.[1] When we speak with Wafa, she tells us of the
deprivations caused by the blockade, the relief that the tunnel system provided, and
the terror of military strikes into Gaza by Israeli jets and drones.*

A LOT OF KIDS SKIPPED SCHOOL TO
DEMONSTRATE OR THROW ROCKS

I was born in a hospital in Gaza City in 1988, during the First Intifada. I'm
from a big family—I have five brothers and six sisters. I'm the youngest.
The town I grew up in is called Deir Al-Balah. It's right in the middle of
the Gaza Strip, about a half-hour drive south of Gaza City.[2]

I grew up used to seeing soldiers in the streets while I played. They'd
always be chasing someone who'd thrown stones. Especially by the start
of the Second Intifada around 2000, there were so many soldiers around
all the time. I remember Israeli soldiers came into our home once to arrest

---

[1] For more on the rise and fall of Gaza's tunnel system, see Appendix IV, page 292.

[2] Deir Al-Balah is a town of about 55,000 people located nine miles south of Gaza City.
The vast majority of residents in Deir Al-Balah are refugees who settled in the town after
the war in 1948. The town is known for its date palms, and it has a history that stretches
back to fortifications used by pharaohs in the fourteenth century BCE.

two of my brothers. One brother was seventeen at the time, and the other was just thirteen. They banged on the door until my mother opened it, and then the soldiers hit her on their way in to get my brothers. I was so scared. The soldiers claimed my brothers were throwing stones, but really they might have arrested my brothers just for looking at them funny. That happened a lot. I cried and cried after they left, it was so frightening.

My seventeen-year-old brother was studying for his *tawjihi* exams at the time, and after he was sent home after being detained for a couple of months, he was too frustrated to continue studying.[3] My younger brother was released right away, but he stopped going to school. During the Second Intifada, a lot of kids skipped school to demonstrate in the streets or throw rocks. But I stayed in school and continued to high school during the Second Intifada. Then suddenly, in 2005, Israeli soldiers left Gaza.[4] For the first time we didn't see the soldiers in the streets, only Gazans. But at the same time, Israel was sealing the borders, so it was hard for people to go to work. Then Hamas got elected, and a lot of aid into Gaza was cut off.[5]

Not long after that, I passed my *tawjihi* exams and got accepted into Al-Aqsa University in Gaza City.[6] I began studying education at Al-Aqsa around 2006, and then after my first year of school, the blockade started,

---

[3] *Tawjihi* is the exit exam for high school.

[4] Israel unilaterally decided to disengage from Gaza in 2004, and the plan went into effect in the late summer of 2005. Under Israel's plan, twenty-one settlements in the Gaza Strip would be evacuated, and the settlers compensated. The Israeli military would leave Gaza completely and leave the entire strip to the administrative and security control of the Palestinian Authority.

[5] After Israel unilaterally withdrew from Gaza, parliamentary elections were held in 2006, and Hamas won the majority of the seats. For more information, see Appendix I, page 267.

[6] Al-Aqsa University is one of a half dozen or so colleges and universities in Gaza. It serves around 6,000 undergraduates.

in 2007.[7] The first thing I remember was the blackouts. Suddenly, we only had power a few hours a day at most. And there was no propane gas to cook with anymore, so we had to hoard it. Really basic things—formula and diapers, for instance—weren't available, at least at first. But then so much of what we needed started coming through the tunnels. Before long you could get just about anything you wanted—European chocolate, designer clothes, anything.

EVERYWHERE I LOOKED I SAW SMOKE

I was nineteen and still a student during the air strikes in 2008 and 2009. The first day of the strikes, December 27, 2008, was quite memorable. I left the university early because I only had one lecture that day. Just before I reached my house, I heard many explosions. I said to myself, *Oh my God, what's happening? There's so much smoke, and I can't see.* I ran home and went upstairs to see what was going on from our roof, and everywhere I looked I saw smoke, but I didn't know exactly what was happening—there was no electricity so I couldn't find out what was going on from the TV. I tried to call out to my brothers and my sisters, but they were out of the house and nobody replied.

I was so worried. My neighbors said that Israeli fighter jets had targeted a place in Khan Younis, but some other neighbors said that they targeted a place in Gaza City, and then some others said, no, it was in the south.[8] Everyone had a different idea about what was going on. I thought,

---

[7] Economic sanctions began in 2006 after the election of Hamas, but the full blockade wasn't imposed until a year later, after skirmishes between Hamas and Fatah in June 2007 drove Fatah out of Gaza. Egypt, which also considered Hamas a terrorist organization, closed its Rafah border as well.

[8] Khan Younis is a major city in Gaza located about twenty miles south of Gaza City. It has a population of around 250,000 and sits near the Rafah border crossing into Egypt.

Oh my God, who should I believe? When I looked up, the sky was full of airplanes and helicopters.

The first day, the fighter jets bombed hundreds of places, including mosques. They must have targeted every mosque in the Gaza Strip. Our house is close to a mosque, and some of our neighbors were so afraid, because the Israelis could have attacked the mosque at any time and destroyed our building in the process. So our neighbors wanted to go to another, safer place. But we told them there was no safe place in the Gaza Strip. Wherever you went, you would find danger there. The jets ended up bombing the mosque and our house shook violently during the explosion, but nobody was hurt. Only the windows of our building were damaged.

It's a funny story, actually. Okay, it's not funny, but our relatives lived near the border with Israel, and they came to live with us near the coast where it was a little safer. But unfortunately, the night they came to our house, the Israelis targeted the mosque. They were so scared! Our relatives left our house saying, "Oh my God! No place is safe to live! We'd rather die in our own house than die in yours!"

I remember the drones showing up. They buzzed through the skies, and the sound they made was like they were whispering, "I'm going to attack you, I'm going to target your house, your family, your friends." But now we're used to the sound of drones. They never really went away after the attacks started in 2008.

The last war, in 2012 was more difficult, actually, because in 2008, to some extent, the Israeli army was coming into Gaza. But in 2012, it was just planes. They hit many places, not just police stations and mosques, but houses—really everything in the Gaza Strip.

By 2012, I had graduated and become a teacher. I was a substitute, and would fill in where I was needed. When I was a teacher, I had a very smart student, and I loved her so much. She was an excellent student. She was in the first grade when I taught her. But just about five months after the air strikes in 2012, I met her again, and I was shocked when I saw her. She had lost her mind, and she was walking down the street as if she didn't know anybody. I went to her and asked, "Do you remember me? I was at your school. Do you remember?" The girl looked at me and laughed. She didn't remember anything. I spoke with her mom and she told me the girl's uncle was killed in front of her eyes. The Israelis bombed the place where he was sitting. He was a civilian, not involved in the resistance at all. He was just sitting in front of his house. And, unfortunately, they also traumatized this girl. And really, I was so shocked and so sad when I saw her.

WHEN THERE WAS NO ELECTRICITY, MY MIND WOULD FEEL SO SLEEPY

Since 2007, we've suffered a lot from power cuts. We might get six or eight hours a day on good days. And power might be on in the morning or at night. Every week we get a new schedule, published in the papers and announced on TV or radio. Everything is affected by the power cuts. So it's hard to establish a daily routine.

We never had a generator at my family's house, because I have a lot of nieces and a lot of nephews, and we were so afraid that one of them would touch it and get burned. You know, you hear many stories of generators blowing up and whole families dying. So we preferred to live without electricity than to see our families injured. We wouldn't use candles either because they're dangerous. Instead, we had battery-operated lights that can be charged during the limited time that power is on. They're safer.

I lived in my parents' household until this past year. There were about twenty-five, twenty-six people in our household—mostly my brothers' families. All my sisters had married and moved out. I was the last to get engaged. During that time, when the power went out, we'd go to the upstairs of the house. I'd sit with my extended family, chatting and having fun.

Sometimes if most of the rest of the family was out, I'd read books or write. But when there was no electricity, my mind would feel so sleepy! This was always a major problem for me. I'd lose concentration for reading or studying for my exams, for example. When I was still a student, I'd have to prepare an assignment for our professor at the university, but I couldn't rely on an internet connection because power would go in and out, so maybe I wouldn't finish in time. Plus, many times the lights wouldn't last for more than two hours, so I had this tiny window to do all my studying. It was a lot of pressure.

As for housework, I couldn't use the washing machine much of the time. I couldn't even make tea with the electric kettle. And I really suffered from not being able to iron my clothes. After I graduated and started teaching, I'd be late to work many times because I was waiting for the electricity to come on to iron. Sometimes I'd go to my friend's house in another city where they had power that day, just to do some ironing.[9] Since the blockade began, we've had a shortage of cooking gas too. This is really a problem. I cannot make sweets or bake a cake. Every time I want to make one, I can't because I don't have any propane gas.

Then there are the water problems. The water is affected by the electricity. There is a water pump in town, so when there is no power, for sure there will be no water. Then the water is polluted. It's saltwater, not for human use. We buy what we call sweet water, or clean water, and use that for drinking and cooking. The other water cannot be used for even

---

[9] The electricity outages rotate throughout the Gaza Strip, so different cities lose power at different times of the day.

animals.[10] We only use it to wash our dishes, clean the house, and wash clothes. Even in the shower, the water ruins our hair. We wash our hair with the sweet water, but not all the time. We can't manage to have a shower with only sweet water. It's not free. So maybe for a wedding, we'll wash our hair well. We have to pay for everything, and a lot of people here in Gaza are unemployed. So they can't pay for the electricity, they can't pay for the gas or the water.

We depended on the tunnels to bring us our basic needs—our food, our clothes, our medicine, everything. When the tunnels were open, we'd go to the store and find all sorts of things. But Egypt and Israel have destroyed the tunnels now, so there's hardly anything in the stores.

MY WEDDING DRESS MIGHT HAVE BEEN BROUGHT THROUGH THE TUNNELS

This year I got married. Planning for the wedding in the current situation was a bit of a challenge! One thing I remember was visiting the market to buy my wedding dress. I asked the merchant if all the dresses had been made in Gaza, and he said he didn't know which ones had been made here, but that many had been sewn in Turkey or Egypt and brought through the tunnels. It's amazing to think of these beautiful dresses being carried fifty feet under the ground through dark, muddy tunnels.

My husband and I were married on March 24, 2014. The day of the wedding, we had to improvise a little. Normally families would prepare food themselves for a wedding in Gaza, but cooking gas was too hard to find. We had to hire a restaurant to cater the wedding for us, since restaurants had an easier time finding cooking fuel. Of course it was all very

---

[10] The other water Wafa refers to is what comes out of the tap when anyone in Gaza turns on the faucet. It's not only too salty to drink or wash with but also polluted with chemical runoff and sewage.

expensive. We rented a wedding hall, but nobody could afford to take a taxi to the wedding hall because gasoline is expensive, and cabs are nearly unaffordable. We had everyone coming from the neighborhood meet at the bus stop, and we all went to the wedding hall from there. Still, it was a beautiful wedding, and I was happy even in my wedding dress that might have been brought through the tunnels.

Now that the tunnels are closed and nothing can get through Egypt, things are getting harder. Nobody has any money, and basic necessities like food are more expensive than ever. There is so much that needs to change in Gaza, but if I could change just one thing, I'd fix the poverty that's making life so difficult for so many Gazans.

SILWAN, EAST JERUSALEM

AHMED AL-QARAIN

Community center volunteer, 42
Born in Silwan, East Jerusalem &
interviewed in Silwan, East Jerusalem

After the Arab-Israeli War in 1948, Israel took possession of Jerusalem's mostly
Jewish western half, while Jordan administered the mostly Arab eastern half,
which included the Old City of Jerusalem, the hill that houses the Temple Mount
(the holiest site in Judaism, where the Second Temple was located), and the
Al-Aqsa Mosque (one of the holiest sites in Islam, where, according to the Quran,
the Prophet Mohammed was miraculously conveyed from Mecca to pass along the
word of Allah). In 1967, during the Six-Day War, Israel took possession of East
Jerusalem along with the rest of the West Bank. In 1980, Israel declared the
whole of Jerusalem the undivided capital of Israel, while the Palestine Liberation
Organization, led by Yasser Arafat, maintained that the city was the capital
of Palestine.

The East Jerusalem neighborhood of Silwan has 30,000 residents and sits
in the shadow of the Temple Mount and Al-Aqsa Mosque to its north. Numerous
archaeological excavations in the nineteenth and twentieth centuries have provided

evidence that Silwan was the original Bronze Age site of the city that would become Jerusalem. Though the majority of the population is still Arab, since the 1980s, hundreds of Jewish settler families have moved into the area, and the tension between settlers and Arabs often boils over into violence.

The first time we walk through Silwan in 2012, a playground and a community center have just been demolished by the Jerusalem police and Israel's National Parks Authority. A few dozen children play in the rubble where the playground was. Without play equipment, they're throwing onions at each other as though they're snowballs. The community center was razed to make room for a new visitor center for the City of David National Park, a massive archaeological museum and dig site that is privately operated by Elad, an East Jerusalem settler organization.

We then visit the nearby Wadi Hilwah Information Center and inquire about people who might be willing to share their stories. There, we meet Ahmed Al-Qurain, who is showing a video about Silwan's troubles to a group of tourists.

Ahmed is ruggedly handsome, with light eyes and a scruffy voice. He begins telling us the story of why he walks with a cane, and we sit with him for a couple hours before making a date to come back. Over the course of half a dozen meetings, Ahmed tells us of his sense of connection to the neighborhood and the problems he has struggled to overcome since being shot twice by a settler outside his home in 2009.

ALL OF MY DREAMS START FROM HERE

I was born here in Silwan in 1971. All my family was born here—my father, my father's father's father's father, as far back as I know. Silwan, it's part of my life. I am part of Silwan. All of my dreams start from here. I've only left Silwan one or two times in my life. My neighborhood, my friends, everything here is made for me.

I was working in the streets here by the time I was six, seven years old. I've learned everything from these streets. So much of the community was supported by tourism when I was young. My parents and neighbors worked in coffee shops, restaurants, as guides. When I was a child, I sold souvenirs, cold drinks, and ice cream to tourists. I learned English before I even started school. I spent a lot of time at the Silwan pool.[1] I'd sell things to tourists in the parking lot there, and I'd help give little tours when I was twelve or so, just showing people around and talking about the history of the place. I knew it well—I could walk from end to end in the dark at night, without a flashlight.

For me, things began to change at the time of the First Intifada in 1987, when I was seventeen.[2] My school was closed during the fighting. It was closed for more than a year, and I never went back. Instead, I started to work. I got a job working in a factory shaping metal. I did that for two years. One day I asked my boss, "What is this metal going to build?" He said, "It's for the Israeli tanks and airplanes." I had no idea, and I quit.

Around 1991, after the whole world started to talk about peace and the end of the Intifada, things really started to change in my neighborhood. Jewish settlers were moving in. There were police everywhere then, and private security as well to protect the new settlers.[3]

One day a group of settlers approached my father and tried to get him to sell our house. They said, "Put whatever figure you want on this check, and that's what we'll buy it for." But my father wouldn't sell—he helped build the house himself when he was just a teenager in the 1940s. Settlers tried the same with other houses in my neighborhood, and they got maybe a few houses that way. In other cases, they'd try to forge papers that were

---

[1] The Silwan pool is an attraction for both Jewish and Christian tourists visiting holy sites. It is said to have been the springs that fed Solomon's gardens and is also the site of a miracle performed by Christ that is described in the Bible. It has been a source of fresh water for the city of Jerusalem for millennia.

[2] For more information on the First Intifada, see Appendix I, page 267.

[3] By the mid-eighties, approximately 75,000 settlers lived in East Jerusalem. By the end of the First Intifada, the population had doubled to over 150,000 and has since increased to over 200,000.

supposed to show that the house had already been sold generations ago, way back in the 1930s. And the more settlers moved in, the more things changed. Suddenly, there were private security guards with big guns at the Silwan pool, and they'd charge visitors money. When my neighbors and I would try to go there, they'd say, "Palestinians aren't allowed."

During this time, I worked installing carpeting. And after that I started to work for a furniture company, assembling furniture, and then I was a truck driver. Around 1998, when I was twenty-seven, I got married. My wife's father is my father's cousin, so she was my second cousin. She was seventeen at the time, and after she finished school, I helped her pay for university for six years. We had two sons a year apart, Asif and Wadi, in 1999 and 2000. Around this time I also bought a truck for myself, and I started my own business as a mover. I worked for Palestinians, for Jewish people, for everyone. In a month I was making 7,000 or 8,000 shekels—enough for my family.[4] For many years, life was good.

YOU SENSE THE SMOKE INSIDE YOU

My story, it's one of thousands of similar stories. I don't like to talk about it. But I have to talk about it. I want people to know what happened to me.

It was September 11, 2009, maybe five-thirty, six in the evening—it was a little before sunset. It was Ramadan, and I was dozing at home, waiting for the sun to go down so that my family could break fast for the day.[5] Suddenly, I heard some people shouting outside, so I went to see what it was about. In the street, dozens of people were shouting at a few private Israeli security guards and a couple of settlers. I asked someone, "Why are you shouting?" And he said, "These two settlers were hitting

---

[4] At the time, 8,000 shekels equaled approximately US$2,000.

[5] During the month of Ramadan, observant Muslims fast from sunrise to sunset each day.

children in the street, and we're demanding that the security guards get these settlers out of here." Since it was Ramadan, all the people in the crowd shouting just wanted peace. It wasn't time for fighting.

My own children were out on the streets at the time, and they were only nine and ten, so I was worried about them. I began to look for them to get them into the house. I also kept my eye on the settlers. They were young, maybe in their early twenties, and dressed in street clothes. They were shouting and pushing at a group of children in the street. Suddenly, I saw one of the settlers put an M-16 in the air. Then he pointed his gun at something, and I saw that he was aiming at a child. And then I realized the child was my son Asif. At the same time, I saw my son Wadi getting hit by the other settler. I was horrified, and realized my neighbors were shouting about my own sons being attacked by the settlers.

I moved toward the settler with the gun and demanded, "Why are you doing this?" He turned to me and said that he could do what he liked. He started to walk away, and I said, "Wait, I want to talk to you. I know you can do this, but why?" He said, "No, you will not touch me." I said, "I want to talk to you—if we do something wrong to you, you can call your security guys. You can call the policeman to come to help you. But I will not allow you to touch my son." As I spoke, the settler was backing away and looking at me and my son, and suddenly, he stumbled backward onto the ground. The other settler yelled, "You have to shoot." So the settler who had stumbled stood up and fired. The people in the crowd started shouting, and I fell down.

I felt like someone had stabbed me with a knife. I had this taste in my body. When you get shot, you sense the smoke inside you. I felt it, and I smelled it in my body. I could taste the bullet in my blood. I saw my right leg was bleeding, and it was twisted beneath me. The bullet was in the thigh.

The people in the crowd asked me where I'd been hit. I said, "I don't know exactly, don't touch me." My two sons ran to my side and asked why it had happened. I was sitting on the ground. I couldn't feel my leg. I started to ask for an ambulance.

I heard the people shouting, and then I heard another shot. The man who shot me had shot another boy in the crowd who was on a bicycle. The boy was about fifteen. Then the man came back and he shot me a second time, this time in the left knee. Why, I don't know. Even the Israeli security guards asked him, "Why are you shooting?" But after that, the shooter and his friend just ran away.

Some people in the crowd called for the ambulance to come and help me. I was bleeding on the street for five minutes. A neighbor brought over some towels, and she packed them on my leg, while a man tied them with a belt to try to stop the blood. They told me, "Someone with a car wants to take you to the hospital." We didn't think an ambulance was going to come any time soon.

They took me and put me in the car. I saw that the boy from the bicycle was already in the car. The man and woman lifted me up under my arms. I felt as though my leg had stayed behind in the street. I told them, "Wait, wait!" I couldn't move my muscles, so I had to lift my leg by the pants and put it in the car. I still couldn't feel it. It was not mine. After that I sat in the car, bleeding. The blood soaked my T-shirt, my shoes, everything in the car.

Then we took off, but on the way to the hospital, the car was stopped twice by Israeli police, and the driver was almost arrested. It was a Friday, and he was probably the only Muslim driving that day, since it's prohibited on Fridays during Ramadan. Once the police realized the situation, they let us go, but they followed us to the hospital.

At the hospital, while the doctor was checking me, a policeman came. He told the doctor, "You have to leave now. You can check on the boy who came in with him, but I want to ask this man some questions." So he interrogated me about the incident, even as I was bleeding.

After I was questioned, my wife showed up. She said that my family, my cousins, they thought that I had died; they were already discussing the funeral.

The doctors got me ready for surgery, and then I was on the operating table for five hours. I later learned that they'd told my wife, "Maybe he has a chance, maybe not." I'd lost eight units of blood and I was very weak.

Later, my sons showed up at the hospital. They looked so sad, and they just said, "We are sorry." I asked them why, and I learned that they'd been interrogated by the police. The police had told them that they provoked the fight with the settlers, and that they were responsible for me getting shot. I told them, "No, no, no, don't think about that. It's not your fault." But even now, they believe that if they hadn't gone out in the streets, I wouldn't have been shot. They still feel guilty.

The police wanted to charge me with assaulting a soldier. The settler who'd shot me was in the Israeli military, but he hadn't been wearing his uniform that day. But luckily, someone in the crowd had taken photos of everything that happened, so it was easy to prove that I hadn't physically attacked the settler in any way.

MY SONS NEED MORE FROM ME

Three months after the operation, I went to get a check up, and my leg still wasn't healing. They performed another surgery to clean out fragments and repair the bone. For maybe eight months, I stayed at home after the shooting. I was in a wheelchair. And after eight months, I started walking again with a walker. After the first year at home, I started to have more pain, and it turns out I needed even more surgeries. Eventually, I was able to replace the walker with a cane.

All of this has changed my life. As a truck driver, part of my job was to move furniture. Also, I would help my family, help out around the neighborhood, play soccer—I can't do any of these things anymore. I have had five surgeries so far. I have two more scheduled. And I have pain whenever I try to do anything physical, even something simple, like helping my son fix his bike. I just can't do it.

For my older son, Asif, the disaster has changed everything in his life. After he was attacked and he saw me get shot, he started to feel like his father couldn't protect him. And when he saw that his father couldn't protect him, he wanted to protect himself. Now, if someone starts picking on him or says something nasty, my son fights with him. These last two years, I've had him in three different schools because of his fighting. Before the shooting, he didn't have any problems in school. Both boys are fighting in school, with other children and with the teachers. And they get angry at the settlers. My sons, they need more from me. As their father, I cannot help them.

One day at home, my sons came to me and said, "Oh, we saw the settler who shot you." I told them, "No, no, he's in jail." I was lying to them. I'd learned that he only spent a day in jail before he was released. They said, "No, we remember him, we saw him." The truth is that the guy who shot me was taken by the police, but he was only questioned for a couple of hours and stayed in jail for twenty-four hours. They picked him up that night. It was Friday when he shot me. Friday night there's no court, and Saturday during the day there's no court, so Saturday evening he went to court and he said that he was defending himself. That was it. They closed the file.

I believe in non-violence. And I tell my children what happened. They ask me, "Why did this Jewish guy shoot you?" I tell them that it's settlers, not all Jewish people. I tell my boys that the difference between the settlers and Jewish people is that the settlers have come here from all over, and they don't really know or understand the land like the Jewish people who have lived here their whole lives do. We visit my friends from Jewish families, and they visited me when I was injured. I've worked with many Jewish people, so I speak some Hebrew. My sons know the difference between the settlers and the other Jewish people. They know. I have told them many, many times. But I also tell them that this is our village, we have to stay here. I tell them to be non-violent, because it's better. If you want to fight something, if you use violence, you will lose.

MUHANNED AL-AZZAH IN FRONT OF HIS ARTWORK

MUHANNED AL-AZZAH

Artist, 33
Born in Bethlehem, West Bank &
interviewed in Bethlehem, West Bank

*The Al-Azzah refugee camp in Bethlehem is barely more than an alleyway
bordered by dozens of small houses jammed closely together. As one walks through
the tight corridors, it's hard to miss the haunting murals painted on the walls of
the houses. These paintings are taken from the Handala cartoon series created by
the late Palestinian artist Naji Al-Ali.[1] In one mural, a girl's hair is twisted
into barbed wire. The painting on another house shows gaunt refugees packing their
bags and preparing to flee. On another house farther down the street, fat politicians
wag their fingers at an emaciated man in rags.*

*The artist behind these graffitied murals is Muhanned Al-Azzah. With
dark eyes and a pronounced beard on his lean face, Muhanned looks the part of an
artist. He's soft spoken but funny, and laughter accompanies all of our interviews.*

---

[1] Naji Al-Ali (1938–1987) was a political cartoonist who criticized Palestinian politicians
and the state of Israel. A recurring character in his artwork was Handala, a ten-year-old
Palestinian boy whose storyline represented the Palestinian refugee experience.

Muhanned's family gave the Al-Azzah refugee camp its name when they led the flight from their village in what is now Israel to Bethlehem during the Arab-Israeli War in 1948.[2] For Muhanned, as well as many other refugees, the dream of returning to lands lost in 1948 (and during the Six-Day War in 1967) persists, even if little remains today of those farms and villages. This dream of a right to return to property long ago claimed by Israel drives much of the politics of resistance within Palestine and is a major roadblock to most two-state solutions.[3]

Muhanned is a prolific painter, and his work can be found both on the sides of buildings and in galleries around the West Bank. On the day of our first interview, he is preparing a collection of abstract paintings for a show in London. Muhanned's paintings explore different subjects, but his recurring focus is the three years he spent in an Israeli prison and the ways the experience have shaped his art. Later, he shows us his rooftop studio, his paintings, and the bullet holes in the walls from the night of his arrest.

MY FAMILY HAS BEEN
IN THE CAMP SINCE 1948

I was born here in the camp, in September of 1981. My parents were born here too. In 1948, my grandparents on both sides left our land, our original village, Beit Jibrin, which is between Hebron and Gaza.[4]

---

[2] Members of the Al-Azzah family had been leaders in the region of their former village ever since revolting against Ottoman rule in the nineteenth century. After many of the residents in their community fled to Bethlehem in 1948, the refugee camp was named after them, in recognition of their prominence. For more on the Arab-Israeli War, see Appendix I, page 267.

[3] For more on the two-state solution, see the Glossary, page 276.

[4] Beit Jibrin was an Arabic village located thirteen miles northwest of Hebron and twenty-five miles southwest of Jerusalem. Before the Arab-Israeli War in 1948, the population was a little under 3,000. The village was depopulated during Israeli raids in the 1948 war, and there is currently an Israeli settlement on its former location called Beit Guvrin.

Even though I've never visited Beit Jibrin, I feel I'm from there. I know all its details, since I've heard so much about it from my grandparents. I know that it's our village.

I know the story of how my grandparents fled the village in October of 1948.[5] One day the soldiers came with guns, planes, and tanks, and everyone in town fled to nearby caves. But some people came back to the village in the night to sleep inside their houses or get things they needed. Then Israeli soldiers entered each house. The first adult male they found inside a house, they brought him to an open space and shot him in front of everyone. The men knew that if they were caught, they might be arrested or shot, so they fled right away. The women followed with whatever they could carry. They didn't have much money, and they couldn't carry much with them. The most important thing was to bring documents to prove that they owned their houses and keep them someplace safe. Most villagers fleeing Beit Jibrin then came here to Bethlehem, where they set up a camp and named it Al-Azzah, after my family.

I have a twin sister, two younger brothers, and one younger sister. Life in the camp has been the same since I was a child. On a typical day, we wake up and the adults go to the main street to eat and talk, to speak about things that are important. Really, it's like cocktail conversation—the news of the day, what's happening with different families, what's happening with the houses in camp. We have political discussions every day, but only in the evenings. In the morning, politics will destroy your brain.

This camp has a little over 1,500 people living in maybe 120 buildings, all packed close together. Everyone knows each other—people spend a lot of time outside because we have such small houses. On the one hand, it can be useful that the community is so close. If a family needs work done on their house, people from the neighborhood will just show up and

---

[5] For more information on the 1948 Arab-Israeli War, see the Glossary, page 276.

help. If a family is hungry, a neighbor always has food for them. But you can't expect any privacy here. If you make something good to eat, people are going to know about it and show up for a meal. If you just want some time to yourself, forget about it. You could be sitting in your pajamas trying to rest or think, and someone will show up at your house and say, "Hey, you wanna go get coffee?" Even if you have something you're trying to hide—like you get a bottle of alcohol—neighbors will know somehow and show up and ask, "Hey, what've you got?" And it was especially hard for my sisters growing up. If they came home in the evenings even just a little late, everyone in the camp would know they were out late and gossip about them. The girls have an even harder time here than the boys, I think.

THE SOLDIERS WENT CRAZY WHEN
THEY FOUND WRITING ON THE WALLS

I grew up dreaming of Beit Jibrin as a paradise. My grandparents always told us about how great life was for them there. Their home and garden in Beit Jibrin were as big as the whole refugee camp where my family lives now. All of my family has hoped that one day we'd be able to return there and live again in our own home.

That's why we were against the Oslo Accords in the mid-nineties.[6] The accords officially made the land that Beit Jibrin was on part of Israel. For us, we preferred a single state between Israel and Palestine so that we could return to Beit Jibrin. We didn't want to accept the Oslo Accords, and some parties in Palestine didn't either. The PFLP opposed the accords and the idea of two separate states that took our land in places like Beit

---

[6] For more on the Oslo Accords, see Appendix I, page 267.

Jibrin and just gave it up to Israel.[7] They supported the right of return.[8] So as I grew up, although there wasn't really a single time or event that led me to it, I came to join the PFLP. There were other things I liked about them too—they weren't a religious party. Hamas, that's the big religious party. And Fatah, that's the big party within the Palestinian Liberation Organization, they were always looking for compromise and were willing to accept two states.[9] But the PFLP seemed like a fit for me—they represented my interests as a refugee from 1948. I'm not going to say much more about their beliefs, though, because I don't want this story to sound like propaganda!

As I grew up, I got more and more into art. My father was an Arabic Literature teacher, and my parents sent me to classes and workshops in Palestinian art at a young age. I grew up seeing art as a way of resistance, through graffiti. During the First Intifada, in 1987, there was no media, there was no radio to cover all that was happening in Palestine.[10] But there were the walls of the houses. They were the only place for media. For example, if there was to be a strike the next day and everyone had to close their shops, there was no simple way to get the message out. So in the night, some people with masks would go into the street with spray paint and write, "Tomorrow, August 9, will be a day of strike for all the shops, the houses, and the schools." So in the morning, everybody could see it.

And every day, when the people went outside, the first thing they did

[7] The Popular Front for the Liberation of Palestine (PFLP) was formed in 1968. For more information, see the Glossary, page 276.

[8] The "right of return" refers to a political position that Palestinian refugees and their descendents should be permitted to reclaim land and property that they were driven from in the wars in 1948 and 1967. For more information, see the Glossary, page 276.

[9] For more information on Hamas, Fatah, and the Palestinian Liberation Organization, see the Glossary, page 276.

[10] For more in the Intifadas, see Appendix I, page 267.

was look at the walls. Sometimes the message was, "Next week, we are gathering for a demonstration on Tuesday." Sometimes there was writing about a martyr, someone who was killed in Bethlehem.[11] The soldiers, when they came in the camp, they'd go crazy when they found this writing on the walls. They would arrest people, and every day there was a fight over who should clean it up. Some people cleaned it, some people refused. And it was very dangerous when artists went out at night to write on the walls.

I was doing some of the same sort of thing even as a teenager. Art was my own individual way of resisting, but we can't do much just as individuals to resist—that just leads to chaos, so that's why I joined the PFLP. More than anything I wanted a chance to go back some day to live in Beit Jibrin, and so a lot of my art has been about being a refugee, about wanting to return home.

After high school, I went to Al-Quds University in Abu Dis to study painting.[12] I also had a chance to study traditional arts in Morocco—decoration, Andalusian art, mosaics, and writing.[13] When I returned home, I continued to study Palestinian art and culture, and I stayed politically active as well.

I was part of the PFLP through 2004, when I was around twenty-two. I met with other members and organized protests and other campaigns on campus. The Israelis considered the PFLP terrorists and an illegal political

---

[11] Palestinians use the term "martyr" generally for anyone killed by Israelis, not necessarily someone who died while fighting. Although originally a religious term, it is now used by religious and secular Palestinians alike.

[12] Al-Quds is a university system with three campuses in the West Bank, including one in the town of Abu Dis, which together serve over 13,000 undergraduates. Abu Dis is a town of around 12,000 people just east of Jerusalem. *Al-Quds* is the Arabic name of the city of Jerusalem.

[13] Muhanned is referring to the art and culture from Spain during the 800 years when it was under Muslim influence. In 710, Islamic armies succeeded in conquering large areas of Spain within a short span of years. The conquerors gave the country the name Al-Andalus.

party, and so I knew that I could be arrested one day, and maybe even killed. But at that time I was feeling that we were under occupation and somebody must do something to change this situation, and anything anybody can do was for the good.

SOMETIMES PEOPLE JUST DISAPPEAR

Late on the night of April 15, 2004, I was home asleep. At home, I slept in the attic where I also had an art studio. My whole family was there, and they stayed on the second floor of the building. We had a friend staying with us as well. My uncle's family lived on the ground floor. Suddenly I woke up hearing megaphones. I knew it was the Israeli military. They were ordering everyone out onto the street, demanding that everyone on the block come out of their homes.

I got out of bed quickly and my first thought was how I could escape. I went to the window and looked out. I saw my neighbors filing out of their homes, and Israeli soldiers were there with jeeps and vans—it looked like they were circling the entire camp. As I watched, the soldiers were moving toward our house, starting to circle it. Then they called out my name through the megaphone. They spoke directly to me in Arabic: "Muhanned Al-Azzah. You cannot escape. Put your hands up and leave the house."

I took my time, if I can speak freely, to hide whatever I didn't want them to take when they searched the house. I hadn't been part of planning any big operations or doing anything violent, but it was against Israeli law to even promote or be part of the PFLP. I guessed they were arresting me because someone had let them know I was organizing for the party.

All I could think was that I might die in a moment, and I asked God for just a few more moments to live. My adrenaline was so high, it wasn't a matter of being strong or not strong, just wanting to survive. But I took my time and put on warm clothes. I knew if I went outside, there would be no time to come back and get clothes. After a few minutes, they started shouting into the megaphone again. By this time, the rest of the people in my house were already outside. I started to see the red laser lights of their guns all over my room and heard shots. They kept demanding that I come out, even as they were shooting at my window. I hid as best I could while I decided what to do next.

After some more time, they brought my mother from the street to my bedroom door. She told me to open the door, that it was safe to go outside. So finally I opened the door and went out with five laser sights hovering over my body. I was terrified.

My neighbors were all outside their houses sitting in the street in the middle of the night. There were maybe fifty people, my family and neighbors, watching and waiting for me.

The soldiers didn't tell me why they were arresting me. They told my family they needed to speak with me for five to ten minutes and then I'd come back. My mother was crying, but she couldn't move because there were a lot of soldiers surrounding her. She couldn't tell me goodbye. My family knew I would come back, but not when—in one hour? One day? One hundred years?

After the soldiers handcuffed me, they put me in one of their jeeps, and we drove for what seemed like a couple of hours. We ended up at Al-Muskubiya in Jerusalem.[14]

The room where they took me was small—maybe eight feet by eight feet, white, with air conditioning. There was a white light, a table, and computer—these were the only things in sight, other than a chair in the middle of the room. The chair was fixed to the ground. They cuffed my

---

[14] Al-Muskubiya ("the Russian Compound") is a large compound in the Old City of Jerusalem that was built in the nineteenth century to house an influx of Russian Orthodox pilgrims into the city during the time of Ottoman rule. It now houses a major interrogation center and lockup as well as courthouses and other Israeli government buildings.

hands behind the chair and chained my legs and hands to it. I couldn't move a millimeter.

Then they questioned me for two days straight. They'd be asking me questions for twenty or more hours a day, with three or four officers asking the same sorts of questions. They weren't really about anything particular—just questions about my life. They didn't even accuse me of anything. I started to get very confused and disoriented. I fell asleep hundreds of times, but just for a second each time. When they saw that I was nodding off, they'd throw water on me to wake me up. They pushed me very hard. Twice a day, they brought me beans and released one of my hands. They said I had two minutes to eat. After two days of being awake, sitting upright, not moving, my legs and hands became numb.

They'd also tell me things to break me down. They told me that my house had been demolished, that my family had been killed. They brought pictures of my younger brothers and told me they'd been shot. I didn't really doubt them, and I assumed I'd be killed too. Sometimes people just disappear, and I thought I'd be one of those people. I started to feel lost, just completely out of focus.

Finally on the third day, they let me know I was being held because of my association with the PFLP and because they suspected the PFLP was planning an attack on Israel. They wanted me to talk about it. I didn't know anything about an attack, but I also didn't want to give them any names of other people in the PFLP that I knew, so I stayed quiet. Sometimes they'd interrogate me for just a few hours a day, sometimes for twenty hours or more. When I wasn't being interrogated, they sent me to a small, gray room—less than six feet by six feet. If I tried to lie down to sleep, my head and legs would be pressed against opposite walls. If I caused a problem in this room, like making too much noise, they'd cuff me and leave me bound up for five or six hours. They gave me just enough food to keep me alive. After a week, they gave me a few cigarettes but no lighter.

Sometimes in between long sessions, they'd put me in a cell with other Arab men. These men would tell me their stories, say they were from Hebron or whatever, and then start asking a lot of questions about me. It was pretty obvious that these men were informants, part of the interrogation, and that their job was to get me to talk when I was feeling less scared, more relaxed. They'd say things like, "I told the Israelis everything, and now I can sleep. If you tell them everything, they'll be easier with you."

I never saw sunlight. I never knew what time it was—evening, morning? I would sleep for a few hours, and I didn't know whether I slept for one hour or for one hundred hours. I didn't know which day it was. I didn't know anything. I spent a lot of time alone, and my mind was going, but I had something inside that pushed me to stay strong.

JAIL IS A TIME TO MAKE AN EVALUATION OF YOUR LIFE

After about four months in Al-Muskubiya, I was taken to military court.[15] There were around twenty soldiers there, all with guns. I felt alone and threatened, and I think this was part of the game. They wanted to scare me in any way they could. But I felt strong, because I was not just one person, I was one with the Palestinian cause. I was a civilian, I had the right to resist occupation, and I didn't care about what they would accuse me of. I didn't listen to what they said, really. They charged me with political activism, activity against the Israeli state, and being a member of an illegal political party—the PFLP. They had no evidence against me that I was part of any attacks on Israel, just that I had promoted the PFLP. They gave me three years.

---

[15] Up to this point, Muhanned was being held in administrative detention, a system that allows Israel to indefinitely detain Palestinians without specific charges. For more information, see the Glossary, page 276.

I was taken to a prison near Be'er Sheva around August of 2004, not quite four months after my arrest.[16] The amazing thing was that the route that the prison bus took to get to Be'er Sheva took me right through the site where my home village, Beit Jibrin, used to be. I had never seen it before, so I tried to see as much as I could as we passed through. When I saw the village, I was shaken. My grandparents had said so many good things about it, about the good old days. I had dreamt of it as a paradise. But the land was barren except for a few trailers that make up an Israeli settlement. There was an old mosque, and lots of ruins—old stones and parts of buildings that were thousands of years old.

My grandparents had been driven from their home by force, and here I was seeing it, again only by force. It was hard. I was alone. It reminded me that I wasn't with my family, and I always imagined I'd see the village some day with them. It was a bad, lonely feeling. It was almost like I had woken up from a coma—I couldn't make sense of everything that must have changed from that time before 1948, a time I knew only in my dreams.

Life at the prison at Be'er Sheva took some time to get used to. I spent most of my days inside my cell. The cells were about ten feet by fifteen feet, and there were seven people living in each one. There were bunk beds for each of us, but we couldn't come down from the beds all together at the same time because there wasn't enough space to stand. For example, when we wanted to clean the room, only two people could do the cleaning.

Everyone was from different places. Some people were very old, some people were young. Some had ten or twenty years in jail, and some had one year. If you wanted time alone, you had to pretend you were sleeping. From the first day, I began to get to know the other prisoners pretty

---

[16] Dekel Prison, near the city of Be'er Sheva, is a maximum-security facility that was opened in 2003. Be'er Sheva is a city of over 200,000 people located sixty miles southwest of Jerusalem.

well. Social relations in Palestine are very close—there are strong connections between Palestinian people. So you can find somebody in jail whose brother or friends you know and you can speak with him.

We had two opportunities to leave our room: once in the morning and once for an hour in the evening. We walked outside in the prison courtyard. In my section there were a hundred and twenty people, but only forty people could fit in the courtyard. So forty people entered and walked in a circle in rows, four to a row. We had one hour, so we walked half an hour clockwise and half an hour counter-clockwise. One of the prisoners would clap when half an hour was up and then we'd walk in the opposite direction. As we walked, I thought, *This is the circle of our life, of every day. And when we start at this point, after one hour we will be back at the same point.*

The courtyard was mostly covered, so there was barely any sunlight even on bright days. Most of the prisoners started to feel sick, just from lack of sun. There were some small windows in the hallways outside the rooms, and if you wanted to get sun, you had to go there in the morning. But there was a pecking order. I was new to the prison, and there were older people who had been in jail for twenty years and they were sick, so it was more important for them to be in the sun than me. I didn't really see any sun for over a year.

Slowly, my mind started to bend and adapt to life inside cell walls. Jail is a time for each Palestinian to sit with himself, a time to make an evaluation of his life. And it's an important, powerful experience to have the time to learn and share stories with people in jail.

Sometimes we found somebody sitting by himself in the room with his mind on the outside world, and we knew we had to keep him from feeling alone. If any of us prisoners began to live with our mind outside the jail, we would start to feel down, depressed. So we would give each other a little time to think those thoughts, but if we saw someone looking pensive, we would go to him after maybe half an hour and start joking, discussing things, anything, just to keep him from getting lost within himself.

I was in isolation a few times—sometimes for a few days, sometimes for one week. This could be for something like having contraband, like cell phones. It was very bad. There was no bed, just a small room with a mat on the floor that you slept on. You had five minutes to go to the bathroom and do what you want, shower, clean—just five minutes. And then you came back to the small cell. Some people spend years in isolation.

There were often conflicts with the guards inside the jail. We would begin to shout or knock on the door and they would come and shoot us with pepper bullets.[17] The bullets cut your skin and the pepper goes in.

The guards searched the room several times each day. When they did these searches, they would bring at least nine or ten soldiers to every room. Sometimes they came just to search. Sometimes they came to bother us. They might come at three in the morning, when we were sleeping. Within a second they'd open the door and nine soldiers would enter with their guns, shouting, "Get down! Put your hands up!"

Still, we were able to hide things sometimes. One thing that was important to us was a cell phone. We used the phone to get news, to talk to our families. At one point, it was my job to hide the phone every evening. We would take it out at six o'clock in the evening and use it until ten, twelve at night, and then hide it. I hid it in a lot of places—for example, we put it in the floor. We cut out a little bit of tile and put it underneath. But you had to be very fast and careful because when the guards came, they searched everything, even the floor sometimes. One time, they brought in a metal detector, and they were able to find our phone that way. They took it, and as punishment they took away visits for two months.

---

[17] Pepper-spray projectiles are weapons sometimes used to incapacitate and control crowds. Each projectile ball fired from the weapon contains chemicals such as capsicum, which is also used in pepper spray. Though they are intended to be non-lethal, deaths have been reported from the use of pepper-spray projectiles.

THEY WANTED MY FAMILY TO
FEEL LIKE THEY WERE IN JAIL TOO

During the whole time I was under interrogation in Jerusalem, my family had no idea where I was or what was happening to me. Toward the end of my time in Jerusalem, someone who knew me from the camp spotted me as I was being escorted down the halls to or from interrogation. This guy told his mother about me when he got out, and then his mother told my mother where I was. Then my mother and father went to the International Red Cross to ask for permission to see me.[18] Finally, two months after I was transferred to Be'er Sheva, they came to visit me.

When I first saw them, my mother had been crying. She was behind a pane of glass and we spoke into telephones. It was difficult for me and it was difficult for her, because we knew she was going to leave after forty-five minutes.

During the visit I told them, "It's okay, I'm good. We have a big space, and TV, and the food is good. We have meat, we have chicken every day, we have juice, we can drink what we want." And all of that was a lie to make her feel better about the situation. It wasn't easy, because I knew if anybody was released from jail, they would tell her what was really going on. And I knew that she knew I was lying, but she didn't want to say it.

But she wanted to keep my spirits up as well. I kept asking about what was happening outside, and she told me everything was good—this friend was getting married, this one was about to graduate from college. There were a lot of bad things she didn't tell me about. I know she lied because she wanted to give me a nice picture of the outside. So we were lying to each other just to keep each other happy.

---

[18] The International Committee of the Red Cross (ICRC) is an organization that monitors prisoner rights around the world, among other functions. For more information on the divisions of the Red Cross/Red Crescent, see the Glossary, page 276.

My parents came twice a month. It was hard for them to visit the jail. They'd get on the bus at four in the morning and wouldn't arrive until noon, and the visit is forty-five minutes. They wouldn't get home until at least seven or eight at night. Sometimes when they came, the prison guards told them, "He's not here, we took him to another jail," or "He's in court." It wasn't true. Once, another prisoner coming back from a visit told me, "Muhanned, your family is waiting outside." I changed my clothes for the visit and waited for my turn. But every time I asked the soldier about it, he said, "Not now, not now." Finally, visiting hours ended and the soldier said, "Your family didn't come." I told him my family was outside, and he went to check. When he came back he told me they had been there, but that they had to leave because visiting time was over.

You know, I didn't want my family to come. I didn't want them to spend all these hours just to come for forty-five minutes and sometimes not even see me. It was a punishment for my family. The Israeli authorities wanted to make my family feel like they were in jail too. So, one night, I used the mobile that we had hidden to tell them not to come.

A couple of months after my parents first started visiting, my two younger brothers were arrested as well. The older of the two was sentenced to two years. He was nineteen. My youngest brother was given administrative detention for a few months—he was just sixteen at the time.[19] I was the first, but my father and mother now say the Israelis have a map of the house since they've visited so many times.

When I was arrested, it was hard for my family. My mom didn't leave the house for a while. But after she came to visit me the first time, she began to meet people and she began to see there were people who would spend all their lives in jail. They had families, wives, and children that they'd never see. So this gave her some perspective. She thought, *My son,*

---

[19] For more on administrative detention, see the Glossary, page 276.

at least he will get released. And she felt the same way about my brothers. I felt the same way, too. There were a lot of people who had twenty-year sentences. So I felt I was just in prison as a tourist.

After a year and a half, in the spring of 2006, I was moved again, this time to the prison in Naqab.[20] There I lived in a tent in the desert for eight months. There'd be maybe twenty of us in each tent, and huge walls around each section of tents. The walls were the same height as the apartheid wall.[21] We were in the desert in June and July, the hottest time of year, under the sun all the time. It was like 104 degrees Fahrenheit, but we were just out in the sun. All the prisoners, they spent their time close to the wall trying to get shade. And there were so many bugs—mosquitoes, bed bugs. It was terrible. The only good thing was the other people, the other prisoners I met.

After the prison in the desert, I was transferred again to Shate Prison, near Nazareth, not long before my release.[22] I spent a few months there. Then finally, in 2007, I was released.

---

[20] The Ktzi'ot Prison is a large, open-air prison camp in the vast Negev desert (Naqab desert in Arabic), located forty-five miles southwest of Be'er Sheva. Ktzi'ot was opened in 1988 and closed in 1995 after the end of the First Intifada, and then reopened in 2002 during the Second Intifada. Today it is Israel's largest detention facility and is being rebuilt to include an immigration detention facility. According to Human Rights Watch, one out of every fifty West Bank and Gazan males over the age of sixteen was held at Ktzi'ot in 1990, during the middle of the First Intifada.

[21] This is a reference to the barrier wall separating Israel from the occupied Palestinian territories, which is twenty to twenty-six feet high and made of triple-reinforced concrete.

[22] Shate Prison (*shate* means "hot pepper" in Arabic) was opened in 1952 and houses 800 prisoners.

I MADE MY ROOM
LOOK LIKE THE ROOM IN JAIL

I knew the date I would be released, but not the place. They released me in Jenin.[23] It was very far from home, and I didn't have any money. I didn't have anything. In 2007, the situation in Jenin was not easy.[24] I borrowed a phone from a taxi driver to call my family and tell them to come and take me back to Bethlehem.

When I got home, I found a hundred friends, family, and neighbors waiting for me at the camp. All of them wanted to carry me on their shoulders or to hug me. I had spent the last three years speaking and living with a maximum of seven people, and to be around so many people all of a sudden, so much commotion, was overwhelming. I was happy, but it was a little too much. Everyone seemed to be talking at once, and I couldn't focus.

The first day I slept in my own house, I woke up at six in the morning, alone. I had gone to sleep at four or five o'clock in the morning because I was celebrating with my family and friends, but I woke up at six because every day while I was in jail, we woke up at six to do the count.

For three or four months, I wanted to be alone. I didn't want to speak with anybody. I didn't want to meet anybody. I made my room look like the room in jail—I filled it with some boxes to make myself a smaller space, and I had coffee and everything I needed around me in that one room.

---

[23] Jenin is a city of almost 50,000 people on the northern border of the West Bank. It's located over sixty miles north of Bethlehem.

[24] Muhanned was released in 2007 just after the Second Intifada, a time of violence and unrest across the West Bank, but especially in Jenin, the location of one of the largest refugee camps in the West Bank. For more on the Second Intifada, see Appendix I, page 267.

Everybody who goes to jail has a lot of problems when they get released. For me, I had trouble speaking with more than one person at the same time, and sometimes I needed a long time to focus on all the details of a conversation. Also, sometimes I had a problem with—I don't know how to say it—feeling secure. For example, if I heard a voice outside, I had to go and see who was talking. If somebody opened the door to my family's house, I had to go and see who it was. Sometimes I'd be sitting in some public space with friends and I'd notice a person sitting behind us, staring at us. My friends, who hadn't been to jail, wouldn't notice that.

But still, I tried to get back into my life. I wasn't as active anymore with friends or politics. But I started school at Abu Dis again in 2008. I was going back to my old art program, the one I'd been in when I was arrested in 2004. My family is educated, as are many people in the camp. Work is not easy to find, and we are not in a normal country. So you must study to have something to do. Having a B.A. here in Palestine is like the same level of qualifications as finishing high school somewhere else. I have four uncles: one has a Ph.D. from Rice University, one has a Ph.D. in education, one is an engineer, the other finished his master's. Two of my aunts are getting their master's. It's the only way to make a living. My twin sister finished her master's and is working for her Ph.D. So getting a degree was very important to me.

Still, it sometimes felt like the hardest thing in my life to go back to university. I had been out of university for almost five years, and when I came back, all my old friends were gone. People who had been studying with me, they were now my professors at the school. I couldn't spend time with other students to discuss anything because they were five or six years younger than me. They felt the things they were discussing were very important, but I didn't care if I had Ray-Ban sunglasses or how much my watch cost or whatever. So I found a distance between myself and others. To be honest with you, I skipped a lot of classes.

I wasn't like that before jail. Before jail I was happy and proud to go in the morning to lectures, to attend university. I was proud of the books I was reading. But after jail, I was ashamed. I didn't want anybody to see me going to school. I felt too old and that this time was finished for me.

But I also met someone, a woman who was about six years younger than me named Aghsan. Before long, we got engaged. But for me, having a girlfriend didn't change much—it was still hard to adjust to being out of prison. For the Palestinian, the occupation changes everything, controls everything: your mind, your life. Aghsan is from Ramallah, and it should have taken me one hour to go and visit her coming from Bethlehem.[25] But at the checkpoint, Palestinians are stopped for hours, even if you are just going to meet your girlfriend. At the checkpoint you don't know how long you will stay.[26]

I had to tell the soldiers at the checkpoint that I had been in jail because if I had answered no, they would have checked and it would have been a problem for me. They asked a lot of questions. And sometimes they didn't ask anything, they just told me to get out of my car and made me wait. It depended on the soldier. If the soldier had a problem with his girlfriend, if he was having a bad day, he would make it a bad day for me. So during our engagement I would just go from Bethlehem to Ramallah to see my fiancée for a couple of hours and then head the opposite way to come back, and this was my whole world. After a while, I started to think the story of Romeo and Juliet was easier than my story. I thought, *Why am I in love with a girl in Ramallah? London and Ramallah seem like the same distance. Is this really worth it?* Sometimes I think the occupation will even stop love.

I also have had trouble at work because of my time in prison. I got

---

[25] Ramallah is the de facto administrative capital of Palestine. It is about thirteen miles north of Bethlehem.

[26] For more on checkpoints within Palestine, see the Glossary, page 276.

a job at an organization called Addameer a little after I started school.[27] It's difficult for me when I feel I'm under someone else's control. I don't want to be under control. This is a problem I have at Addameer. I don't like signing in every day, having my actions determined by someone else.

I BELIEVE ART IS RESISTANCE

When I came back to university at Abu Dis, I spoke with my art teacher. I told her that I wanted to make art about the jail. She supported me because she said there were few artists like me who had experienced jail, even if there were a lot of artists who made prison the focus of their work. Palestinians and international organizations are always speaking about political prisoners in Palestine. Some Palestinian artists make posters, drawings, paintings, and they often depict prisoners as very big and strong, as guys who can destroy the walls of the jail. But I wanted to do something different. I wanted to speak about prison, about life from the eyes of a prisoner. My art was about how the prisoners see the outside world. I painted the bars of the windows, because that's the view we knew. We never saw a view without the fence, without the windows. And when I went to visit my family, my mother, she was on the other side of the glass. So when I was looking at my mother, I saw my mother, but her face was never completely in view. I've painted glimpses of faces and people and houses and cars on small square canvasses to represent the way the outside world appears to prisoners, seeing the world through these little screens, through small glimpses.

I had an exhibition in London in 2011, and also one in Jerusalem, and a third one in Bethlehem. I am proud of that. But I know these paintings I made, somebody can take them for money and put them in his house

---

[27] Addameer is a nonprofit organization working to protect the rights of Palestinian prisoners.

and close them up. So the maximum number of people who will see these paintings is ten people, twenty people. But I believe that art is for all levels of society. I am from a refugee camp, and I am drawing for the poor people in Palestine, not for the bourgeoisie. I'm not doing a painting to keep it inside the house.

After I was released from jail, I started doing graffiti. Sometimes I and a couple of other artists used stencils, because we did a lot of painting in places where we are not allowed to paint, so we had to go fast. I did graffiti in the main street to let everybody see the drawing.[28] If we're caught painting the walls, we will have trouble from the Israeli military.

I believe art is resistance. The graffiti in Palestine, it's not like the graffiti in any other place in the world. Because when you write something on the wall, this means it has a connection with the First Intifada and the revolutionary time.

When I make my art, it feels that I am giving something to my homeland and sending my message to the rest of the world. I paint because I'm speaking for thousands of people nobody knows about: the people in jail. Many of them have been living for thirty years or more in jail. Few people speak for or about them. There are 12,000 people living inside military jails who are civilians. Why people don't know about them, I don't know.

If you live in Palestine, you have big problems: much pain, much suffering. I am painting to change that, to help ease the pain. Many of us are not fighting with guns, but we find our own way to resist. We may lose our lives or freedom, but we are working for the lives of our next generation.

---

[28] Most of Muhanned's murals are done with the permission, and even at the request, of the property owners.

PROTESTERS NEAR BIL'IN, WEST BANK

TALI SHAPIRO

English-Hebrew translator, 31
Born in Jerusalem, Israel &
interviewed in Ramallah, West Bank

The West Bank village of Bil'in is located two miles east of the Green Line demarcation boundary and seven miles west of Ramallah. It's well known for weekly
protests against the occupation of the West Bank and the construction of the West
Bank barrier wall.

    Construction of the West Bank separation barrier began during the Second
Intifada, and the proposed route of the wall crossed through the western edge of
Bil'in, effectively annexing a broad swath of land that included private property
and much of the village's grazing land. In 2005, people from the village began
protesting every Friday afternoon against the incursion into village lands. These
regular protests quickly became a focal point of the Palestinian protest movement,
with hundreds showing up each week from throughout the West Bank, Israel, and
the international community. Celebrities and international leaders have joined in
the protests, from Richard Branson to Jimmy Carter. Human rights lawyers have
taken up the cause as well, and in 2007, Israeli courts ordered that the wall be

dismantled and moved closer to the Green Line, stating that there was no pressing security concern to justify the route of the wall through Bil'in. That same year, however, Israeli courts declared legal the construction of thousands of additional buildings in the Israeli settlement of Modi'in Illit that would occupy land privately held by residents of Bil'in. The territory between Bil'in and the Green Line remains strongly contested.

Tali Shapiro has been attending these protests since 2009. We meet Tali at a weekly protest amid a barrage of teargas and percussion grenades. She wears jeans and a T-shirt with a bandanna around her neck, and she passes out alcohol wipes to soothe the eyes and sinuses of people unfortunate enough to get a face full of noxious tear gas.

Tali agrees to meet with us later at a café in Ramallah. Ramallah is in Area A, and Tali is legally forbidden to visit as a citizen of Israel.[1] However, like many other Israelis, she seems to be able to enter the city without too much trouble from Israeli or Palestinian Authority police. In fact, when we speak to her again in 2014, Tali explains that she has relocated to Ramallah, a move she'd been planning for years.

AS A KID I WAS VERY SHELTERED

My parents were born in Israel. Their grandparents came from Poland, Russia, Ukraine, and Lithuania. I was born in Jerusalem in August 1983, and I have one brother, Benjamin, who is a few years older than me. My parents worked in medicine—my father was an anesthesiologist, and my mother was a psychiatric nurse. We were in Israel for the first five years of my life, and then we moved to the States, to Seattle, for two years while my father had a residency there.

---

[1] Area A territories are administered and policed by the Palestinian Authority. For more information on Areas A, B, and C, see the Glossary, page 276.

The impact of living in the States on me was huge. Before living in the U.S., I'd never had questions about who I was or where I was from. One of the things I specifically remember in the States was the Pledge of Allegiance. Having to stand up every morning and pledge allegiance to a flag that was not my own was very suspicious to me. I'd think, *Oh wait, I can't really do this, can I?* But then, interestingly—and I was like seven years old at the time—I began to think, *If I feel strange pledging allegiance to this flag, what should I be feeling when I sing the Hatikva?*[2]

And then after Seattle, we came back to live in a small town called Omer, outside Be'er Sheva.[3] Omer is a really affluent town, maybe one of the three wealthiest in Israel. It was really lovely and really boring—pleasant, a lot of greenery, all the houses pretty much the same. There wasn't much to do, but it was a nice place to grow up.

As a kid, I was very sheltered. There was so many terrible things going on all around, but my parents shielded me from confronting anything difficult or complicated. For example, my mother wouldn't take me to funerals when some aunt died, because she didn't even want me to see that. And my family had this history of being part of the Zionist movement. My grandparents helped start towns—they had streets named after them. So I grew up in this sheltered, patriotic world. So much in our culture was about Israel, Israeli security. During holidays, I remember teachers sending us home with little chocolates wrapped in foil with Israeli flags sticking out of them.

And everyone loved soldiers. They were idols. Everyone had been a soldier and therefore a hero—my mom, my dad, uncles, aunts, everyone.[4]

---

[2] The *Hatikva* is the Israeli national anthem.

[3] Omer is a suburb of over 7,000 northeast of Be'er Sheva. Be'er Sheva is a city of over 200,000 south of Jerusalem.

[4] Military service starting at age eighteen is compulsory for most Israeli citizens. For more on the Israeli Defense Force, see the Glossary, page 276.

But of course, we were fed the idea in school and in the media that by the time my generation was old enough, there wouldn't be a need for everyone to do military service, that it was just a temporary problem that would be solved. That isn't something you hear anymore, but when I was growing up in the nineties, after the Oslo Accords, there was this idea that Israel wouldn't need this big military any longer.[5]

IT'S SORT OF LIKE
SUMMER CAMP WITH GUNS

As a teenager, I didn't really think about service that much. I was just a typical bored teen in a small town. And I didn't understand the politics of Israel and Palestine at all. I'd hear terms like "settlers" in the media from time to time, but I think girls, especially, were shielded from knowing about those sorts of issues. I didn't really know what a settler was, even in high school.

At age sixteen I got my draft registration in the mail. I was confronted with the possibility for the first time that I'd probably have to be a soldier. The way the registration order works is that you start going through the process of figuring out what sort of unit you'll be in, in what capacity you'll be serving. I got a pretty sad-ass order that basically let me know I was going to be a secretary or something, while some of my friends were going to be scouts out in the wilderness or doing other interesting assignments. The summer when I was sixteen, I went to Gadna camp for a week.[6] This is something that most Israeli teens do—it's sort of like

---

[5] The Oslo Accords marked the end of the First Intifada and established a tentative plan for Palestinian governance of the West Bank and Gaza. For more information, see the Glossary, page 276.

[6] *Gadna* is short for *Gdudei No'ar*, or youth battalions. The Gadna tradition dates back to before the formation of Israel.

summer camp with guns. We stayed in tents in the desert and female IDF officers taught us how to take apart a rifle, took us to the firing range, that sort of thing. It was my first experience with weapons.

Then, right after I turned eighteen, around 2000, I enlisted. Up until then I wasn't sure if I'd have to serve or not. Only about 40 percent of the Israeli population ends up serving, even if everyone is supposed to enlist. So what happens is you're in a situation where you don't want to do it. But you feel an obligation to do it, there's a social pressure to do it. It's considered very selfish within Israeli society if you refuse to serve in the army. People just look at you like, *Oh, you're just a big baby.*

My one month of basic training was done in the north, near Haifa. Basic training was a strange experience. It didn't seem like we were learning anything. Other than practicing at the firing range, we were just dealing with the discipline of day-to-day life, like making our beds the right way, dressing the right way, handling kitchen duty. We all slept in tents in the cold weather and ran a bit during the days. We'd get yelled at if we messed up and would have to run extra laps. I think basic was a little easier for me, because I wasn't going to be assigned to combat duty. Like I said, I was selected to be a secretary.

After my month of basic, I was transferred in September to the biggest military base in Gaza at the time, which was right on the edge of Khan Younis.[7] I served during the Second Intifada, and there was a lot of fighting at the time.[8] I remember the sounds of shots fired and explosions all through the night. I remember the rumble of buildings collapsing. It could be so loud, and it was hard to feel like I wasn't in danger, even though I wasn't involved in combat. In fact, most enlisted female soldiers

---

[7] Khan Younis is a city of over 250,000 residents in southern Gaza. It's the second largest city in the Gaza Strip and close to the Rafah border crossing into Egypt.

[8] For more on the Second Intifada, see Appendix I, page 267.

weren't allowed to carry weapons—only female officers and female field medics. I remember a commanding officer telling me that female soldiers with guns were more likely to cause damage than do anything useful with them. That seemed like a pretty common attitude in the military.

I still didn't understand the situation between Palestine and Israel at the time. I'd hear all sorts of things in the media. For instance, I remember hearing about these crazy settlers who decided to jump the border and cross into Gaza, and then the military had to send people out to protect them. I'd think, *Why don't we just pull back, and then the settlers will pull back too?* It just all seemed weird to me, mostly. But I didn't think of it much.

THE WAR CAME TO ME
IN SMALL OBSERVATIONS

I was stationed in Gaza for one year and eight months. Most of my days were fairly routine, actually. I'd file personnel reports every morning on who was on the base, who was off the base, what they were doing. And then after doing that, I'd still have time to go eat, work out in the gym, take a nap, read. I'd see friends who were in combat, and they'd have been out for fourteen hours and simply exhausted. Meanwhile, I was just trying to fill up my days.

But a few moments are embedded in my mind—I guess they were in the back of my head until I could deal with them. We were stationed on a hill that was overlooking the beach, and there was a pathway where the kids would go to school. So I'd see them, you know, walking hand in hand or running after a donkey cart and catching a ride to school and I remember thinking, *That's the enemy? Hmmmm, okay.*

And then another moment was when I was with some soldiers at the border crossing, and there was a guy on his knees without his shirt on. He was cuffed with his hands behind his head. And there were other soldiers who were pushing him into the jeep rather roughly. All I could think was, *Why isn't he wearing a shirt? Did they make him take it off, rip it off, why?* I couldn't face what was really going on, the possibility that he'd been beaten, stripped to humiliate him. So the war came to me in just these small observations that lodged in the back of my mind.

And I remember one surreal moment later in my service. It was a little shocking to me. My commanding officer, who I wrote up reports for, had a map of Khan Younis spread out on his desk. One day he called over his deputy and asked, "How many houses did we demolish this year?" The deputy told him that we were up to 297 houses. So my commanding officer took a black marker and made three Xs on the map. He showed his deputy the locations he'd marked, and said, "It's almost the end of the year. Let's do a few more and round it up to a nice, even 300."

Nobody ever said anything about the morality of what we were doing. I think most soldiers were really just preoccupied with how shitty life was. Because the army was like prison, with occasional leave to go home. But it's high-discipline bullshit, wearing the uniform, having to work from morning to night.

I JUST WANTED TO DO
SOMETHING TO STOP THE WAR

After my military service was up at the end of 2002, I moved back home with my parents for most of 2003. I was just trying to figure out what to do, how to get out of Omer. I applied to a fine arts program in Tel Aviv and was accepted, so I moved there to go to school in the fall of 2003.

For the four years I was in school, I didn't think about politics much—I was just focused on my art. But in my last year, I switched from fine arts to animation, and I started dating another student in my program. He was much more political than I was. He challenged me to defend all the stuff I'd grown up hearing through the media. We probably had a political conversation every day for the three years we were together, just naturally while watching the news on television or reading the paper. I slowly started to move away from the sort of blind patriotism I'd grown up with.

During this time I was also trying to make a life in Tel Aviv. I was able to make some money selling prints of my art, and I also supported myself by doing online marketing work. I broke up with my boyfriend in 2008, but I didn't stop thinking about the relationship between Israel and Palestine. I remember a documentary I saw that was made by the BBC. The larger narrative in the documentary was about activists and journalists that had been killed by the Israeli military—Rachel Corrie, Tom Hurndall, James Miller.[9] At one point in the documentary, there was a story about a twelve-year-old girl who was shot in the head by an IDF soldier during the Second Intifada. The girl went into a coma, and the documentarians were there in the hospital when she regained consciousness, and they captured the moment when she realized that she was blinded by the shooting. I remembered what I was like at twelve, and I just couldn't separate myself from this girl's experience. Then a little later in the documentary, the filmmakers interviewed the commanding officer of the unit responsible for shooting the girl, and I recognized the officer as one of my former commanders. I realized that I had served in that unit around the time the girl was shot. I didn't understand my feelings at the time, but it was the first time I had felt this emotional sense of responsibility in some way for what was happening between Israel and Palestine.

---

[9] Rachel Corrie was an American pro-Palestinian activist who was killed by the Israeli military in Rafah in 2003 during the Second Intifada. She was crushed to death by a bulldozer while trying to defend a Palestinian man's home from demolition. Tom Hurndall was a British photography student who was shot by an Israeli sniper in Rafah in 2003 (after a nine month coma he died in 2004). James Miler was a British filmmaker who was shot and killed by Israeli military in Rafah in 2003. The story of the three deaths is investigated in the BBC documentary *When Killing is Easy* (2003).

And then late in 2008, Cast Lead came.[10] When the media started reporting that it was likely that Israel would invade Gaza, I started having a panic attack. I remembered my own experiences there in Gaza, some of the things I saw, and I just knew a lot of people were about to die. And then when the invasion happened, and I watched it all unfold on the news, I felt I was going crazy. I just wanted to do something to stop the war. I suddenly found I couldn't do my art any more. It just didn't seem important. I joined a protest march against Cast Lead in Tel Aviv, but it didn't feel like I was doing enough.

A few weeks after Cast Lead began, my ex-boyfriend called me up and he said, "Hey, you want to go to Bil'in?"[11] By that time I had already seen the protests from the village on TV, and I said, "Yeah, I want to go, I want to meet these people."

So I started coming to the West Bank in 2009. We used to meet at Levinsky Park in Tel Aviv to carpool to the protests.[12] Just going to the park and starting to talk to the other activists there, I knew I was where I belonged. We went to Bil'in every Friday—that's when the protests against the wall took place. There was a lot of tension at the time because of the operation in Gaza. People in Israel had flags up on their cars, and it was the same with Palestinians. There was a lot of nationalism on both sides. But what I remember first about the protests in Bil'in is just what a festive atmosphere it was. There was dancing, joking. It felt like a celebration—of resistance, of continued existence. The protest I'd gone to in Tel

---

[10] Operation Cast Lead was a military invasion of Gaza from December 2008 to January 2009 in response to rocket fire into Israel and the militarization of Hamas. Approximately 1,400 Palestinians were killed during the invasion. For more information, see Appendix I, page 267.

[11] Bil'in is a village of around 1,800 people.

[12] Levinsky Park is located in south Tel Aviv. The surrounding neighborhood is home to many North African immigrant communities.

Aviv was solemn, serious, like a funeral. That was fine, since it seemed respectful, but I much preferred the feeling in Bil'in.

Of course compared to the march from Bil'in to the barrier wall, the protests at the barrier itself were intense. Teargas, rubber bullets. Of course I knew something about what was going to happen. I'd seen videos of the weekly protests, and I'd been carefully briefed about the dangers by other protesters. But being there in person, I felt so vulnerable. Probably the most important thing for me about those first few trips to Bil'in were just meeting Palestinians, talking to them casually even during a time when tensions were so high. Their situation went straight to my heart.

I'VE BEEN ARRESTED
PROBABLY TWENTY TIMES

I've been to the weekly protests in Bil'in over 250 times now. I go just about every week, unless there's a wedding or other big event I have to be part of. Before activism, I felt I just had a complete estrangement from society. And now I feel deeply part of it, as complex as it is. So now at least I have some kind of context to who I am and where I belong and why I had so many issues with the identity, my Jewish identity. I'm an atheist, so the whole Jewish identity is kind of strange to me. It's in my ID cards. My nationality is Jewish. I have to deal with this. So at least I have some kind of prism from which I can deal with it.

Getting to Bil'in was never much of a problem. We'd often go by bus. Only twice over the last five years have any soldiers at checkpoints boarded the bus we take and checked everyone's IDs. Lucky for me, I have two passports—my Israeli passport, and also a European one. I have Polish citizenship, passed down from my grandfather, and if I need to I show the European passport to checkpoint guards to help me get into areas restricted to Israelis. The checkpoints are all run by Israeli guards, so there's no risk if they catch me anyway. Once, when I had to show my European passport, a guard asked to see my visa as well. Of course I didn't have one. But the guard just reminded me that I was going into an area that could be dangerous, that I should consider turning back.

I've never had any trouble with Palestinian security.

When we get to Bil'in, we start by congregating in the center of town.[13] Then we start marching toward the wall. Usually, we don't have the chance to start demonstrating at the wall, because the army will start dispersing us even before chanting begins. And the dispersal is brutal. Most commonly, it's through tear gas. It's a terrible experience, the choking, the sore eyes, the whole thing, you know. It's an extreme physical experience. I think after four, five, six times, you kind of become desensitized—you're prepared to get gassed.

It hasn't been easy. I've been arrested probably twenty times. But I haven't been physically assaulted during arrest. The soldiers treat me differently, because I'm female, because I'm small, because I seem feminine. I'm kind of reaping the rewards of machismo. As a woman, I feel I should be the human shield for men, because many times they get treated very brutally, and if I'm there, then it softens things. Sometimes I can keep men from being arrested—not just Palestinians, Israeli men as well. My presence helps ease tensions sometimes.

I've seen some terrible things, though. Beatings happen often. Rubber bullets. And sometimes people are hit by teargas canisters. That's one of the ways people are killed during protests. A friend named Iyad, who I knew from the protests, was hit in the face by a canister once. He wasn't even that close to where it was fired, but it crushed his face. I didn't see it happen, but I saw him getting dragged to an ambulance. His face was bloody—I couldn't even recognize him, other than his clothes.

---

[13] Bil'in is about thirty miles from Tel Aviv.

He survived, but he has a big Y-shaped dent in his forehead now, and he has a little issue with memory loss. But he's going to be okay, I think.

I remember another friend, a young guy, who was struck in the knee with a canister, and his kneecap was broken. It hurt him a lot—he was writhing in pain when he was struck, but we decided not to take him to an ambulance, because he didn't want to get arrested. After the protest, he basically grew a second knee while we were driving home—it was that swollen. He was still in so much pain. We ended up calling his mother and meeting in the parking lot of an IKEA. She had no idea he was at the protest and would have been very much against it. I remember trying to calm her down as we got her son out of the car. She was calm about it, but I think quite worried, and after she took him to the hospital and he was treated, she gave him a lot of shit about being part of that kind of protest.

A lot of Israeli protesters have trouble with their parents. Mine are definitely not supportive of my politics, but they support *me*, so we're at peace. And I've never been injured or spent any real time in jail, so they haven't had to face that sort of thing yet.

I don't necessarily think protests are the most effective sort of action we can take. I think boycotts are a lot more useful in terms of leverage on the Israeli government. But it's important for me to meet people face to face and understand what's going on in the West Bank and make friends. And I think it's good for forming friendships, especially between Israeli citizens and Palestinians, where we agree politically that their rights are being infringed on.

I FEEL MORE LIKE I CAN BE MYSELF
IN RAMALLAH THAN IN TEL AVIV

For years I planned to move to Ramallah. Then I finally did it at the start of 2014. I had a lot of reasons for making the move. For one, my partner is here. And I'm closer now to the protests. I'm learning Arabic, and living in Ramallah really helps me pick it up quickly.

I still go back to Israel every couple weeks, to visit friends in Tel Aviv or to see my parents in Omer. I still get a little nervous at checkpoints, but I never have any real problems. And I haven't had any issues in Ramallah because of my Israeli citizenship. I don't go around telling everyone I'm Israeli, but I don't try to hide it either. For the most part, my life here is completely normal. I go shopping in the market, I'm comfortable in the streets. There are moments here when I'll meet someone new, maybe with a group of friends, and I'll talk to them for a while and they'll think I'm nice. Then I tell them I'm Israeli, and they sort of have to recalibrate a little. So I do find myself hiding my identity a little bit. But I still feel comfortable here, even if I have to be a little circumspect about where I'm from.

In many ways, I was less comfortable living in Tel Aviv. In Tel Aviv, I can sit in a coffee shop and watch a building going up across the street and know that all the workers at the building site are probably from the West Bank. I could talk to those guys if we were in the West Bank, but it would be weird for me to talk to those same people in Tel Aviv. It's just sort of taboo for Israelis to chat with Palestinians working in Israel. And I remember times when I'd be out with a friend of mine in Tel Aviv who is very outgoing. We'd be at a restaurant and she'd strike up a conversation at with people at the next table over. I found that sort of thing made me so tense. I'd be so worried something political would come up, and I'd end up getting into an argument about something stupid. I don't really feel that way here in Ramallah. It's a little ironic because I'm hiding my identity a bit here, but I feel more like I can be myself in Ramallah than I can in Tel Aviv.

UNRWA MURAL IN RAMALLAH, WEST BANK

KIFAH QATASH

Homemaker and student, 42
Born in Al-Bireh, West Bank &
interviewed in Ramallah, West Bank

Both Kifah Qatash and her sister Hanan love black coffee. Their ritual is to make
a big pot and then sit on the overstuffed sofas in Hanan's living room in Ramallah
and talk late into the evening while drinking cup after bitter cup. It is in that same
living room and with that same coffee pot that we sit down with Kifah for her
interview. She speaks mostly in English, with Hanan translating when she falters.

Kifah was born and raised in the neighboring town of Al-Bireh. Although
it is called Ramallah's twin, Al-Bireh is calm and traditional compared to
Ramallah's crush and bustle. Al-Bireh is a largely Muslim community with
elegant nineteenth-century Palestinian houses made of local white limestone. It
hosts a sizeable community of refugee families, including Kifah's family.[1] Though
now peaceful and sedate, Al-Bireh has not always been so. Kifah lived through the
two Intifadas there, which meant years of Israeli soldiers on the streets, imposing

---

[1] For more on the United Nations Relief and Works Agency (UNRWA) and Palestinian
refugees, see the Glossary, page 276.

curfews and raiding houses. Though she's built a life in Al-Bireh, Kifah longs to return to Yazur, the village her family fled in 1948, although she has only seen it during a few short visits as a child.

When we meet, Kifah is dressed simply in a black abaya and white head scarf.[2] She is quiet but speaks with a clear self-assuredness, and is quick to laugh. Kifah is looked up to as a leader in her community through her years of working on behalf of prisoner rights. She believes that this advocacy work, along with her leadership in a network of Palestinian activists in her mosque, may have brought her to the attention of the Palestinian Authority, the governing administration in much of Palestinian-controlled West Bank. The Palestinian Authority is especially concerned about the rise of fundamentalist and Islamist political factions such as Hamas, the party that won elections in the Gaza Strip in 2006 and subsequently drove Fatah—the party that controls the PA—out of Gaza. Kifah believes that information likely passed from the PA to Israeli police led to a raid on her home in 2008, and to her arrest in 2010. She was imprisoned for a year without charges.

I'D WATCH EVERYTHING
THROUGH THE WINDOW

My family is originally from Yazur Village,[3] but I was born in Al-Bireh.[4] I still live in Al-Bireh. It has affected me hugely that I'm not on my land in Yazur. I still want to return to my village someday.

---

[2] An *abaya* is a long, robe-like garment that covers the entire body except for the face, feet, and hands.

[3] Yazur was an ancient town just east of Tel Aviv and Jaffa that had a population of over 4,000 Arabs prior to 1948. It was destroyed and depopulated in the lead-up to the Arab-Israeli War. For more on the conflict in 1948, see Appendix I, page 267.

[4] Al-Bireh is a town of over 40,000 people just outside Ramallah. Though it doesn't house any refugee camps within city limits, the town has become populated by refugee-status families in recent decades, so that now more than 50 percent of the town's population has refugee status under UNRWA.

When I was a child, it wasn't always easy being a refugee in Al-Bireh. On the one hand, people loved us. They saw refugees as an important part of Palestinian history. At the same time, the residents of Al-Bireh were sort of a closed community. A lot of landlords wouldn't rent to refugees—only to people who were from the town. And in a lot of cases, girls from refugee families had a hard time marrying boys from Al-Bireh families. Those families wouldn't be interested in having their sons marry refugees. When I was a child, we were actually one of the few refugee families in Al-Bireh. My father had moved here from the refugee camps near Ramallah after he started a carpentry business here. Later, he started a small grocery as well. But refugees were rare then—now we're more common in Al-Bireh.

Still, Al-Bireh was not a bad place to grown up. It was very quiet. The neighborhood we lived in was peaceful. I was the third child—I had an older sister, older brother, and two younger sisters. My older sister, Hanan, was a year older than me, and we were best friends. We played in the hills nearby, we rode our bikes, climbed trees, played charades. We played with the neighbors. It was safe, and we felt free. We could even stay out at night. My parents wanted to make us feel like we had a normal life. They had grown up in the camps, and life was much harder for them there—especially my father, who is deaf.

When I was a child, I was most aware of the occupation when my family traveled out of Al-Bireh. Travel was difficult. For example, when I was a young child, my family would often visit relatives in Nablus.[5] Quite often, we would start our journey to Nablus, and all of a sudden, we'd hit a roadblock set up by Israeli soldiers.[6] They'd stop our car and

---

[5] Nablus has a population of over 120,000 and is one of the major urban areas of the West Bank. It's located thirty miles north of Ramallah and Al-Bireh.

[6] For more information on the West Bank closures system and checkpoints, see the Glossary, page 276.

send us back the way we came. So they deprived me of those visits, and that really affected me, especially when I was a child. And I remember visiting the site where Yazur had been. There weren't any homes there any more—it was an industrial zone. That affected me as well, to see that this place where my grandparents used to have a big home was now a bunch of factories.

From what I remember, there were always Israeli settlers around, though we didn't have a big settlement near us until 1981. That's when the Psagot settlement was built up.[7] But when I was a child, it didn't seem like such an exceptional thing. We'd see settlers pass through town because we shared a main road. For the most part, we didn't worry too much about the settlers or about Israel.

Then, when I was a teenager, the First Intifada started, and things changed rapidly, even in our quiet neighborhood in Al-Bireh.[8] Suddenly, we could expect to hear of friends or neighbors who were killed by soldiers. We had to worry that soldiers would come in the middle of the night. When they wanted to find someone, soldiers would break into houses in the middle of the night—sometimes they'd break into everyone's house in the neighborhood. I admit I was curious, and I'd watch everything through the window. My older sister, she was more afraid, and she said she refused to see young men being humiliated in the street. Sometimes soldiers would arrest men and have them strip down to their underwear in the middle of the road. Sometimes soldiers would laugh at the men, make them sing songs. It was all terrible, but I needed to see for myself what was going on. Our house was on one of the main streets in town, so we had this happening outside our window quite a lot.

---

[7] Psagot is an Israeli settlement of around 2,000 people located just south of Al-Bireh and just east of Ramallah.

[8] The First Intifada lasted from roughly 1987 to 1993, ending with the signing of the Oslo Accords. For more on the First Intifada, see Appendix I, page 267.

Sometimes the soldiers would make every male in the neighborhood come out of their house. I remember my brother being forced into the street, and he was still just a child. For more than a month after the Intifada started, there was a curfew—we couldn't leave the house even to go to the garden. My father ran a mini-mart on the ground floor of our building, and we were afraid to even go downstairs to get things to eat. We knew if soldiers saw us through the windows, they could do anything—we could be taken. Anyway, that's what we were afraid of as girls. And it wasn't just soldiers. Armed settlers from Psagot, men in civilian clothes, would be in the streets as well. Suddenly, we realized just how close Psagot was to us, and just how scary it was to have a settlement so close.

As the Intifada continued over the years, I started to get more involved. I started to go to demonstrations. During that time when demonstrations happened against the occupation, it could seem like everyone dropped what they were doing to join—people would leave work, strike, whatever. The same with students—we'd march out of the classrooms for demonstrations sometimes.

When I was around sixteen, I was at school one day, and we heard about a big demonstration that was happening in town. Many students got up and started walking out of the building to join in. But when we got to the front entrance of the school, a captain from the Israeli army was there blocking the way, trying to lock up the school. He didn't want us students in the streets.

I filled up a bucket with water, marched up to the captain, and soaked him with it. He got mad. He arrested me and brought me to his jeep. Then he drove around with me handcuffed in the back seat. He said he was going to exile me from Palestine for what I did to him! We drove through Al-Bireh and Ramallah for maybe four hours while he patrolled, and then he took me to the police station where they called my parents. At the time, it was rare for girls to be in demonstrations or out in the streets. When I saw my parents, they told me that friends and neighbors had been calling them all day, saying that they saw me in the back of an Israeli Jeep! It was unusual then to see a female get arrested. I think my parents were probably more scared than I was. I just felt like the Intifada was in my blood. It was my duty to resist.

WE TRY TO DRAG THE MEN BACK

The empty half of the glass is that the occupation is crazy. But the good half, the full half, is that I met my husband, Hazem, and got to know him because of the occupation. He was my brother's friend. It was in the early nineties, during the Intifada. My brother had come back from abroad, and he'd invited his friend Hazem to our house for a visit. Because our house was on the main street in town, there were Israeli soldiers constantly in the road. Palestinian boys would throw stones at the soldiers in their tanks from windows, and the soldiers would sometimes come down from their tanks to search the houses for the boys who struck their tanks. So just as Hazem was arriving at our house for a visit one day, some Israeli soldiers stopped him and started to arrest him.

It wasn't uncommon during the Intifada for girls and women to try and stop arrests—it was rare for soldiers to arrest or beat up women. So women would sometimes try to intervene, argue, and drag men who were getting arrested into their houses. So I went out to help when I saw Hazem get picked up by the soldiers. Just as I started to argue, the soldiers let him go. So it was that moment when he saw me helping him, endangering myself for him, that he noticed me. And after a couple of months, he came to my family and proposed. I ended up leaving school just before graduating to marry Hazem.

We got married in 1992, when I was around eighteen, and I had a son in 1993 named Moad and a daughter in 1994 named Duha. My husband studied at a vocational school, and he got a job as a maintenance man at a factory in Ramallah that made sweets, cookies, chocolates, that sort of thing. It took me some time to learn to cook, but I eventually became very good at it.

Marriage didn't really change me in terms of activism. Not a bit. I went to demonstrations even after I was married. One thing that did slow me down, though, was that I was diagnosed with lupus when I was twenty-six. I was pregnant, and I had a miscarriage. When I went to the hospital for tests, that's when they discovered that something was wrong. I would get pain in my hands and feet, and swelling sometimes as well.[9] The pain was constant, and the doctors tried a lot of medicines and did a lot of tests before they diagnosed me with lupus. The pain was especially bad in cold weather. Doctors tried to treat it, but the pain didn't go away. I had to develop tricks to deal with the pain, just to keep going. I had to have faith in God. I stayed involved too—I could take my mind off the pain by seeing friends, seeing family, being out in the community.

After the First Intifada and the Oslo Accords were signed, the Palestinian Authority took over.[10] There were fewer demonstrations, and I also had my kids, so I wasn't as involved in street protests. But through our mosque, I started getting to know people whose family members had

---

[9] Lupus is a chronic autoimmune disease that can affect the heart, lungs, kidneys, and joints. Those who suffer from the disease may have symptoms such as fevers, rashes, and fatigue. Kifah has also been diagnosed with Raynaud's syndrome, which is a chronic condition sometimes associated with lupus that causes restriction of blood vessels in the extremities in response to cold or stress. The hands and feet of those with Raynaud's syndrome are often discolored, and the disease can lead to tissue damage and infections such as gangrene. Kifah has been more recently diagnosed with Sjogren's syndrome, another autoimmune disorder, which destroys the salivary and lacrimal glands, causing chronic dry mouth and eyes.

[10] The Oslo Accords took place in 1993 and led to the formation of the Palestinian Authority, an interim government that was designed to administer parts of Palestine until the peace process was finalized. For more information on the Palestinian Authority and the Oslo Accords, see the Glossary, page 276.

been killed in the Intifada, and many who had family members still in prison. So between the First Intifada and the Second Intifada, I spent a lot of time helping families who had been affected by the conflict. A lot of us did—we all felt it was right to help each other. That's when I started getting involved with prisoner rights. I would go and see the families of prisoners to make sure they were doing well. So many young men were arrested in the Intifada, and it was really hard on the families. This is one of the things that helped keep me active and involved even after I contracted lupus.

I was involved in supporting families with prisoners especially after the start of the Second Intifada in 2000, and I became very well known in Al-Bireh and Ramallah. I got out as much as I could. I couldn't do everything around the house that I wanted because of my disease, but luckily, my family helped out so much. My husband helped to take care of the house when I couldn't, and my two kids were helpful from a young age as well. So I did my best to maintain my home, and I stayed involved in the community as much as I could as well.

I BECAME A SUSPECT

I am 100 percent sure that the Israeli police target religious people like me. If you want to go to the mosque and pray, that's okay with Israeli soldiers. But after prayer in the mosque, I like to sit down and listen to a lesson or lecture and Islamic teachings. If it's a lesson in the mosque about women's issues, such as our periods, that's okay. But if I wanted to learn something about what's happening in Egypt or another political issue, for the Israelis, that's not okay. Islam has two parts: your relationship with God, and your relationship with society. So if you want to focus on your relationship with God and pray, that's okay. But once you focus on your relationship with society, that's not okay, and it will probably get you noticed by the authorities. I think any mosque where there are lectures about politics—whether about Palestine or other countries as well, like Egypt or Syria—Israeli authorities will be suspicious about what's going on.

Israel is an occupying country, and the most important thing for them is security. Therefore, if they suspect for a split second that someone is active against Israel, they don't hesitate to go and arrest them. I think between my work with prisoners and my attendance at political lectures in the mosque, PA or Israeli police started to monitor me. The Israelis don't want anyone to have anything to do with the prisoners because they want to cut the prisoners off from the community. So if you're working on behalf of the prisoners, giving comfort to them, you become someone working against Israel; the Israelis saw this as if I was doing something against them. So I became a suspect.

And unfortunately, the Palestinian Authority is actually the same way. I think sometimes they take their lead from the Israeli government in monitoring what goes on in mosques. This is especially true since Hamas took over in Gaza.[11] The PA supervises lectures and monitors what gets said at mosques in the West Bank. They don't want a religious party like Hamas to gain influence. They even target young men just for going to the mosque too much. They'll watch and see who goes to the mosque in between the five daily prayer times. If they see people talking at the mosque in between prayer times, the PA will wonder if they're conspiring to do something bad. They see Islam as a threat.

In 2005, there were municipal elections throughout the West Bank,

---

[11] Hamas is a political party that was elected to power in Gaza in 2006 and subsequently forced the Palestinian Authority (largely controlled by Hamas's rival party, Fatah) out of Gaza. Hamas is considered a terrorist organization by Israel and other countries, and is generally considered an Islamic fundamentalist political party. For more information on Hamas, see the Glossary, page 276.

and many of the families I worked with encouraged me to run for office in Al-Bireh. I submitted my name under the Change and Reform List.[12] The party I was running with was interested in challenging Fatah, which controlled the PA. We thought they were too corrupt. I didn't win the elections, but running for office made me more visible to authorities, I think.

The PA was worried about religion and politics, about Hamas, and about any challenge to their power. Sometime after the election, I began hearing from people I knew at the mosque that PA authorities had been asking questions about me. In fact, they seemed very interested in the network of women in the mosque who stayed connected to prisoners and worked with families of martyrs. I wasn't the only person they were asking about.

Around that time, I decided to go back to school. First, I had to pass the *tawjihi* exams,[13] and I had to be disciplined about studying material I'd been away from for so long. It was hard. I had my sister, who was a teacher, help me study. I passed in 2006, and in 2007 I enrolled in psychology and social work courses through Al-Quds Open University.[14] I had ambitions for myself—I wanted to be a social worker. I didn't have

---

[12] The Change and Reform List was a political bloc made up of parties that opposed Fatah, including breakaway factions within Fatah itself. Though the Change and Reform bloc was not synonymous with Hamas, Hamas was the majority party within the bloc, which ran under the name Change and Reform Party in the 2006 legislative elections that brought Hamas to power in Gaza.

[13] The *tawjihi* exam is the exit exam for high school in Palestine. They determine not only whether students graduate but also what schools they can attend and even what they can study. The year spent preparing for this exam is very stressful for students, who must commit an enormous amount of information to memory, and many parents are very involved in supporting their children and helping them pass the exam.

[14] Al-Quds Open University is a distance-learning public institution with over 60,000 students enrolled. It is not affiliated with Al-Quds University, a university system with three campuses throughout the West Bank.

the time to be a full-time student, but I took classes for years and really enjoyed them.

Then, in April of 2008, Israeli officers raided my home. Luckily, none of us were home at the time. But they went through all our things, and they took all of our important documents: our passports, our UNRWA cards that allowed us to receive refugee benefits, my children's birth certificates, even my medical records. We had to send requests to get them back, and eventually they returned some of my medical files and my children's birth certificates. That was it.

GOING INTO THE UNKNOWN

I was arrested on August 1, 2010. Israeli soldiers came to our house at around one a.m. My family was sleeping. The soldiers knocked on the building door, and one of the neighbors let them in. And they came up to our floor and started pounding on the door— there were at least twenty soldiers.

I asked them to wait because I needed to put on my hijab and get dressed.[15] After I opened the door, they told us to gather in the living room, and they took everyone's IDs. My children were around sixteen, seventeen years old at this point. There were many soldiers, and they started searching the house. And then the one in charge came to me and told me, "Kifah, I want to talk to you in person," and he took me into another room.

We sat down, and he told me he was going to start investigating me there. He asked questions about my activities, my affiliation with Change and Reform, connections I might have to Hamas. He was threatening me,

---

[15] The *hijab* is a garment that covers the head and neck and is worn by many Muslim women throughout the world.

saying if I didn't answer him, he would arrest me. He really wanted to know if I knew anyone associated with Hamas. Then he told me, "I know you're sick. You have a disease, and that's why we have a doctor to oversee your situation." After around thirty minutes, he told me to get ready to go with them. And so they arrested me, and they told me I was going to the station. The soldier in charge said, "We're going to respect your disease and your age, and we're going to let you bring your medicine with you," and they didn't handcuff me. But I was not allowed to talk to my family before I left. They allowed me to say goodbye very fast, and that's it.

The officer who led me away told me, "You're going to be in jail until your daughter gets married." My daughter, Duha, was around sixteen and a half, and what he meant was, *You're going to be in jail for a very long time.* Duha told the commander, "Bring my mom back soon because my brother's a senior in high school, and he needs help preparing for his exams." The captain told her, "You're strong enough to take care of your brother."

I mean, we're Palestinians. Maybe we're used to these things. You find that you have patience you didn't know about. My children were strong, thank God. As a Muslim believer, I just thought, *This is in God's hands.* I was afraid because I was going to the unknown. I didn't know what was going to happen, but I had my faith in God.

As the soldiers were driving me to the station in the car, they were very focused on the fact that I was sick. The commander kept saying, "Don't think that because you're sick it's going to stop us from taking you. We're going to take care of you, but we're still going to take you." They took me to Al-Muskubiya, in Jerusalem.[16] Once there, they strip-searched me. The one who searched me was a female soldier, but it was

---

[16] Al-Muskubiya ("the Russian Compound") is a large compound in the Old City of Jerusalem that was built in the nineteenth century to house an influx of Russian Orthodox pilgrims into the city during the time of Ottoman rule. It now houses a major interrogation center and lockup, as well as courthouses and other Israeli government buildings.

still a strip search—I was mortified. And then after the search, they took me directly to the doctor. He took a look at my medicine and asked me about my disease. Then they took me to the investigation room. At around six a.m., the interrogation started.

They took general information about me and my family. They asked me again if I knew anyone in Hamas, who they were, how I knew them. I know a lot of people in Al-Bireh because I live here, I'm active in the community, and I stay connected to families that have suffered in the Intifadas. But my connections to people in town are all social, not through some political affiliation. I kept asking them, "Why are you afraid of these social relationships?" They wanted to know about my work with prisoners' families, and they were trying to get me to confess that I had helped transfer money from Hamas to the families of political prisoners and martyrs. But I hadn't done anything for Hamas, and they didn't have any evidence. They interrogated me for two hours before I was allowed to rest.

They kept investigating me for four days. They had three shifts, so they would change the officer, but the questions would remain the same. I studied some psychology at university before I left to marry, and I knew that folded arms meant there's something you don't want to say. I know that all the investigators studied body language, so I would sit with my arms uncrossed because I didn't have any secrets. I'm an open page.

They knew that, because of my disease, I am affected by the cold, and they had the air conditioning on the whole time in the cell. I'm sure they did that on purpose.[17] It wasn't just uncomfortable, it was very painful.

One of the times they interrogated me, an officer tied my hands to the chair and left for around fifteen minutes. When he came back and untied

---

[17] Leaving the air conditioning on is a common technique used during interrogations to keep those being questioned in a state of alertness and discomfort.

my hands, they had become almost black. My lupus causes a lot of circulatory problems, and I just wasn't getting any blood to my hands. I told the officer, "You know that I'm sick and I have a problem with my hands." So when he went out the next time, he told me he wouldn't tie me up if I promised not to move. I was allowed to sleep during the investigation. At nighttime, they took me to the cell, and I slept there and then went back to the investigation room during the daytime.

I still had this feeling of going into the unknown. I didn't know where they were going with their questions, and they kept threatening me, saying they were going to put me in jail. The interrogating officer kept threatening me with administrative arrest if I didn't confess to connections with Hamas.[18] That was the thing that scared me most because even with no charges, they could put me in prison. At that point, my faith in God kept coming back to me.

WE'D RACE TO WASH THE DISHES

After the four days of investigation, they took me from the station to the prison in HaSharon.[19] When they took me to prison, they didn't tell me it was administrative detention. I never had any charges.

It was very hard to be in prison because it's a new place with new people you've just met. And it was very hard for me, as a mother, to leave my children behind. And another thing was that my disease made it very hard for me, and I suffered a lot. During the four days that they were investigating me, they showed some concern for my disease. They didn't

[18] For more on administrative detention, which is detention without formal charges, see Glossary, page 276.

[19] HaSharon Prison is in Kfar Saba, a suburb of Tel Aviv/Jaffa. It is one of the larger prison complexes in Israel and houses Israeli and Palestinian prisoners in separate wards. There are few female Palestinians in the prison, however—perhaps a dozen at any given time.

leave my hands bound, and they let me take my medicine. But after those four days, they didn't pay any attention to my disease.

In prison, we were four women in a room. There were about seventeen women in the prison in total. In our room we had our cots, a few shelves for our clothes, and a couple of chairs. We were able to get a space heater as well, since it could get so cold in the winter.

We were together all the time, and we became friends. There was a woman there who I was friends with before, but we became better friends in prison. The fact that we knew each other before prison was the only thing that was lucky about my time there.

Our day started with the *Fajr* prayer.[20] After that we would stay in our beds and put on our head scarves and veils, and then the officer came in and counted us. After that we would stay in our beds, praying and reciting from the Quran until noon, because there was not much to do. We couldn't even spend much time cleaning up because it was a really small room. I remember I would keep the small shelf for my clothes unbelievably tidy because there was nothing else to do.

After twelve, we would say the noon prayer. We would pray all together. And after that we would prepare ourselves for the break, when we got to go for a walk outside. The break would be three hours. Break time was the worst, because it was between noon and three p.m., which, during the summer, is unbelievably hot. In the winter it would be cold and raining, and the thing is you can't go out and then come back. If you go out, you must stay out for three hours, so sometimes we would be soaking wet in the rain or be very hot. Or you just stay inside for the whole day. But most of the time, you would go out because it was the only change you would get. It was the better of two evils.

---

[20] *Fajr*, which means "dawn" in Arabic, is the first of five daily prayers said by practicing Muslims.

In my case, I would go out if it was sunny. If not, I wouldn't take my chances. I would stay in my cell. I asked for gloves so I could protect my hands from the cold, but the guards denied them. For the whole three hours of the break, I would keep walking. I wouldn't sit down. The courtyard was only about thirty feet long, and we kept going back and forth in those thirty feet the whole time. But that was the only activity we got for our legs, so we kept doing it.

After that we would go back to our cells and start preparing for our main meal, which was lunch. They would bring us food three times a day: breakfast, lunch, and dinner. We had a hot plate that we were allowed in the cell, and we would re-cook the food. We would never keep it the same way they brought it. The food they brought was often potatoes or spaghetti.[21] And it was not completely cooked. We Arabs like our food well done, and we like our spices, so we would spice the food up and make it better.

After we had lunch, we would race to see who was going to do the dishes. Not because we love doing them, but because we wanted to keep busy. After that we would say the *Asr* prayer, and then we would go back to our recitations or watch some TV. The only channels available were Israeli TV channels and PBC because Israel and the Palestinian Authority have to approve what's broadcast.[22] Or we would just sit on the bed and read. In my case, I would keep walking so I could keep my blood circulating, and I would read books from the small library in the prison. I read almost fifty books while I was in prison. Some of the books were religious, but I really enjoyed the ones about social work or psychology.

---

[21] Neither of these foods are common in Palestine.

[22] The Palestinian Broadcasting Corporation (PBC) was established in 1994 after the formation of the Palestinian Authority.

MY DISEASE CAN BE FATAL,
BUT IT DOESN'T KILL FAST

After three months, my daughter came to visit me. She came with my sister, and they were able to visit every couple of weeks. And after six months, my husband was allowed to visit once. But my son wasn't allowed to visit me. My family needed permits to visit me because the prison was in Israel, and my family had to apply to visit. My son wasn't granted a permit, maybe because it was harder for young Palestinian men to get permits to get into Israel. I also had contact with some human rights organizations, such as Addameer, a prisoner rights organization. They tried to get me a doctor, a specialist for my disease, but it was denied by the prison administration.

The main reason for my sickness is that I have a lack of immunity, and it's difficult for me to fight off viruses. And I have a lack of sensation in my extremities. For example, one day when I was first in jail, I was cutting potatoes—not with a knife because you can't have a knife, but with a can-opener. So I was using that to cut the potato, and I cut off part of my finger without even feeling it.[23] It bled a lot, and I fainted because I was so worried about the situation. And the other women talked to the officers and asked them to take me to the infirmary. That did not go well at all. My finger took almost three months to heal. It became infected with gangrene and turned completely black. It was very, very painful. After that, the other women would not allow me to touch anything, especially that can-opener, or anything wet because I needed to heal. Of course, life then was very boring for me.

When I got sick, I would sometimes have to wait two weeks to see a

---

[23] Several of Kifah's fingers are damaged or partially missing from cold or infections. When she told this story, she held up one of the damaged fingers to show why she couldn't feel the pain from the cut.

doctor. All the different prescriptions that I gave them, they never filled them and I didn't get any medicine. The thing is, even if I get a flu, it's really hard to recover because of my lack of immunity. So it wasn't necessarily just emergencies, it was the simplest diseases, coughs or colds. That made me suffer. It took its toll on me. So one time I started screaming in the infirmary, and I told them, "You keep saying you're all about human rights and treating people right, and you're not giving me even minimal medical care."

I also had a problem with my legs. They were very swollen for a month. I couldn't even walk. It was very painful. And they gave me no treatment whatsoever at the beginning. The nurse passed by every day just to check on the prisoners, and one of the prisoners who was our representative with the prison administration kept pushing the nurse and told him, "If anything happens to this inmate, we will blame you." And after almost a month they took me to the doctor, to see what was wrong with my legs. I got medicine for the swelling, but they still wouldn't fill my prescriptions.

My disease can be fatal, but it doesn't kill fast. It takes time. If I don't take medicine, especially for infections, I could die. When I was in prison, my eyes were hurting a lot because I had an infection. It was almost three months before I could see an eye doctor. When I went to him, he didn't take me seriously. He didn't even check my eyes. He just treated me based on my complaints, and gave me eye drops that were only meant to moisten the eyes. I left the drops on his desk and told him, "I'm not using those." I was scared, and the other prisoners were really worried all the time because I didn't get the treatment that I needed.

I filed complaints with various human rights organizations in Israel. They would respond and do their best. But I was cautious about filing complaints, because the other prisoners explained to me that since I was under administrative detention, the Israeli authorities could extend it as long as they wanted if they thought I was causing problems. They would use a complaint as a reason to give you more time in prison under administrative detention.

I HAVE ALL THE POWER NOW

I stayed in prison for a year. The authorities renewed my detention three times. They finally released me in Tulkarm in August of 2011, and my family members were waiting for me there.[24]

The hardest meeting was with my son Moad, because he hadn't been allowed to visit me in prison. Seeing him again was very emotional. From the first moment that I entered prison, I had been waiting for that moment, I had been picturing it, all of the time. And now it was not my imagination, it was really happening. When I saw him after my release, he was eighteen, a grown man. It had been very hard for him that year—he'd needed his mother because he had the *tawjihi* exams.[25] When I got out, he was already finished with the exam, and he had registered for school. So many women came to visit me at the house, but he wanted to stay with me all the time. So when I was sitting with my visitors, he would keep calling for me, "Mom, come see this, come see that," as an excuse to talk to me.

The positive thing is that when I got out of prison, I felt that my children really did mature in that one year. Also, when I wasn't home, Hazem saw the huge role that I play in organizing everything with the kids, the family, and the house. So he appreciates my role way more than he used to! He's always helped out because of my lupus, but he was even more appreciative of what I could do when I got out.

Psychologically speaking, my time in prison still affects me. Now, when I get sick, I always go back to that period of time in my head and

---

[24] Tulkarm is a city of over 60,000 people on the northwest border of the West Bank, about sixty miles north of Al-Bireh.

[25] The *tawjihi* is an exit exam for high school.

remember how it was to be in prison. For example, I'm very careful about having my medications nearby because I was deprived of them when I was in prison. When I'm sick, I go the very next morning to the doctor, and I have the feeling that I've been deprived of the medications for a long time. Now when I go to the doctor and he smiles at me, I really do feel it and appreciate it. I used to take many little things for granted. For example, just having pins to hold my head scarf in place. In prison, we couldn't have them, so now I appreciate them.

After being released from prison, I didn't change my activities, such as visiting the families of prisoners. I continue because I believe in my work. They can't stop me from having my convictions, so I've stayed the same. And I'm a very social person. They can't change my character, you know.

One thing really opened my eyes. When you're in suffering, it's completely different from being the one outside of the suffering. All the time, I would go to the wives of the prisoners and try to comfort them and tell them to be patient and do this and do that. They would keep saying, "It's hard, it's hard," and I would comfort them.

But what I found out is that it's a million times harder for the prisoner himself than his family, and I tried it firsthand. I used to think that prison would just be somewhere you rest. There's no responsibility, you just sleep, and there's nothing to do. Everyone has all these errands that we have to run, and we have no time. And we're just busy all the time. This is a bliss that we don't appreciate. You have to appreciate every day, even though it's tiresome. And once I was in prison, I really saw it differently. Now, every time I feel I'm in a tough position or it's hard, I just remind myself of my time in prison, and it's more than enough to bring me up again and motivate me. I have all the power now. I can do whatever I want.

NADER AL-MASRI RUNNING BY BARRIER WALL

NADER AL-MASRI

Runner, 34
Born in Beit Hanoun, Gaza &
interviewed in Gaza City, Gaza

Nader Al-Masri is the only Palestinian man we interview who doesn't smoke—the absence of a cigarette in his hand is striking to us. Dressed in a faded plaid shirt, he sips a fruit cocktail as he answers our questions. Everything about Nader is neat and trim, from his chiseled face to his clipped answers during the interview. His stern, focused manner perhaps comes from the force of will it takes for him to pursue running in Gaza, a place where it's difficult to earn recognition for following a dream, much less get paid for it. With an unemployment rate of 30 percent, most Gazans are focused on getting by, but Nader has scraped together a way to support his family of seven while keeping up a demanding training schedule and traveling to competitions.

We first interview Nader during our trip to Gaza in the spring of 2013. He explains to us why, despite the lack of support, Gaza's legendarily hot summers, difficulties traveling, and even Israeli air strikes, he has kept running.

I WAS ALWAYS FASTER
THAN THE OTHER BOYS

I grew up in Gaza, in Beit Hanoun.[1] I was always faster than the other boys. In Gaza when I was a child, the only sport kids played seriously was soccer. So when I was very young, running meant running back and forth while chasing a ball. Really, though, I didn't care about the ball—I just enjoyed running. One day when I was fourteen, my teacher Saoud Hamed—he taught Arabic and sports—announced that we'd be having a foot race. That wasn't something we'd ever done before in school. I prepared for it by running whenever I could for a few days, and then I won the race easily. My teacher told me I had a special talent, and offered to help me train.

From that first race, I wanted to be a runner, to be the fastest there is, but my family didn't support me. My dad thought there were better things for me to do, such as help out with his business as a grocer. So I had to train secretly while I was a teenager. Then one day, I was away from home for a long time, running, and when I came back, my father asked me what I had been doing. I said, "I was training to run, and running is the thing I want to do with my life. That's all there is to it." Later, my uncle visited our house and was able to convince my dad to let me train.

Training for me took a lot of extra effort. There weren't any great places to run in Gaza City. I didn't have good shoes. And I had to work long hours at my family's produce market a lot of the time. It was routine for me to leave the house with my father at two in the morning for work. I'd go to markets in Gaza City to pick up shipments of produce, and he'd

---

[1] Beit Hanoun is a town northeast of Gaza City with over 30,000 residents. The town is on the northeast border of Gaza and close to the Erez crossing, one of three crossing points from Gaza to Israel. Beit Hanoun is a frequent target of Israeli invasions, especially since the rocket attacks on the Israeli town of Sderot, which is only three miles away.

go into Israel through Erez to buy produce there.[2] Then my brothers and I would run the market, which was right next to our home, until my father returned from Israel. So there were many days when I didn't have a chance to start running until the afternoon, when it could be hot, and when I was already tired from a long day.

During this whole time, my teacher, Saoud, was very supportive of me. He helped me train, and he also worked to get the attention of the Palestinian national running team, which was based in the West Bank. I got stronger and stronger as a runner, and then I joined the national team in 1999, at nineteen years old. I remember telling my family that I was on the national team and that I was going to travel to Ireland for a race. They didn't believe me. They asked me, "What are you talking about?" They went and asked my coach, Saoud, and he said, "Yeah, your son made the team and we're leaving in a few days." My family was shocked that this was something I could actually do with my life.

So in 1999 I left Gaza for the first time through the Rafah border into Egypt. Saoud was with me. I remember him saying, "You are about to have an amazing experience, Nader." We flew to Ireland out of Cairo. When I got on a plane for the first time, I was a bit worried, but I was calm as soon as the plane took off.

In Ireland, I saw a very different life than the one I knew in Gaza. People there had so much, there were times I felt like what we had back in Gaza couldn't even be called "life." But one of my best memories from Ireland was just meeting the other runners on the Palestine national team, getting a chance to talk about shared experiences. I'd never met them before, since I'd never had the chance to travel to the West Bank, and there weren't any other members of the team from Gaza. The coach of

---

[2] The Erez crossing was one of the major border crossings between Israel and the Gaza Strip before the border was closed in 2007. Today, Gazans are allowed to pass through Erez only for humanitarian reasons.

the national team was Majed Abu Maraheel. He was the first runner to represent Palestine internationally when he ran in the Atlanta Olympics in 1996. The national team had just been formed the year before in 1995, just after the Palestinian Authority was first recognized internationally. It was great to feel like there were others like me, other Palestinians who had devoted themselves to running.

After I finished the championship, I insisted on going back to Gaza and training there, so that I could represent Palestine again and again in other countries. I didn't want to be a Palestinian runner living somewhere other than my home, and I wanted to stay in Gaza, where people were just starting to notice me and realize that running has a purpose.

I'VE ONLY BEEN TO THE WEST BANK ONCE

In international competitions, I'm a runner, and I throw shot put. As a runner, I participate in the 5,000-meter race. My proudest moment as a runner so far was at the Asian Games in Doha, Qatar, in 2006, when I got eighth place in the 5,000-meter race. All together, I've been in forty international competitions, including the Beijing Olympics in 2008. I was just under the qualifying time to run in Beijing, but I still got a chance to represent my country on the national stage.

In the past thirteen years since I joined the national team, I've been to twenty-five countries, but I've only been to the West Bank once. That was in 2008, when I had to cross to Jordan. It wasn't easy. It took seven months for me to get the permit to travel through Jordan. It was because of the media, because I got many interviews with Israeli TV channels and news-papers. At the end of the day, the Israeli government gave me the permit.

I also ran the UNRWA Marathon in 2011 and 2012, and I received first place both times. [3] Then in 2013, it was canceled. In 2013 and 2014, Gazan runners were also banned from going to Bethlehem to participate in the new marathon there. [4] Israel would not grant us a permit to go. In 2013, I applied four times. They didn't give reasons. The Bethlehem Marathon meant a lot to me, because I wanted to run in Palestine against other top Palestinian runners.

I've never been to Bethlehem or Jerusalem. It would have been my first time. Even if I get a permit to the West Bank, I won't get a permit to Jerusalem this year because of my age. The Israelis only give permits to men older than thirty-five to travel to Jerusalem, because they see young men from Gaza as too dangerous to even consider allowing in the city.

IT GIVES ME THE SENSE OF BEING FREE

I'm married with five kids—four girls and one boy. I was married to my wife Sawsan in 2007, and I supported my family for a time as a security officer with the Palestinian Authority. But after Hamas took over shortly after I got married, they drove the PA out of Gaza and I was left without any job. Still, I continue to be paid by the PA, which is true of many Gazans who had worked for the Palestinian Authority. I'm paid around

---

[3] The UNRWA Marathon is an annual marathon that was started two years ago and brings people from around the world to Gaza. In 2013, it was canceled because Hamas didn't allow women to run.

[4] The 2013 Bethlehem Marathon was the first marathon ever organized in the West Bank. The Israeli government denied passage of twenty-six Gazan applicants into the West Bank to participate in the race on the grounds that the applications didn't meet criteria for extreme humanitarian need, such as medical urgency, which are currently the only criteria for permitting Gazans to travel into the West Bank.

$500 per month.[5] That helps to feed my family, and I also need the money for vitamins and supplements, when I can afford them.

I train alone because no one can compete with me. There is no sense in competing with people slower than me. I have to compete with people who are like me, and that doesn't exist in Gaza yet. I usually train at a playground near my house. It's 400 meters, like a normal track, but it's a sand track, so the sand slows me down. It takes more time. It also hurts my legs, so I don't train there all the time. Sometimes I train on the beach, sometimes on the sidewalk. I wake up at six a.m. and train for two hours in the morning, and then I go back home, have lunch, and take a nap. Then I train again at six p.m. I have a program. I train all summer, even when it gets extremely hot.[6] It's harder, but I never stop, because when I stop I feel like my legs need to move. I run even during Ramadan, after I break the fast. I usually start at six a.m., but during Ramadan I start training after we eat at seven or eight p.m.[7]

I regularly go to Europe and other countries to participate in competitions. If you visit my home, you can see the many medals and prizes I've received over the past thirteen years. Sometimes, host organizations that invite me to races pay for my travel. But I still have to figure out how to get to Cairo, which can be impossible when the borders are closed.

Soccer players are sponsored and supported by the government and the Palestinian Authority more than runners. I feel isolated because I am not supported and I don't have facilities. Sometimes I stay for six months

---

[5] The Palestinian Authority governed Gaza from 1995 until 2007, when the political party Hamas took full control of Gazan governance. Though employees of the Palestinian Authority in Gaza were replaced by Hamas loyalists, the Palestinian Authority continued to pay former government employees in hopes of an eventual return to power in Gaza.

[6] Average temperatures in Gaza City in July and August are over 90 degrees Fahrenheit.

[7] For the month of Ramadan, observant Muslims refrain from eating between sunrise and sundown.

or so outside Gaza to train, since I don't have the facilities to help improve my running here. I have the proper shoes, but I can't run with them in Gaza. They have spikes, and I can't run with them on the sand, so I only use them when I travel. But then when I wear them, they give me problems because I'm not used to them. I can run 5,000 meters in fourteen minutes, but the international qualifying standard for a number of top-level competitions is just over thirteen minutes. So I'm training so I can participate in international competitions and make money. I can't make money until I reach this goal. But becoming better with the facilities I have available here in Gaza is difficult.

My running doesn't make money. Not in Gaza. In other countries around the world, I could be sponsored, the state could pay for it, but not in Gaza. I've thought about leaving Gaza to have more support as a runner. I have a wife and kids who I would have to leave behind, but I would be paid, so they would have a better life and I would be achieving my dream.

I go running while people are sleeping, and I do all these things partly because I want to get first place when I run and show that Palestinians have something to be proud of. I'm proud to be representing Palestine, no matter how hard it is for me to keep training. When I go to represent Palestine in championships, I try to focus on the idea that Palestinians are a peaceful people. And I draw attention to the fact that we can't move around easily because we don't have an airport and we have to go through Egypt to travel, and not even that is reliable.

Unfortunately, not many Gazans know about what I've done as a runner. Usually, when you say you are on the official team of your country, it means something, but here there isn't much appreciation of that sort of achievement. There was a movie I saw about a runner who died, and as the ambulance pulled away, people were clapping like he was something great. But in Gaza, if I died while I was in the middle of a training run, probably nobody on the street would notice.

I've thought of quitting many times because of the lack of support, but running is still the thing I want to do at the end of the day. It takes all of my time, but it's what I want to.

I also keep running because it basically means freedom to me. It's not like soccer, where I have to play with eleven others. I run on my own. I go wherever I want, do whatever I want, and it gives me the sense of being free. The second I start running, I feel free to fly and go wherever I want. When I was young, before I had a family, I'd even run when there was an Israeli invasion or bombing in Gaza City. Today, I stay with my family when anything like that happens. But whenever I feel stressed out by everything that's happening here, I can still leave the city and go running in the country, where there's nobody else in sight, and it gives me the feeling of being free.

APPENDICES

I. TIMELINE OF MODERN PALESTINE

The history of the lands west of the Jordan River is vast, complex, and contentious. We've composed the following brief timeline as a guide to understanding the history of the region that has significantly shaped the lives of our narrators.

8000 BCE—The first permanent human settlements appear in the land between the Mediterranean Sea and the Jordan River. These settlements develop into the city of Jericho.

8000 BCE–1000 BCE—Control of the land between the Mediterranean Sea and the Jordan River (known in the ancient world as Canaan) passes through control of numerous empires, including Egypt and Babylon. Parts of the region are controlled by autonomous Canaanite city-states at times. The earliest settlements around what will become the city of Jerusalem are formed as early as 4000 BCE. Around 1200 BCE, a coastal Canaanite people known as the Philistines form a defensive alliance around the cities of Gaza, Ashdod, and Ashkelon near the Mediterranean coast. Egyptian writers describe the land of the Philistines as "Peleset." Later, Greek writers refer to the entire area between the Mediterranean Sea and the Jordan River as "Palestine," or "land of the Philistines." The earliest known historical reference to the people known as the Israelites is from an Egyptian inscription from 1209 BCE.

1000–850 BCE—The Kingdoms of Israel and Judea emerge from confederations of autonomous tribes of the Israelite peoples after attempts of total unification by Israelite rulers. The Kingdom of Israel has its capital in Samaria (near modern Nablus), and the Kingdom of Judea makes Jerusalem its capital.

853 BCE—The earliest recorded use of the word "Arab" appears in Assyrian text and refers to a people that the Assyrian army has battled west of Mesopotamia. Other early references to Arabic peoples describe them as a large coalition of desert-dwelling tribes between Mesopotamia and the Mediterranean Sea.

722 BCE—The Kingdom of Israel is conquered by the Assyrian Empire.

586 BCE—The Kingdom of Judah is conquered by the Babylonian Empire. The Babylonians destroy much of Jerusalem including Solomon's Temple, the central holy site of Judaism. The temple is rebuilt after the Persian Empire conquers Jerusalem in 538 and invites Israelites back into the city.

332 BC—Alexander the Great conquers Jerusalem and Palestine on his way to defeating the Persian Empire. After Alexander's conquest, Palestine passes through control of numerous Hellenistic Greek dynasties as well as periods of relative autonomy for Israelite dynasties centered around Jerusalem. Semi-autonomous city-states of other Canaanite peoples develop throughout Palestine.

73 BCE—The Roman Republic asserts control over Palestine. The Romans appoint a client ruler, Herod, as the "King of the Jews" in Palestine from 37 BCE until his death in 4 BCE.

70—Roman Emperor Titus sacks Jerusalem, destroying the Second Temple and dispersing Jews and early Christians from the city.

324—Roman Emperor Constantine moves his capital from Rome to the city of Byzantine (renamed Constantinople). He establishes Christianity as the religion of the new Byzantine Empire, which includes all of Palestine. Christian churches begin to appear throughout Jerusalem and Bethlehem.

324–634—Palestine passes through Byzantine rule to Persian rule, then back to Byzantine rule. During this time period, much of the population of the region is Christian.

610–632—The religion of Islam is established in the Arabian Peninsula under the leadership of Prophet Muhammad. By the time of his death in 632, Muhammad has established Islam as the accepted belief of many Arabic-speaking peoples in the region.

634—Two years after the death of Muhammad, Islamic Arabs defeat the armies of the Byzantine Empire and begin to take control of Palestine. In subsequent years, Arabic-speaking peoples move north into Syria, west into Egypt and Africa, and east into Mesopotamia.

691—Builders complete the Dome of the Rock in Jerusalem at the site of the former Second Temple. The Al-Aqsa Mosque is completed in 705. According to Islamic tradition, the two structures mark the spots where Muhammad received instructions on how to pray and later ascended to heaven.

634–1516—During the Middle Ages, Palestine is ruled by a number of dynasties, Sultanates, and Christian armies. Jews, Christians, and Muslims all have varying levels of autonomy and religious freedom depending on the ruling power of the day. In 1453, Constantinople falls to an Islamic Turkish people known as the Ottomans. After renaming the city Istanbul, the Ottomans push beyond Turkey and establish the Ottoman Empire.

1516–1918—Palestine is ruled by the Ottoman Empire for over four hundred years. During this time Jews and Christians in Palestine have varying levels of freedom to practice religion. The peoples living in the region include nomadic Bedouin Arabs with marginal loyalty to the Ottoman Empire.

1800—By this year, there are as many as 250,000 people living in Palestine, including Christian and Jewish communities. Though the majority population is Muslim, there may be as many as 7,000 Jews living in the region and 20,000 Christians.

1850s—The roots of the modern Zionist movement first appear in Europe and Russia, in the context of growing anti-Jewish sentiment and secular nationalism. Some religious and secular Jews seek a homeland free of persecution. Many other Jews see assimilation as the best path to avoiding persecution. In the following decades, 1.5 million Jews emigrate from Europe and Russia—some to Palestine, but many to the United States.

1896—Austrian journalist Theodor Herzl publishes *The State of the Jews*, calling for the creation of a Jewish state. The book establishes Herzl as the world leader of Zionism, although it does not commit to a specific location for its proposed Jewish state. The next year, the World Zionist Organization forms, declaring the goal of Zionism to be a home for Jewish people in Palestine, then still an Ottoman territory.

1900—The World Zionist Organization and Jewish leaders in Europe sympathetic to the Zionist movement begin buying land in Palestine from the Ottoman Empire. Jewish colonies are established. By 1900, the population of Palestine is over 500,000, with as many as 50,000 Jews and 60,000 Christians living among nearly 400,000 Muslims. As Zionist activities increase, some Muslims and Christians living in Palestine begin to identify communally as Palestinians.

1914—World War I begins. The Ottoman Empire joins Germany and the Central Powers against Britain, France, and Russia.

1915—Britain's high commissioner in Egypt writes letters to Arab leader Sharif Hussein bin Ali and promises British support for Arab independence if Hussein revolts against the Ottomans. Hussein plans for a unified Arab state that stretches from Palestine and Syria to Yemen.

1917—Britain issues the Balfour Declaration, promising Jews a national home in Palestine. British officials hopes to encourage war support among Russian and American Jews.

1918—World War I ends. The British army defeats the Ottoman army in Syria, and British forces occupy Palestine, Transjordan, and Iraq while French forces occupy Syria and Lebanon.

1921—The first serious conflict between Jewish and non-Jewish Arab communities erupts on May 1. Dozens are killed near the neighboring cities of Tel Aviv and Jaffa.

1923—Through the League of Nations, Britain receives a mandate to administer Palestine. Transjordan is established as a semi-autonomous kingdom called Jordan, while Britain and the League of Nations agree to work toward a Palestine divided between a Jewish Nation and an Arab one.

1924—European banking heir Edmond James de Rothschild establishes the Palestinian Jewish Colonization Association, an organization that helps fund the construction and maintenance of new Jewish colonies in the region.

1929—Further armed conflict erupts between Jews and self-identified Palestinians throughout Palestine. Sixty-seven Jews are killed in the city of Hebron. Zionist settlers develop the Haganah, a paramilitary group established to protect Jewish interests.

1931—A paramilitary group called the Irgun splits off from the Haganah and begins to organize military strikes against the British and non-Jewish Arabs.

1936—British forces kill Sheik Al-Dinn Al-Qassam, a leader of the anti-Zionist Arab movement. The killing sets off an Arab revolt in Palestine that lasts for three years.

1939—World War II begins. Britain bans land sales to Jews in Palestine in an effort to obtain Arab support against Germany.

1946—The Irgun orchestrates the bombing of the King David Hotel, then the British mandate headquarters.

1947—The General Assembly of the newly formed United Nations recommends partitioning British-mandate Palestine into a Jewish state and an Arab one. Under the proposal, Jerusalem will be shared by the two states under a United Nations peacekeeping force. The vote represents international community approval of the Zionist aspiration to an independent state and lays the groundwork for the state's establishment. Still, many Christian and Arab residents of Palestine resist the planned partition. Their argument is that the land granted to the Jewish State doesn't reflect the demographic distribution of Palestine. At this time, the population of Palestine is approximately one-third Jewish.

—Beginning soon after the UN vote, paramilitary groups such as the Irgun begin expelling Palestinians from their homes and demolishing their villages. The mass migration of Palestinians that begins in 1947 during the emergent civil war comes to be known as the Nakba, or "catastrophe." Over the next year, 750,000 Palestinians are displaced from their homes and pushed toward the coastal land around Gaza City, Egypt, the lands east and west of the Jordan River, Syria, and Lebanon.

1948—On May 14, David Ben-Gurion declares statehood for Israel, with borders largely following the UN plan, and becomes its first prime minister. The next day, U.S. President Harry Truman instructs a member of the American delegation to the UN to recognize Israeli statehood. The same day, military units from Iraq, Syria, Lebanon, Egypt, Jordan, and Saudi Arabia invade the new state of Israel.

—May–June: Coordinated Arab forces battle the Israeli military until both sides accept a truce proposed by UN peacekeeping forces.

—July: Syria and Egypt opt to end the UN truce. Subsequent Israeli military victories lead to Israel expanding the territory under its control. After Israeli invasions later in 1948, Israel expands from the UN partition borders to include parts of western Galilee, the Negev desert, and access to the Red Sea.

—December: After capturing part of the West Bank of the Jordan River in the 1948 war, King Abdullah I declares the union of Arab Palestine and Jordan.

1949—The UN mediates armistice agreements between Israel and Egypt, Lebanon, Jordan, and Syria, ending the conflict. The armistice establishes new boundaries between Israel and bordering nations, though no formal border. The UN boundaries come to be known as the "Green Line" and are used as a point of departure when Israel and Palestinian representatives discuss borders in future peace negotiations. Since the armistice, 750,000 non-Jews have been displaced from the land declared to be Israel while as many as 150,000 remain and receive Israeli citizenship.

—The peace agreement creates the Gaza Strip and the West Bank as distinct political regions. The Gaza Strip comes under Egyptian control, and Jordan, the only Arab state to grant citizenship to these Palestinian refugees, gains control of part of the West Bank including East Jerusalem. Jewish immigration to Israel increases, bringing Israel's population to one million people by the end of 1949.

1950—Israel passes its Law of Return, allowing any Jewish person (with a few restrictions) to live in Israel and receive Israeli citizenship. From 1949 to 1952, Israel's Jewish population more than doubles.

1964—**January:** Arab League leaders meet in Cairo and decide to sponsor the creation of the Palestine Liberation Organization (PLO), an organization with transnational aims of representing Palestinians and "the liberation of" Palestine.

—**May:** The PLO holds its inaugural conference.

1965—Syria becomes dissatisfied with the PLO and begins discreetly supporting Fatah, a smaller organization founded in 1959 by Palestinian refugees in Gaza. Fatah seeks military action against Israel and begins raids on Israeli targets in mid-1965. The organization carries out more than three dozen attacks by the end of the year.

1967—Israeli military forces clash with Fatah and Syrian armies. With regional tensions mounting, Egypt sends troops near its border with Israel in May. In response, Israel mobilizes troops to the Sinai border and calls up its reserve soldiers.

—**June 5:** Israel launches an air strike on Egypt's airfields in the Sinai, destroying nearly all of the Egyptian air force and beginning what will become known as the Six-Day War.

—**June 7:** Israel secures East Jerusalem and moves further into the West Bank as fighting continues.

—**June 8:** Egypt accepts a UN cease-fire.

—**June 9:** Syria accepts a UN cease-fire, but Israel begins an assault on the Golan Heights.

—**June 10:** Israel occupies Qunaitra, a key position in the Syrian Golan Heights. The Six-Day War ends. At the war's end, the borders marking the edges of Israeli military and administrative control begins inside Jerusalem, the West Bank, the Gaza Strip, the Golan Heights, and the Sinai Peninsula.

—More than 100,000 new Palestinian refugees leave the newly occupied territories for Jordan. Soon after, Arab heads of state attempt to find diplomatic solutions to regain the territory Israel occupied in the war. Fatah continues attacks in the West Bank as well as in land within Israel's pre-1967 borders, and new factions organized around Palestinian liberation and Arab nationalism emerge.

1969—February: Yasser Arafat, a Fatah leader, is elected head of the PLO.

1973—The Israeli government builds settlements in the West Bank, the Golan Heights, and northern Sinai, suggesting an eventual turn from temporary military occupation to a permanent Israeli civilian presence.

—**October 6:** On the Jewish holiday of Yom Kippur, Egyptian and Syrian forces attack Israeli forces in the Golan Heights and the Sinai Peninsula.

—**October 22:** A cease-fire agreement officially ends attacks on both sides, but some attacks continue as Egypt attempts to gain territory in the Sinai. In postwar negotiations brokered by the U.S. early the next year, Syria regains much of the Golan Heights, and

Egypt and Israel agree to new borders on either side of the Suez Canal. Israel continues to occupy a portion of the Golan Heights despite international legal restrictions on the occupation.

1974—November: Arafat speaks before the United Nations and asks for international recognition of Palestine as the home of an independent people. In response, the UN grants the PLO "observer status." The designation allows limited participation in the UN General Assembly by certain non-state organizations.

1978—September: U.S. President Jimmy Carter meets in secret with Israeli Prime Minister Menachem Begin and Egyptian President Anwar Al-Sadat at Camp David, resulting in the Camp David Accords. These agreements set the principles for an Egypt–Israeli peace treaty that ends three decades of hostilities between the two countries. Under the agreement, Israeli soldiers are removed from the Sinai Peninsula, and the region is returned to Egypt. Largely in reaction to this agreement, the Arab League suspends Egypt for the following decade.

1981—December: Israel votes to annex the Golan Heights, which it had captured from Syria in the Six-Day War.

1982—June: After the PLO attempts to assassinate an Israeli ambassador, Israel invades Lebanon, where the PLO is based. Defense minister Ariel Sharon's raids exceed the limits of the state-approved defense plan, taking Israeli forces into Beirut and incurring civilian casualties. By the end of the summer, a multinational peacekeeping force arrives to protect Palestinian civilians and oversee the departure of the PLO. The PLO leaves Lebanon and settles in Tunisia.

1987—December: An Israeli tank-support truck crashes into civilian cars in Gaza, killing four Palestinians. Shortly after, Palestinian frustrations erupt into demonstrations in Gaza and the West Bank. Known as the *Intifada* or "casting off," this uprising begins without direction from the PLO or any other external organization. By January 1988, Intifada leaders adopt proposals calling for the creation of a PLO-led Palestinian state that would coexist with Israel. Leaders also attempt to initiate a UN conference to address Israel/Palestine issues and end the taxes imposed on Arabs living in Israel.

—Over the next few years, the center of Palestinian politics shifts from exiled Palestinian populations in neighboring Arab states to the occupied territories. Israel responds to the uprising with violence targeting demonstrators and Arab prisoners, and begins large-scale arrests of protesters; during this period its per capita prison population climbs to the highest in the world. In the first five weeks of the Intifada, almost 200,000 Palestinians are imprisoned, more than 250,000 are wounded, and 33 are killed; Israel's response receives criticism from the international community and creates solidarity across Palestinian factions.

—As Intifada violence escalates, members of the Egyptian Muslim Brotherhood looking to influence politics form Hamas, an armed group calling for a theocratic Palestinian state in the territory of former Palestine. With diplomacy failing to end the conflict and PLO corruption scandals on the rise, the appeal of Hamas and other Islamic groups grows.

1991—October–December: Leaders from Israel and Arab representatives from Lebanon, Syria, and a combined Jordan-Palestine delegation convene in Madrid for peace and land negotiations, at a conference sponsored by the U.S. and the USSR. The conference is the first attempt at direct peace talks between delegates from Israel, the Arab states, and the Palestinians.

1992—October: Jordan and Israel announce that they have drafted a peace treaty, to be ratified if a larger, comprehensive regional peace treaty is established.

1993—March: Following a series of attacks in Gaza, Israel closes the Gaza/Israel border, preventing people who live in Gaza from going to work in Israel. A number of experts attribute subsequent violence in Gaza to poverty induced by economic isolation.

—September: After months of talks in secret, Israel and the PLO sign the Oslo Peace Accords. For the first time, the PLO formally recognizes Israel's existence as a state, and Israel formally recognizes the Palestinian people and the PLO. Israel and the PLO agree to negotiate the withdrawal of Israeli forces from the Jericho area and most of the Gaza Strip. The agreement also establishes the Palestinian Authority, which will govern Palestinians in Gaza and the West Bank on an interim basis. Israel also promises to freeze settlement construction in the occupied territories. While there is some disagreement among historians about where to mark the end of the First Intifada, most place it at either these Oslo Accords or the 1991 Madrid conference.

1994—May: The Palestinian Authority begins governing in Gaza and Jericho, months beyond the original deadline set in the Oslo Accords.

—October: Israel and Jordan ratify a peace agreement.

1995—September: Israeli Prime Minister Yitzhak Rabin and Palestinian Authority Chairman Yasser Arafat sign another peace accord, known as Oslo II, that solidifies some of the principles set out in the 1993 Oslo Accords. Oslo II sets deadlines for Palestinian elections, negotiations on permanent status, and land concessions from Israel.

—November: Amid unrest from the ultra-Orthodox and extremist Israeli settlers in reaction to Oslo II's proposed land concessions, Israeli Prime Minister Yitzhak Rabin is assassinated by Israeli citizen Yigal Amir. The assassination and its fallout disrupt the peace process severely.

1996—Israel's next elected prime minister, Benjamin Netanyahu, lifts a four-year freeze on settlement expansion in the territories without consulting Yasser Arafat, signaling a change of direction from the principles of Oslo II. Settlements expand rapidly. Over the next decade, the population of settlers in the West Bank alone doubles from roughly 125,000 to 250,000.

1999—May: The deadline for the end of negotiations on Palestine's permanent status, as set by the Oslo agreements, passes without talks having been resumed.

2000—July: U.S. President Bill Clinton hosts Israeli Prime Minister Ehud Barak and Palestinian President Yasser Arafat for negotiations at Camp David, though no agreement is reached.

—**September:** The Second Intifada begins soon after Ariel Sharon, an Israeli opposition leader and former military commander, visits an East Jerusalem site holy to both Judaism and Islam known as the Temple Mount, or the Al-Aqsa Mosque. While visiting, Sharon publicly declares that the holy site will remain forever under Israeli control. Palestinian protests begin in Jerusalem and spread throughout the West Bank and the Gaza Strip. Compared to the First Intifada, the Second Intifada is marked by increased violence: greater incidence of shootings, suicide bombings by Arab militias, and targeted assassinations of Palestinian political leaders by the Israeli Defense Forces.

2001—Ariel Sharon is elected prime minister of Israel.

2002—Israeli military forces invade and occupy parts of the West Bank in Operation Defensive Shield, their largest military drive into Palestinian territory since 1967. Israel begins construction of a barrier separating the West Bank and Israel, which divides communities, blocks travel routes, and remakes the geography of the West Bank. Nearly 85 percent of the proposed barrier between Israel and the West Bank cuts through territory delineated as Palestinian by the 1949 Armistice "Green Line."

2004—**April:** Israeli prime minister Ariel Sharon announces a "Disengagement Plan," calling for the removal of all Jewish settlers from the Gaza Strip and parts of the West Bank. Intifada violence dwindles, although experts mark no clear end point.

—**October:** Yasser Arafat falls ill, and dies in November.

2005—After the death of Yasser Arafat, Mahmoud Abbas is elected president of the Palestinian Authority.

—**August:** Evacuation of Jewish settlers under Sharon's Disengagement Plan begins, and all 8,000 settlers in the region are relocated by the following September. While the Palestinian Authority governs within Gaza, Israel stays in control of Gaza's borders.

2006—**January:** Ariel Sharon suffers an incapacitating stroke. Soon afterward, Hamas wins a surprise majority in elections for the Palestinian Authority's legislature. In response, international donors including the U.S. and the European Union suspend aid to Gaza. Israel also begins withholding the taxes it collects for the Palestinian Authority.

—Soon after the election, Hamas drives political rival Fatah out of Gaza and begins firing rockets into Israel. It also captures Israeli soldier Gilad Shalit from a Gaza border post. His safe return becomes a focus for Israel's politicians and citizens.

2007—With support from Egypt, which shares a small border with Gaza, Israel imposes a comprehensive blockade on Gaza, restricting the movement of people, goods, electricity, fuel, and water. This pressure brings international sympathy to Hamas, while placing it under severe economic and humanitarian pressure. By mid-2008, imports to Gaza are reduced to 30 percent of their pre-blockade levels.

2008—Israel launches Operation Cast Lead, a campaign into Gaza with the stated aim of destroying Hamas's rocket capabilities. Casualties are widespread, including the deaths of 1,200 to 1,400 Gazans. Israel also damages much of Gaza's internal economic infrastructure, leaving it reliant on outside aid that has been restricted by the blockade.

2009—October: Israel releases twenty female prisoners in exchange for a video proving that Gilad Shalit is still alive.

2010—April: Palestinian President Mahmoud Abbas signs a decree promoting a boycott of products made in the Israeli settlements. The decree stipulates punishments for Palestinians who sell settlement goods.

—June: Israel eases import restrictions of the Gaza blockade after a failed raid on a flotilla of six ships bringing aid to Gaza. During Israel's raid nine Turkish activists on the ships are killed and dozens injured, causing an international outcry.

2011—After five years, Hamas releases Gilad Shalit, in exchange for the release of more than 1,000 Palestinian prisoners held by Israel. Rocket attacks and armed conflict between Israel and Hamas continue, as does the Gaza blockade.

2012—November: The UN General Assembly overwhelmingly approves Palestine as a non-member observer state, the same status held by the Vatican. Also, in response to Hamas rocket fire, Israel launches Operation Pillar of Defense, mobilizing 75,000 reserve soldiers and increasing operations into Gaza. An informal cease-fire agreement is reached after eight days.

2013—U.S. Secretary of State John Kerry announces renewed Israel–Palestine peace talks. Plans to construct housing for settlers in areas of the West Bank and East Jerusalem under Israeli control increase.

2014—In response to increased settlement construction, the Palestinian Authority unilaterally applies for membership in fifteen international organizations and treaties. The peace talks initiated by John Kerry are called off. In April 2014, political parties Hamas and Fatah announce a reconciliation and begin to negotiate a reunion between Hamas and the Palestinian Authority. The reconciliation plan includes new elections scheduled for the end of 2014.

II. GLOSSARY

administrative detention: A legal procedure under which detainees are held without charges or trial. Some forms of administrative detention is legal under international law during times of war and while peace agreements are negotiated between opposing factions. Many of the detainees in Guantanamo Bay, Cuba, are held by the United States in administrative detention indefinitely, and the procedure has also been employed in Northern Ireland against the Irish Republican Army and in South Africa during the apartheid era. Administrative detention was employed by the British against Jewish insurgents during the British Mandate of Palestine, and the Israeli military adopted the practice at the formation of Israel. In 2014, Israel holds as many as 300 Palestinians in administrative detention. Though each term of detention is limited to a set number of days (usually a single day to as many as six months), detention can be renewed in court, meaning detainees can be held indefinitely without trial or charges. Though article 78 of the Fourth Geneva Convention grants occupying powers the right to detain persons in occupied territories for security reasons, it stipulates that this procedure should only be used for "imperative security reasons" and not as punishment. During the Second Intifada, Israel arrested tens of thousands of males between fourteen and forty-five without charges.

Al-Aqsa Martyrs' Brigades: The informal military wing of the Fatah party. Though some members of Fatah disavow the brigades, they have been actively associated with the party since the Second Intifada. The brigades are considered a terrorist organization by Israel, the United States, Europe, and others.

Al-Quds Brigades: The military wing of the Islamic Jihad in Palestine movement. The Al-Quds Brigades were especially active around the city of Jenin during the Second Intifada, but the strength of the organization has been diminished since the end of the Intifada.

Arab: A designation that is defined by broad cultural and linguistic ties rather than by ethnic, geographic, or religious affiliations. Most Arabs speak some version of Arabic, of which there are numerous dialects. Approximately 80 to 90 percent of Arabs identify themselves as Muslim. Most of the rest are Christian. There is some disagreement over whether or not Jews living in Palestine before the Zionist movement were considered Arab or not, even those who spoke Arabic.

Arab-Israeli War: A conflict between newly formed Israel and neighboring Arab nations that has shaped Israeli–Palestinian relations since 1948. Tensions between Jewish and Arabic residents of the British Mandate in Palestine (1923–1948) were high leading up to the 1947 United Nations announcement of partition of the region into a Jewish nation (Israel) and a state for the region's non-Jewish Arab population (Palestine). The Arab League, an organization of neighboring Arab countries, opposed the partition plan, and invaded Palestine in May of 1948 after Israel officially declared statehood. The war between the Arab States and Israel lasted until armistice agreements in the spring of 1949. During the war, more than 750,000 Palestinians were displaced from their homes, and Israel annexed 60 percent of the land that had been demarcated as Palestinian territory under the 1947 U.N. partition plan. Palestinians refer to the war and its aftermath as the Nakba, or "catastrophe," and much of Palestinian politics today is driven by the claimed right of families to return to lands they were expelled from in 1948.

Arab League: An organization of Arab countries that was formed in 1945. It originally included Egypt, Iraq, Jordan, Lebanon, Saudi Arabia, and Syria. The Arab League has grown to include twenty-two countries and is chartered to promote Arab economic and political interests. During the Arab-Israeli War in 1948, the Arab League countries launched a joint attack on newly formed Israel in response to the displacement of Arabs within Israel's newly declared borders.

Areas A, B, and C: Administrative areas within the West Bank that were established following the 1993 Oslo Accords. In Area A, the Palestinian Authority maintains full civil and security control. This area makes up only 18 percent of the West Bank but includes dense urban areas—the cities of Bethlehem, Hebron (approximately 80 percent of the city), Jenin, Jericho, Nablus, Qalqilya, Ramallah, and Tulkarm. Israeli citizens are forbidden to enter territory designated Area A; however, the Israeli Defense Forces conducts raids and arrests in these territories, and in practice, few Israeli citizens have trouble when entering Area A territories. Area B represents 22 percent of West Bank territory and is mapped out around approximately 440 Palestinian villages. Here, the Palestinian Authority maintains civil control while Israel maintains security control. Area B territories are not supposed to have any Israeli settlements, though Israeli citizens are permitted to travel throughout Area B under certain circumstances, such as to visit religious sites. In Area C, Israel maintains full civil and security authority. Area C represents 60 percent of West Bank territories and is the home to as many as 500,000 Israeli settlers within the West Bank. Palestinians are partially restricted from entering Area C. However, approximately 200,000–300,000 Palestinians, including Bedouins and some farmers, live in Area C, though their access to resources such as water and electricity is significantly restricted.

Balfour Declaration: A diplomatic letter publicly released by the British government on November 2, 1917, that declared support for a Jewish nation following the dissolution of the Ottoman Empire in return for Jewish support during World War I. The Balfour Declaration conflicted with a promise made through T. E. Lawrence for support of a pan-Arab nation in the same territory.

Bedouin: An ethnic group with historical ties to the Arabian Peninsula. The Bedouin were traditionally nomadic, desert-dwelling, tribal peoples who spoke Arabic. Today, approximately 40,000 Bedouin live in Palestine, many in Area C of the West Bank.

Black September: The name for a civil war fought in Jordan beginning in September in 1970 and ending in July 1971. The war was waged between the Palestinian Liberation Organization and the Jordanian monarchy. Since the Arab-Israeli War of 1948, the population of Jordan (which included the West Bank) was around two-thirds Palestinian, making Palestinians the dominant force in Jordanian politics. The war led to the end of citizenship in Jordan for Palestinian refugees and forced the base of the Palestinian resistance movement to southern Lebanon.

British Mandate for Palestine: Following the breakup of the Ottoman Empire and the end of World War I, Great Britain assumed administrative control of former Ottoman-ruled territories east of the Jordan River (Transjordan, now the Kingdom of Jordan) and west of the Jordan River (Palestine). Formal British control began in 1923 and was set to expire in 1948 with the formation of independent states, including a national home for the Jewish people and a state for the Mandate's Arab population as well.

checkpoints: Barriers on transportation routes maintained by the Israeli Defense Forces on transportation routes within the West Bank. The stated purpose of the checkpoints in the West Bank is to protect Israeli settlers, search for contraband such as weapons, and prevent Palestinians from entering restricted areas without permits. The number of fixed checkpoints varies from year to year, but there may be as many as 100 throughout the West Bank. In addition, there are temporary roadblocks and surprise checkpoints throughout the West Bank that may number in the hundreds every month. For Palestinians, these fixed and temporary checkpoints—where they may be detained, delayed, or questioned for unpredictable periods of time—make daily planning difficult and can make cities or villages only a few miles away seem like distant points on the map.

crossing points: Crossing points are the gateways into Israel from parts of Palestine, or between Palestine and neighboring countries such as Egypt and Jordan. There are currently five crossing points by land into the Gaza Strip, and most of them have been closed or significantly restricted since the Israeli military blockade was imposed in 2007. There are seventy-three barrier-gate crossing points from West Bank into Israel, and Palestinians with permits have access to thirty-eight of them.

Dome of the Rock: The Dome of the Rock and the Al-Aqsa Mosque ("the farthest mosque") are built on the Temple Mount, considered one of the holiest sites in Judaism. They mark the location where Muslims believe Prophet Muhammad was miraculously transported from Mecca to Jerusalem in a single night to lead other prophets in prayer and also receive instructions from God regarding the rituals of prayer. The site remains a focal point of conflict in Israeli–Palestinian negotiations.

East Jerusalem: The eastern districts of the city of Jerusalem are among the major flashpoints in the Israeli–Palestinian relationship. Both Israel and Palestine have declared Jerusalem to be their respective capitals, and the area is home to some of the holiest sites in Judaism and Islam—the Temple Mount and the Al-Aqsa Mosque and Dome of the Rock. Following the Arab-Israeli War, Israel claimed the western half of the city (which was mostly Jewish) while Jordan negotiated for the eastern half (which was mostly Muslim and Christian Arab). Israel occupied all of Jerusalem following the Six-Day War in 1967 and annexed an area including East Jerusalem itself and a twenty-five-square-mile territory surrounding it that had formerly been administered by Jordan. Arabs living in East Jerusalem following the Six-Day War were granted permanent resident status in Israel and permitted to apply for Israeli citizenship, though few chose to do so. East Jerusalem was made up of over 60,000 Arabs and just a few hundred Jewish residents in 1967, but by the time the Oslo Accords were negotiated in 1993, Israelis outnumbered Arabs in East Jerusalem by about 155,000 to 150,000.

Fatah: A left-leaning political party that makes up the majority of the Palestinian

Liberation Organization coalition. Fatah was founded in 1959 largely by Palestinian refugees who had been displaced by the 1948 Arab-Israeli war. After its founding, Fatah had several militant wings and conducted a number of military actions against Israel, and Israel targeted military and non-military elements of Fatah.

Gaza Blockade: An Israeli military blockade of goods coming into and out of the Gaza Strip by air, land, and sea, which has been imposed since 2006, the year that the political party Hamas won control of the Gazan legislature. Israel (as well as the United States, the European Union, Jordan, Egypt, and others) considers Hamas a terrorist organization.

Gaza Strip: A 140-square-mile territory between Egypt, Israel, and the Mediterranean Sea that is currently independently governed by the political party Hamas. Gaza shares a thirty-two-mile-long border with Israel that is sealed off by the Israeli–Gaza barrier. Gaza has been self-governing since 2005, when Israeli military forces withdrew and Israeli settlements were removed. In 2005, Gaza was administered by the Palestinian Authority. In 2006, the political party Hamas won control of the parliament of Gaza in democratic elections, and then severed its relationship with the Palestinian Authority after violent confrontations with members of the party Fatah, which makes up the bulk of the Palestinian Authority. Following the victory by Hamas, Israel imposed a blockade on Gaza, officially to ensure that weapons such as rockets did not fall into the hands of Hamas, which it considers a terrorist organization. In 2012, the United Nations recognized Gaza as part of the state of Palestine, though Hamas and the Palestinian Authority have never fully reconciled, and the Palestinian Authority has no control in Gaza. Gaza is home to 1.7 million Palestinians, and the vast majority (75 percent) are considered refugees by the United Nations.

Geneva Accord: A peace initiative that took place in Geneva, Switzerland, in 2003, during the middle of the Second Intifada. Israeli and Palestinian representatives agreed on the outlined details regarding borders of two separate states (a two-state solution), compensation for refugees, and land-swap deals for the removal of settlements. The plan was refined and expanded in 2009 and remains the most detailed proposal of a two-state solution to be tentatively agreed upon by many Israeli and Palestinian officials.

Golan Heights: An area along Israel's border with Syria and Lebanon that Israel annexed from Syria in 1981. The region is important as a strategic military position as well as a source of fresh water.

Green Line: The lines of demarcation agreed upon between Israel and its neighbors during the armistice after the 1948 Arab-Israeli War, also known as the 1949 Armistice Line or the "pre-1967 borders." The armistice line is the basis of negotiations for a two-state solution in most major peace initiatives between Israel and Palestine, with some land swaps included. After the Six-Day War in 1967, Israel occupied territory beyond the Green Line, including the West Bank, Gaza, Golan Heights, and Sinai Peninsula.

Gush Emunim: An activist movement founded in 1974 within Israel that sought the fulfillment of Biblical prophesy through the settlement of the lands known in the Bible as Judea and Samaria and today known as the West Bank. Starting in the late seventies, Gush Emunim led numerous settlement groups to establish a presence in the West Bank, sometimes with the cooperation of the Israeli government and sometimes despite legal sanctions imposed by the government.

Hamas: A political party founded in 1987 as an offshoot of the Egyptian Muslim Brotherhood. Hamas is a Sunni Islamist political party, and its stated aims are to liberate Palestine from Israel and establish an Islamic state in the region that now encompasses Israel and the occupied territories. Hamas gained greater influence in the early 2000s, surging to power on dissatisfaction with the Palestinian Authority, which many Palestinians viewed as corrupt and willing to cede too much to Israel in peace negotiations. After winning parliamentary elections in the Gaza Strip in 2006, Hamas solidified its power in Gaza after violent skirmishes with opposition party Fatah. By 2007, Hamas had effectively taken control of Gaza, driving the Palestinian Authority from power there. Because Israel views Hamas as a terrorist organization (conquest of Israel is part of the Hamas charter), it imposed a crippling economic blockade on the Gaza Strip following Hamas takeover. In the spring of 2014, Hamas and Fatah announced a political reconciliation, though to date Hamas remains the sole power in Gaza.

International Red Cross and Red Crescent Movement: A group of international humanitarian organization founded in 1863 with the purpose of assisting victims of disasters and providing developmental aid to strengthen communities in crisis. The movement is made up of three distinct organizations: the International Committee of the Red Cross (ICRC), which safeguards human rights in conflict zones; the International Federation of the Red Cross and Red Crescent (IFRC) which coordinates relief assistance missions around the globe; and National Red Cross and Red Crescent Societies, which address humanitarian needs and are organized on the national level. The Palestine Red Crescent Society is one of the National Red Cross and Red Crescent Societies. It was formed in 1968 and has over 4,000 employees and 20,000 volunteers. Because the Palestinian Authority administers only a patchwork of territory within the West Bank, the Palestine Red Crescent Society provides some essential services to Palestinian citizens, including ambulance service and some medical care.

Intifada: *Intifada* in Arabic means "to shake off," and it is popularly used throughout the Arab world to mean a rebellion or act of resistance. In Palestine, Intifada usually refers to two intense periods of conflict. The First Intifada began in 1987, after increasing tensions between Palestine and Israel, including a number of civilian deaths. It included years of civil disobedience against the Israeli occupation, as well as armed attacks that led to the deaths of nearly 200 Israelis and over 1,000 Palestinians. The First Intifada began to wind down with the signing of the Oslo Peace Accords in 1993. The Second Intifada began in September of 2000, after a conflict between Palestinian protestors and the Israeli Defense Forces led to deaths. In the ensuing violence from 2000 to 2005, approximately 1,000 Israelis and 3,000 Palestinians were killed.

Israel: A state founded in 1948 to be a national home of the Jewish people. Today, Israel has a population of over 8 million, with slightly over 75 percent of the population Jewish and slightly over 20 percent Arab. Its capital is Jerusalem. Hebrew and Arabic are both official languages.

Israeli Defense Forces (IDF): The Israeli Defense Forces were established with the formation of Israel in 1948, and were formed from the paramilitary group the Haganah. Today, there are over 175,000 active personnel and 450,000 reserves in the IDF. Military service starting at age eighteen is compulsory for most Israeli citizens. In practice, only about half of all eighteen-year-old Israelis end up enlisting in active duty. Israel's Arab population, which makes up 20 percent of the total population of the country, is exempt, but Arabs may serve if they wish. A number of other exemptions exist, though they change from year to year. They include physical or mental disability, religious studies, demonstrated moral objections such as a commitment to pacifism, and enrollment in alternative national civil service programs.

Israel–Gaza barrier: A wall between Israel and the Gaza Strip constructed in 1994 following the Oslo Peace Accords. Much of it was destroyed during the Second Intifada, but it has since been rebuilt. An additional wall between Gaza and Egypt was built in 2005. The barrier has only five crossing points. The Erez crossing is a pedestrian and cargo crossing into Israel at the north end of the strip, a couple of miles north of Gaza City. Since the military blockade of Gaza was put in place in 2006, Gazans must obtain permits to pass through the crossing, which are usually only granted for medical or humanitarian reasons. The Karni crossing, just southeast of Gaza City, is a cargo crossing that has been completely sealed since the start of the military blockade. The Rafah crossing is Gaza's main crossing into Egypt. It was closed by Egypt following elections that brought Hamas to power in 2006, and it has been opened and closed numerous times since. The Kerem Shalom and Sufa crossings are smaller cargo crossings in southern Gaza, near the city of Rafah, and are used mostly for transportation of humanitarian assistance into Gaza.

Israeli–West Bank barrier: A wall between Israel and the West Bank that was built starting in 2002. When completed, it will be approximately 430 miles long. The wall deviates from the 1949 Armistice Line (the "Green Line") that has come to define the boundary between Israel and the West Bank. The 430-mile barrier will leave slightly more than 10 percent of Green Line-defined West Bank on the Israeli side of the wall. This land, known in Israel as the "seam zone" is home to most of the Israeli settlers in the West Bank and also as many as 275,000 Palestinians.

Nakba: Means "catastrophe" in Arabic. Commonly used by Palestinians and other Arabs to refer to the results of the 1948 Arab-Israeli War. The conflict displaced more than 750,000 Palestinians between 1948 and 1950. Many Palestinian families fled to Egypt, Jordan, or elsewhere outside the lands claimed by Israel in the aftermath of the war. The Nakba still drives Palestinian politics, with generations of refugees continuing to claim a right of return to properties owned before 1948 that are now part of Israel.

one-state solution: A proposed peace plan that would make all of Israel and Palestine a single state, with equal voting and legal protections for all citizens. Though increasingly popular among Palestinian Arabs as the best possible result of the peace process, the one-state solution is opposed by the majority of Israelis because they would become a demographic minority in a unified state. Current peace process negotiations continue to target a two-state solution.

Operation Cast Lead: A three-week-long invasion of the Gaza Strip by the Israeli Defense Forces between December of 2008 and January of 2009. The stated reason for the invasion was to stop rocket attacks from Gaza and weapons smuggling into Gaza. During the invasion, Israeli jets bombed numerous military and administrative facilities in Gaza, including those in densely populated areas of Gaza City and Rafah. More than 1,400 Palestinians were killed in the invasion.

Operation Defensive Shield: A large-scale military operation by the Israeli Defense Forces within the West Bank in 2002, during the height of the Second Intifada. The stated goal of the operation was to arrest or kill Palestinian militants in the region and halt rocket attacks and suicide bombings in Israel. During a period of a little over a month, the Israeli Defense Forces entered West Bank cities and laid siege to the compound of Yasser Arafat and the Palestinian Authority in Ramallah. Around 250 Palestinians were killed, while 30 Israeli soldiers were killed. The operation represented the most significant military incursion into the West Bank since the Six-Day War in 1967.

Operation Pillar Defense: An Israeli military invasion of the Gaza Strip that lasted eight days, starting on November 14, 2012. The stated goal of the invasion was to stop rocket attacks and disrupt military networks. The Israeli Defense Forces struck over 1,500 targets during the invasion. As many as 133 Palestinians were killed. During the operation, Palestinian rockets launched into Israel killed six Israeli civilians.

Oslo Accords: A series of negotiated agreements between the leadership of Israel and the Palestine Liberation Organization starting in 1993, during the height of the First Intifada. The goal of the accords was to institute a peace plan and create an interim Palestinian government in anticipation of eventual Palestinian statehood. The Oslo Accords led to the creation of the Palestinian National Authority (subsequently called the Palestinian Authority), a temporary governing body formed from the administration of the PLO.

Palestine: The name Palestine is derived from a term used in Ancient Egypt for the region bordering the Egyptian empire along the eastern coast of the Mediterranean as early as 1200 BCE. Today, Palestine may refer to the entire region made up of Israel, occupied territories, and territory under control of the Palestinian people, or it may refer to the areas of the West Bank and Gaza, defined as Palestine under the 1949 Armistice Agreement. It can also refer to the limited areas administered completely by the Palestinian people, which make up all of the Gaza Strip and approximately 27 percent of the West Bank. The Palestinian population in Israel and Palestine is hard to determine but probably numbers around 10 million in 2014. Another 3 to 4 million Palestinians live in Jordan, Syria, Lebanon, and Egypt. Though the Palestinian Authority claims Jerusalem as its capital, its de facto administrative capital is Ramallah.

Palestinian Authority (PA): A governing body for the Palestinian territories that was established as part of the Oslo Accords initiated in 1993. The Palestinian Authority (or Palestinian National Authority) was formed out of the administration of the Palestine Liberation Organization (PLO) and was dominated in its early years by the political party Fatah. Initially, the Palestinian Authority was meant to be an interim governing body while Israel and Palestine worked toward a final peace agreement between 1994 and 1999.

However, an agreement was never reached, and the Palestinian Authority has remained the internationally recognized governing body of the Palestinian people until the present. In 2006, after popular elections in Gaza brought the political party Hamas to power, Hamas militias clashed with Fatah and representatives of the Palestinian Authority, ultimately driving the PA from power in the Gaza Strip. Though a reconciliation between Hamas and the Palestinian Authority was announced in the spring of 2014, the PA's authority continues to extend only to those parts of the West Bank not administered by Israel.

Palestine Liberation Front (PLF): A precursor to the Popular Front for the Liberation of Palestine, the PLF was a Marxist Arab nationalist movement started in 1961 and based in Ramallah.

Palestine Liberation Organization (PLO): The Palestine Liberation Organization is a coalition of political organizations that was formed in 1964 with the aim of creating an independent Palestinian state. The PLO was first formed in the summer of 1964 during a meeting of the Arab League, and was composed of numerous political and military factions, including Fatah and the Popular Front for the Liberation of Palestine (PFLP). Yasser Arafat led the PLO from 1969 until his death in 2004. The coalition was considered a terrorist organization by Israel and the U.S. until 1991. After negotiations known as the Oslo Accords began in 1993, the PLO became the official governing and diplomatic body of the Palestinian people. In 1994, the Palestinian Authority was formed out of the organizational structure of the PLO and chartered as an interim government of Palestine for the duration of peace negotiations between Israel and Palestine.

Popular Front for the Liberation of Palestine (PFLP): A Palestinian political party founded in the wake of the 1967 Six-Day War. The PFLP had origins in the Pan-Arab movement, as well as in secular socialist political ideology. In the seventies and eighties, PFLP was the second largest political organization in the PLO coalition (behind Fatah). The party generally supports a one-state solution and opposes most negotiations with the Israeli government. It is considered a terrorist organization by the United States, the European Union, and Israel and is known for its commercial aircraft hijackings throughout the 1960s and 1970s.

pan-Arab movement: An ideological movement especially influential in the 1950s and 1960s that sought to make predominantly Arab nations a unified political and cultural force. The modern pan-Arab movement originated in the early twentieth century and was partially responsible for the rebellion of Arabic regions against the Ottoman Empire during World War I. The pan-Arab movement has often been seen as a force that directly conflicts with the Zionist movement, which sought a Jewish homeland within a mostly Arabic region within southwest Asia.

permit system: A complex system of identification-card requirements within Israel and Palestine that governs where individuals can live, work, and travel. Residents of the West Bank must have permits to travel on most roads and special permits to enter or work in Jerusalem and Israel. Palestinians in East Jerusalem must maintain IDs to prove resident status. Most Palestinians are restricted by the permit system from using numerous roads, border crossings, and checkpoints in the West Bank that are limited to Israel settlers or the Israeli military. On the other hand, Israeli citizens must obtain special permits to enter a portion of the West Bank under control of the Palestinian Authority and are not permitted to enter the Gaza Strip. Gazan citizens are not permitted to enter Israel, except with certain permits obtained for medical or humanitarian reasons.

refugee camp: There are fifty-eight active Palestinian refugee camps throughout the West Bank, the Gaza Strip, and neighboring Arab states. See entry for the *United Nations Relief and Works Agency for Palestinian Refugees (UNRWA)*.

right of return: A principle of international law that grants peoples displaced from their homes by war or other humanitarian crises to return if so desired. The right of return has been a contentious point between Israel and Palestinians since the Arab-Israeli War, which displaced more than 750,000 Palestinians, and the Six-Day War, which displaced an additional 250,000 or more (some of whom had previously been displaced during the 1948 war). In 1948, the United Nations passed General Assembly resolution 194, which read in part: "[The General Assembly] resolves that the refugees wishing to return to their homes and live at peace with their neighbors should be permitted to do so at the earliest practicable date, and that compensation should be paid for the property of those choosing not to return and for loss of or damage to property which, under principles of international law or in equity, should be made good by the Governments or authorities responsible." Subsequent U.N. statements further supported a Palestinian right of return to lands annexed by Israel in 1948. However, Israel disputes the right, and most major peace initiatives since the Oslo Accords have not included any right-of-return claims.

Sinai Peninsula: A 23,000-square-mile peninsula that separates Egypt from Israel and the Gaza Strip. The Sinai Peninsula was occupied by Israel as a buffer zone with Egypt following the Six-Day War in 1967 and then returned to Egypt in 1967. The Sinai was a major route of goods smuggled into Gaza during the blockade imposed by Israel starting in 2010, though this border route was largely shut down by the Egyptian military in 2013.

Six-Day War: A conflict in 1967 between Israel and Egypt, Syria, and Jordan. At the time, Gaza was administered by Egypt and the West Bank by Jordan. Following heightened tensions, border skirmishes erupted, including with Palestinian guerillas who launched assaults on Israeli military positions from Jordan. The conflict built to a land-war victory for Israel, and Israel occupied the West Bank (including East Jerusalem), the Gaza Strip, the Sinai Peninsula, and Golan Heights.

two-state solution: A proposed peace plan that would create a separate Palestinian state and define clear boundaries between Israel and Palestine. Most peace process plans since the First Intifada between Israel and Palestinian authorities have targeted a two-state solution rather than a one-state solution, which would unify all Palestinian and Israeli territories into one state and grant all citizens equal legal rights and protections.

Temple Mount: One of the holiest sites in Judaism and the former location of the Second Temple of Jerusalem, which was destroyed by the Romans in 70 CE. Today, it is the site of Al-Aqsa Mosque and the Dome of the Rock, making it also one of Islam's holiest sites. It is also bordered by the Western Wall, or Wailing Wall, the last vestige of the Second Temple and perhaps the most important religious site in the world for many Jews. Many

Jewish scholars consider the Temple Mount the site of a prophesied Third Temple. The site remains a focal point of conflict in Israeli–Palestinian negotiations.

United Nations Relief and Works Agency for Palestinian Refugees (UNRWA): The United Nations Relief and Works Agency was established in 1948 by a UN charter to provide material aid to Palestinians after the Arab-Israeli conflict, especially the more than 700,000 individuals that the UN registered as having been displaced from their homes by the war. The organization began providing housing and services such as healthcare, infrastructure, and education in designated refugee camps throughout the Gaza Strip, the West Bank, and neighboring Arab states. That aid has continued to be provided to descendents of those original refugees, as well as refugees from the 1967 Six-Day War. Today, UNRWA operates fifty-eight camps with over 1.5 million residents, and also provides services to millions of designated refugees living outside the camps. In the Gaza Strip, 1.25 million Palestinians are designated refugees (75 percent of Gaza's total population). In the West Bank, 750,000 residents are designated refugees (28 percent of the West Bank's total population). Over 2 million designated Palestinian refugees live in Jordan, 500, 000 designated Palestinian refugees live in Syria, and 450,000 designated Palestinian refugees live in Lebanon.

West Bank: The territory west of the Jordan River that has been occupied by Israel since the Six-Day War in 1967. The peace plan known as the two-state solution would make much of the West Bank part of an independent state along with the Gaza Strip and East Jerusalem. The population of the West Bank is approximately 2,750,000 (including East Jerusalem), with around 2,200,000 Palestinian Arabs, 500,000 Israeli settlers, and a few thousand members of other ethnic groups.

West Bank closures: Transportation routes throughout the West Bank are regulated by obstacles such as checkpoints, roadblocks, barriers, gateways, and other physical restrictions that are officially designed by the Israeli government to protect Israel from violence from Palestinians in the occupied territory. These barriers are either permanently or occasionally manned by the Israeli Defense Forces and significantly inhibit movement within the West Bank for Palestinians. Aside from permanent and spontaneous checkpoints on roads, many roadways require specific permits to enter, with many roads available only for the use of Israeli settlers.

Zionism: A global movement to create and develop a Jewish homeland. The Zionist movement resulted in the formation of Israel in 1948.

III. PALESTINE AND
INTERNATIONAL LAW
by Allegra Pacheco

While more than one hundred United Nations resolutions support the establishment of an independent Palestinian state, Palestine still remains under Israeli military occupation and has been rejected as a full member of the UN. The following essay offers a brief overview of the key international UN resolutions and legal issues affecting Palestine today, as well as Palestine's status as a "state" among the nations of the world.

PALESTINE AND THE UNITED NATIONS

The status of Palestine has been a contentious political and legal issue in the eyes of the international community since the fall of the Ottoman Empire and the establishment of the British Mandate of Ottoman territories in 1923.[1] All of the territories under the British Mandate eventually became fully independent states—except for Palestine. In Palestine, the British developed plans in light of its government's Balfour Declaration of 1917, which supported "the establishment in Palestine of a national home for the Jewish people."[2]

As the British Mandate came to a close in 1947, the United Nations took over responsibility for finding a political solution in Palestine. The UN General Assembly approved the "partition plan"—Resolution 181—which envisioned dividing the former British Mandate Palestine into two independent states, one Jewish and one for non-Jewish Palestinian Arabs.[3] The plan intended for an economic union to be formed between the two states, and for the cities of Jerusalem and Bethlehem to remain open to all sides as autonomous international entities. Many Palestinian Arabs immediately objected to the proposal, claiming that the plan for land division was not proportional to the population of the

---

[1] For more on the Ottoman Empire and the British Mandate of Palestine, see Appendix I, page 267.

[2] For more on the Balfour Declaration, see the Glossary, page 276.

[3] The United Nations General Assembly is the body of the UN comprised of all member states and its resolutions reflect the common position of the international community. It does not have enforcement powers like the UN Security Council.

time. The Jewish population constituted approximately 1/3 of British Mandate Palestine, and yet the partition plan granted the majority of Mandate land to the new Jewish homeland. Objectors also claimed that the partition plan violated the right of Palestinians to decide for themselves the type of sovereign entity that should be established in the region.

After the British ended the Mandate and left Palestine in the spring of 1948, the partition plan was not immediately implemented. Instead, war broke out, and the newly declared state of Israel took over 78 percent of Palestine as defined under the British Mandate. Neighboring states Jordan and Egypt took control of the remaining 22 percent part of Mandate Palestine—the West Bank and East Jerusalem under Jordanian control, and the Gaza Strip under Egyptian authority.

For Palestinians, the Israeli victory was considered a disaster—they called it the *Nakba*, or "catastrophe." Beyond the dramatic loss of land, the disaster was defined by Israel's refusal to allow as many as 750,000 Palestinian refugees who had fled the violence and/or been expelled to return to their homes. Instead, Israeli forces destroyed and/or depopulated 418 Palestinian villages and many Palestinian cities such as Lydda and Ramla. Israel also took ownership of huge amounts of Palestinian refugee rural and urban land, buildings, banks, and other assets (industrial equipment, agricultural stocks, vehicles) valued at billions in today's dollars.

In light of the huge Israeli seizure of land assets and the large number of refugees, the UN General Assembly passed Resolution 194 in December 1948. The resolution called for the return of the Palestine refugees willing to live in peace with their neighbors, compensation for those not wishing to return, and compensation for the property taken by the Israeli government. This resolution established the UN Conciliation Commission for Palestine to facilitate the implementation of the Palestinian refugee repatriation, compensation, and restitution and to "put the Palestinian refugee issue at the heart of resolving the conflict."[4]

Following the 1948 war, the return of the Palestinian refugees and their property constituted the main international legal issue dominating the conflict.

---

[4] UN Resolution 194 reaffirmed the basic international law principle of the right of every person to return to his home. See Article 13(2) of the Universal Declaration of Human Rights, 10 December 1948: "Everyone has the right to leave any country, including his own, and to return to his country."

However, as time passed and the Cold War came to dominate international politics, GA Resolution 194 was never implemented. The Conciliation Commission ceased functioning after several years.

During the June 1967 war between Israel and its Arab neighbors, Israel took by military force the remaining 22 percent of mandatory Palestine—the West Bank and East Jerusalem from Jordan, and the Gaza Strip from Egypt. These areas became referred to as the "1967 occupied territories." An additional 400,000 Palestinians fled the violence and became refugees from this war. In November 1967, the UN Security Council passed resolution 242, which reinforced the prohibition of acquisition of territory by force, and demanded that Israel withdraw from recently occupied territories.[5] However, UN Resolution 242 omitted the right of return for the Palestinian refugees, and instead calling for a "just settlement" to the refugee issue.[6] It proposed a "land for peace" formula leading to a two state solution based on the 1967 borders.[7][8] UNSC 242 states:

> The Security Council, expressing its continuing concern with the grave situation in the Middle East, emphasizing the inadmissibility of the acquisition of territory by war and the need to work for a just and lasting peace in which every State in the area can live in security…, affirms that the fulfillment of Charter principles requires the establishment of a just and lasting peace in the Middle East which should include the application of both the following principles:
>
> • Withdrawal of Israeli armed forces from territories occupied in the recent conflict;

---

[5] The word "all" territories was omitted from the English version.

[6] Notably, UN SC Resolution 237 (14 June 1967) issued right after the war, called on Israel to allow the return of the 1967 refugees. It states that the UN Security Council "calls on the government of Israel to facilitate the return of those inhabitants who have fled the areas since the outbreak of hostilities."

[7] For more on the Six-Day War, see Appendix I, page 267.

[8] The UN Security Council is often considered the highest body of the UN—it is charged with enforcing international law, and its resolutions on peacekeeping, sanctions, and the authorization of international military actions bind member nations to their international responsibilities.

- Termination of all claims or states of belligerency and respect for and acknowledgement of the sovereignty, territorial integrity and political independence of every State in the area and their right to live in peace within secure and recognized boundaries free from threats or acts of force.

As a unanimous decision of the Security Council, UN SC Resolution 242 and the subsequent UN Security Council Resolution 338 in 1974 took over as the new paradigm for international resolution of the conflict and the backbone of all subsequent Security Council resolutions on Palestine. The change of wording in UN SC Res. 242 did not legally constitute a waiver of the refugees' rights; however, many Palestinians were concerned that it reflected a political compromise by external powers on the actual return of refugees to their former land. Nevertheless, the UN General Assembly continued annually to reaffirm UN Resolution 194 and the repatriation and restitution for the refugees.

MILITARY OCCUPATION UNDER INTERNATIONAL LAW

As a general rule, international law does not permit or recognize territory acquired by force. This is stated explicitly by the Geneva Conventions and the original Charter of the United Nations, written after World War II. However, exceptions are made if the invasion is short term—until hostilities end and a peace agreement is set in place.

Typically, when a war ends, so does the related occupation. In most cases, the occupied territory is returned to the occupied state. The right of the people to self-determination—to govern themselves fully—is suspended until occupation ends. During occupation, international humanitarian law delegates the responsibility of restoring order to the army of the controlling power. But international law also recognizes that an occupying force is an enemy/hostile entity, and that the civilians under the control of an occupying force are inherently vulnerable to humanitarian abuse as well as exploitation of economic resources. That is why humanitarian law has established an extensive set of regulations to prevent the occupying force from abusing their power imbalance by exploiting the civilians and their resources.

Because the right to self-determination is a fundamental principle of international law, the laws regulate occupations in a temporary framework. Another principle of occupation under international law forbids the occupying power from ownership of the land and its resources, what are known as sovereign rights. The occupying power is meant as only an administrator of the land and property for the temporary period of military occupation, tasked with preserving resources and maintaining order.

While the occupying power has discretion regarding immediate military necessities it must administer the occupied territories for the interests and the benefit of the local population.[9] Occupying powers are charged with ensuring food, water, and sanitary conditions, and providing or allowing international support for education, health, culture, and religious affairs. The military must preserve the resources in place before the war as much as possible, and cannot change the laws of the occupied territory for their own material advantage.

Israel's prolonged occupation of the Palestinian areas has defied many of these international legal principles. Israel has defended its continued occupation of the West Bank since 1967, and its effective control of Gaza's borders and trade, by pointing to ongoing security concerns. But the entrenched Israeli settlement enterprise, with over half a million Israelis living in these areas of the West Bank, constitutes the major obstacle for Israel to end its occupation. The international community shares this view. The UN Security Council determined in 1979 "that the policy and practices of Israel in establishing settlements in the Palestinian and other Arab territories occupied since 1967 have no legal validity and constitute a serious obstruction to achieving a comprehensive, just, and lasting peace in the Middle East."[10] This position has been reiterated by the Security Council many times since. Settlements are illegal under international law because they make ending the occupation more difficult and lead to discriminatory policies on the part of the occupying power in favor of its settlers.

International humanitarian law has no clear provisions in place to address an occupation that has continued as long as Israel's has over Palestine. Although

---

[9] For example, international humanitarian law permits the occupying power to place people in administrative detention—detention without trial though for short periods of time and not as a substitute to trying people in court. For more information, see the Glossary, page 276.

[10] UN SC 446 (1979) The Resolution was adopted by 12 votes to none, with 3 abstentions from Norway, the United Kingdom and the United States of America. Recently, the Israeli cabinet voted to investigate the possibility of annexing these settlements and parts of the West Bank, and provide Israeli citizenship to the Palestinians living in these areas, as a way to avoid withdrawal from the settlements.

international law prohibits settlements, it does not provide guidance, legal and punitive procedures, and/or remedies for those under occupation after an occupying power has illegally settled its citizens in occupied territories. The Rome Statute, which set up the International Criminal Court, has declared settlement under occupation a war crime—but this cannot be enforced in Israel or Palestine, since neither has agreed to the court's jurisdiction. However, international law is clear that as long as Israel's military remains present in Palestine, or retains effective control over the occupied population, the area is considered occupied. This is also relevant to the Gaza Strip. Though Israel removed its Israeli settlers from the Gaza Strip in 2005, it still retains effective control over the occupied population on all movement and access of goods and people, provision of utilities, and basic resources such as fuel and food.

UN RECOGNITION—STILL INCOMPLETE

In 1974, the General Assembly reaffirmed the inalienable rights of the Palestinian people to self-determination, national independence, sovereignty, and the right to return.[11] It instructed the Secretary General to make contacts with the Palestine Liberation Organization (PLO) on all matter concerning the Palestinian people.[12] In November 1988, the PLO recognized the two state paradigm by declaring the establishment of the state of Palestine in the areas occupied by Israel in 1967—the 22 percent of British Mandate Palestine established by the original 1947 UN partition plan. The UN General Assembly then voted to recognize the political leadership of the Palestinian people under the PLO as representatives of "Palestine" rather than simply representatives of the PLO. Thus, UN recognition of the PLO as a representative political entity became de facto recognition of a quasi-state entity called "Palestine." Delegates from the PLO were granted "observer" status, which meant that they could attend General Assembly meetings but not cast any votes.

Under international law, a military occupation and the occupying power's obligations towards the civilian population end by a declaration of the UN Security Council and, ideally, with a political agreement acceptable to all sides, whereby the occupying power terminates all its effective and residual control over the territory and its population.

---

[11] A/RES/3236 (XXIX) 22 November 1974

[12] For more information on the PLO, see the Glossary, page 276.

The Oslo Accords, first contemplated in 1993, were the closest Israel and Palestine have come to a political agreement. However, they were never designed to end Israel's full control over the territories. The agreements were technically "interim agreements" for five years (effective from 1994 to 1999), designed to set up the Palestinian Authority as a governing body and to "test the waters" of transferring authority over the occupied territories. Under the Oslo Accords, major authorities—including security, land planning, administration of East Jerusalem, water usage, road construction, and the population registry—remained under Israeli control. The planners of the Oslo Accords envisioned that most of the occupied territories would be under PA control at the end of the interim period, and that a final status agreement would be in place to resolve the more difficult political issues still obstructing peace such as return of refugees, the division of Jerusalem, settler movement, water usage, and borders. Fifteen years later, repeated failures to reach a final status agreement have resulted in the "interim agreement" still in place. Neither side has canceled the Oslo Accords, but Yossi Beilen, one of its Israeli architects, has compared the continued application of the Oslo Accords to "keeping a twenty year old in kindergarten."

In 2011, the PLO requested international recognition of Palestine as a member state on the 1967 borders, including East Jerusalem, and sought admission to the United Nations as a full member. The PLO based its request on UN General Assembly Resolution 181 II from 1947 where "sympathetic consideration" was meant to be given to the Palestine application for membership in the UN. It also based its request on the numerous UN General Assembly resolutions affirming the right of Palestinians to self-determination, sovereignty, and independence, and full respect of these rights as an "indispensable element to the establishment of a just and lasting peace in the Middle East."[13]

The UN Security Council rejected the PLO request for full membership to the wider United Nations, stating that the legal threshold to become a state had not been reached—specifically that Palestine had not fulfilled the condition of becoming a "peace loving" entity, and lacked effective governmental control over the Gaza Strip.[14]

---

[13] See UNGA Res 2672 (1970), UN GA Res 3236, UN GA Res 2649

[14] See the the International Court of Justice in 1948 which determined five additional criteria for states seeking full United Nations membership: A candidate must be: (1) a state; (2) peace-loving; (3) must accept the obligations of the Charter; (4) must be able to carry out these obligations; (5) must be willing to do so.

Despite the UN SC rejection, in 2012, the UN General Assembly voted over-whelmingly to upgrade Palestine's position in the UN from "observer entity" to "non-member observer state."[15] The move granted Palestine the power to poten-tially join international organizations and specialized UN agencies such as the World Trade Organization and the International Criminal Court. Two years later in April 2014, Palestinian President Mahmoud Abbas used Palestine's new status as "non-member observer state" to sign letters of accession to fifteen multilateral treaties and conventions as a way to claim fuller rights of statehood under inter-national law. Despite the upgrade of its status by the UN General Assembly, Palestine is still not recognized by the United Nations as a state. It does not have the power to vote within the UN General Assembly, and Palestine's rights to use the International Criminal Court and other international bodies have barely been tested.

However, under international law, the Security Council's rejection of Palestine's full membership in the United Nations does not determine whether or not Palestine is recognized as a country. The United Nations does not have the power to declare statehood as a legal fact on its own. Only full recognition by the rest of the global community has the power to make Palestine a state in both name and fact.

While full membership as a state recognized by the UN remains elusive, international recognition of Palestine as a state has progressed significantly. More than 130 countries comprising 75 percent of the world's population recognize the "state of Palestine," and have accorded it the requisite diplomatic status as a state. Despite these political victories, the most important obstacle to full statehood remains in place—the continued Israeli military occupation of Palestine. The Israeli military has prevented the formation of borders for the Palestinian state and maintains control over Palestine's economy, land use, resource use, provision of utilities, and the movement of its goods.

THE PATH TO STATEHOOD

The legal ambiguities surrounding statehood brought about by the Israeli occu-pation have many ramifications for Palestinian governance and the citizens of

---

[15] The vote was 138 in favor to 9 against (Canada, Czech Republic, Israel, Marshall Islands, Micronesia (Federated States of), Nauru, Panama, Palau, and the United States), with 41 abstentions.

Palestine. The borders of the Palestine state are not under Palestinian control, and their final status has been delegated to political negotiations. The Palestinian president and the Palestine Authority (the governmental body designated by the Oslo Accords to administer parts of Palestine) cannot fully carry out their duties in the face of de facto Israeli control. Palestinian citizens' movements are obstructed by the Israeli barrier wall, checkpoints, and Israeli-controlled crossings constructed inside Palestine. These obstructions also block the Palestinian refugees, numbering 7 million (70 percent of the Palestinian population) today from returning to their homes. For Palestinian refugee communities living in neighboring states such as Syria, Jordan, and Egypt, it is difficult to obtain permission from Israel to move to the West Bank or the Gaza Strip. As many as a half-million Israeli citizens, generally referred to as settlers, have moved into illegal Israeli settlements in the West Bank area of Palestine, assuming control of key land areas, thoroughfares, water, and natural resources. And the declared capital of Palestine, East Jerusalem, is not in Palestinian hands—it has been annexed by Israel, pulled within Israeli borders and behind Israeli barrier walls, leaving Palestine "capital-less."

The reality on the ground demonstrates that from a legal perspective, the "state" of Palestine is not yet fully substantiated. While most of the basic elements that define a state under international law are present—such as a permanent population, a government or political authority, and a (partial) capacity to enter in relations with others states, some critical factors are missing, such as "a defined territory and borders," and the full capacity to carry out the UN Charter.[16]

Palestine might be recognized by other states, but Palestine's ability to perform all the functions of a state remain obstructed due to Israel's control of the areas. Palestine is "almost" a state—semi-statehood under occupation—though inherently this prevents real self-determination and the realization of true independence and freedom.

The harsh reality of Palestine today is that while international law supports the Palestinian cause, and most of the international community has recognized the "state of Palestine," not one member state of the UN, nor the UN Security Council as a whole, has taken any *effective* steps to end Israel's occupation—

---

[16] Also refer again to the International Court of Justice criteria for states seeking full United Nations membership: A candidate must be: (1) a state; (2) peace-loving; (3) must accept the obligations of the Charter; (4) must be able to carry out these obligations; (5) must be willing to do so.

the main obstacle to real Palestinian statehood. Politics has interfered repeatedly in obstructing Palestinian rights grounded in international law. Without an end to Israel's occupation, the large number of recognized Palestinian embassies worldwide will remain a cosmetic achievement. The denial of Palestinian international legal rights not only prevents a viable peace from being established in the Middle East, but erodes the effectiveness of international law and diplomacy, as a principled model of how we want the world to be.

Allegra Pacheco is an U.S.-born lawyer currently working in the occupied Palestinian territories. A graduate of Columbia University School of Law, she is admitted to both the New York and Israeli bars. She has litigated Palestinian human rights cases in front of the Israeli Supreme Court and has worked in the United Nations. She is also married to Abdelrahman Al-Ahmar, one of the narrators in this book. For Abdelrahman's story, see page 75.

IV. GAZA'S TUNNELS

by Nicolas Pelham

This essay is adapted from "Gaza's Tunnel Phenomenon: The Unintended Dynamics of Israel's Siege," which first appeared in the Journal of Palestine Studies *in 2012, and has been updated by the author to reflect developments in the time since its publication. The full version of the 2012 essay can be found on the website of the Institute for Palestine Studies, www.palestine-studies.org.*

Until very recently, visitors approaching the Rafah border crossing from Gaza to Egypt could be forgiven for thinking they had stepped back in time to the 1948 Nakba.[1] On the southern reaches of the town, the horizon was interrupted by hundreds of white tents flapping in the wind. Instead of dispossessed refugees, the tents sheltered the mouths of hundreds of tunnels, which since 2007 have played a critical role in providing a lifeline for Gazans hit by a punishing siege. Beneath the awnings, thousands of workers shoveled heavy materials for Gaza's reconstruction. Front-end loaders plowed through the sands, loading juggernauts with gravel and enveloping the entire zone in dust clouds. Tanker trucks filled with gasoline from underground reservoirs; customs officials weighed trucks and issue the tax vouchers required to exit. The ground that Israel leveled in 2004 to create a barren corridor separating Gaza from Egypt was abuzz with activity on and under the surface, as Gazans operated a tunnel complex that became the driver of Gaza's economy and the mainstay of its governing Palestinian Islamist movement, Hamas.

THE FIRST WALL, THE FIRST TUNNEL

For millennia, Rafah was the first stopping place for merchants crossing the desert from Africa to Asia. Israel's establishment in 1948 did not sever the tie, for Gaza was administered by Egypt until Israel's 1967 occupation. Even after, Bedouins crossed the border unimpeded, continuing to mingle and marry. Only in 1981, when Egypt and Israel demarcated their frontier along Gaza's southern edge as part of their 1979 peace treaty, did separation really set in. No sooner had the agreement's implementation divided Rafah between Israel and Egypt

---

[1] For more on the Nakba, see the Glossary, page 276.

than Bedouin clans straddling the ten-mile border began burrowing underneath, particularly at the midpoint where the earth is softest.

Israel's first recorded discovery of a tunnel was in 1983. To avoid detection, Gazans dug their tunnels from the basements of their houses to a depth of about fifty feet, headed south for a few hundred feet, and then resurfaced on the Egyptian side of the border, often in a relative's house, grove, or chicken coop. By the late 1980s, tunnel operators were importing such basics as processed cheese, subsidized in Egypt and taxed in Israel, and probably some contraband as well, including drugs, gold, and weapons.

Israel's "soft quarantining" of Gaza—the steadily tightening restrictions on the movement of persons and goods into Israel—began with the Oslo peace process and in preparation for the establishment in the Strip of the Palestinian Authority in 1994. After Oslo's signing, Israel built a barrier around Gaza.

Though access continued through Israel's terminals, periodic closures led Gazans to seek alternatives. The perimeter barrier was among the first targets of protestors when the Al-Aqsa Intifada broke out in September 2000,[2] but by June 2001 Israel had replaced it with a higher, grimmer, more impenetrable upgrade. Frequent lockdowns at Israel's terminals and the destruction of Gaza's seaport and airport in 2001, coupled with the militarization of the intifada, intensified the drive for outlets south.

Hence the expansion and upgrading of the tunnels, which for the first time served as safety valves for wholesalers to alleviate the artificially created shortages.

ISRAEL'S BLOCKADE, 2006

Given their quest for weapons and the need for funds to finance operations during the Intifada, Palestinian political factions operated the longest and deepest tunnels. The cash-strapped PA sought to co-opt clans along the border where tunneling was easiest. This fusion of security and business interests, of militia activity and private entrepreneurship, was to become a hallmark of future development.

Successive Israeli military operations aimed at defeating the Second Intifada and widening the buffer zone between Gaza and Egypt also targeted the tunnels. In the lead-up to implementing its unilateral Gaza withdrawal plan, Israel

---

[2] The Al-Aqsa Intifada is also known as the Second Intifada. For more information on the Intifadas, see the Glossary, page 276.

razed some 1,500 Palestinian homes within a 325-foot-wide *cordon sanitaire* (the Philadelphi corridor) between Rafah and the border, and reinforced it with a twenty-three-foot-high wall. Egypt's Mubarak regime largely acquiesced in the wall's construction, hoping it would protect his realm from a spillover of the Intifada and suicide bombing that was threatening its lucrative tourist resorts along the Sinai Peninsula's riviera on the Red Sea. In addition, it feared that Israel's withdrawal risked saddling Egypt with responsibility for Gaza's 1.7 million inhabitants, disconnecting the territory from the West Bank, and thereby ending Arab aspirations for an integral Palestinian state.

In January 2006, four months after Israel completed its Gaza pullout, Hamas won the Palestinian legislative elections. Israel responded by systematically tightening its borders. On March 12, 2006, while Hamas was in negotiations to form a unity government, Israel closed Erez terminal to Gazan laborers in Israel, who once constituted 70 percent of Gaza's workforce. In June 2006, when the Israeli soldier Gilad Shalit was captured by Palestinian militants (and spirited away by tunnel), Israel shut down the Karni terminal, Gaza's primary crossing for goods (already closed for half of the previous six months). Israel also prevented the use of the Rafah terminal for passenger traffic and severely restricted access for the European monitoring mission there.

Israel's array of restrictions on trade, coupled with the need to mitigate the threat of punitive Israeli air strikes targeting the tunnel zone, quickly spurred Palestinians to develop deeper and longer tunnels spanning the width of the Israeli-bulldozed buffer and less vulnerable to sabotage. The tunnel network continued to grow, and infrastructure improved. Even so, the tunnels were ill-prepared for the surge in traffic generated by the near-hermetic seal imposed on Gaza by Israel and Egypt when, in June 2007, Hamas seized control of the Strip, disbanded Fatah's forces, and chased out its leaders.

INDUSTRIAL-SCALE BURROWING, 2007

Hamas's summer 2007 military takeover of the Strip marked a turning point for the tunnel trade. The siege, already in place, was tightened. Egypt shut the Rafah terminal. Israel designated Gaza "a hostile entity" and, following a salvo of rocket fire on its border areas in November 2007, cut food supplies by half and severed fuel imports. In January 2008, Israel announced a total blockade on fuel after rockets were fired at Sderot, banning all but seven categories of humanitarian supplies. As gasoline supplies dried up, Gazans abandoned cars on the roadside and bought donkeys.

Under Israeli blockade at sea and a combined Egyptian-Israeli siege on land, Gaza's humanitarian crisis loomed, threatening Hamas's rule. As the siege intensified, employment in Gazan manufacturing plummeted from 35,000 to 860 by mid-2008, and Gaza's gross domestic product fell by a third in real terms from its 2005 levels (compared to a 42 percent increase in the West Bank over the same period).

With access above ground barred, the Islamist movement oversaw a program of industrial-scale burrowing underground. With each tunnel costing $80,000 to $200,000 to build, mosques and charitable networks launched schemes offering unrealistically high rates of return, promoting a pyramid scheme that ended in disaster. Preachers extolled commercial tunnel ventures as "resistance" activity and hailed workers killed on the job as "martyrs." The National Security Forces (NSF), a PA force reconstituted by Hamas primarily with 'Izz Al-Din Al-Qassam Brigades (IQB) personnel, but also including several hundred (Fatah) PA defectors, guarded the border, occasionally exchanging fire with the Egyptian army, while the Hamas government oversaw construction activity. Simultaneously, the Hamas-run Rafah municipality upgraded the electricity grid to power hundreds of hoists, kept Gaza's fire service on standby, and on several occasions extinguished fires in tunnels used to pump fuel. As Mahmud Zahar, a Hamas Gaza leader, explained, "No electricity, no water, no food came from outside. That's why we had to build the tunnels."

Private investors, including Hamas members who raised capital through their mosque networks, partnered with families straddling the border. Lawyers drafted contracts for cooperatives to build and operate commercial tunnels. The contracts detailed the number of partners (generally four to fifteen), the value of the respective shares, and the mechanism for distributing shareholder profits.

A typical partnership encompassed a cross-section of Gazan society, including, for example, a porter at the Rafah land crossing, a security officer in the former PA administration, agricultural workers, university graduates, nongovernmental organization (NGO) employees, and diggers. Investors could quickly recover their outlay. Fully operational, a tunnel could generate the cost of its construction in a month. With each tunnel jointly run by a partnership on each side of the border, Gazan and Egyptian owners generally split earnings equally.

From enterprises primarily geared to weapons smuggling, the tunnels rapidly turned into what one trader described as "the lungs through which Gaza breathes." By the eve of Operation Cast Lead in December 2008, their number had grown to at least five hundred from a few dozen mainly factional tunnels in mid-2005; tunnel trade revenue increased from an average of $30 million/year in 2005 to $36 million/month.

Mitigating to some extent the Gaza economy's sharp contraction that had resulted from the international boycott of Hamas, the PA's ongoing salary payments to some 75,000 PA employees, including some whom the PA had ordered to stop work, sustained the government's liquidity and purchasing power.

Meanwhile, the area of tunnel operations doubled to five miles, extending along the border from the Rafah terminal west to Tel Zagreb near the coast. So congested were some parts of the border that diggers had to burrow tunnels one on top of the other, using Google Earth to map routes and make sure they stayed on course.

Teams of six laborers working round the clock in two twelve-hour shifts could dig an average of thirty to fifty feet a day. Once functional, tunnels were constantly upgraded to speed deliveries. Over time, they were fitted with internal lighting, intercoms, and generators to maintain operations during frequent power cuts. The tunnels' rough-hewn edges were smoothed to reduce damage to imports.

"Legalized" by Hamas on the Gaza side of the border, the tunnels remained clandestine on Egypt's side. Thus, while in Gaza the tunnel mouths were moved from the basements of private homes to the open terrain fronting the Philadelphi corridor, in Egypt the tunnels extended deep inside Egyptian territory. Up to three-quarters of a standard half-mile tunnel was on Egypt's side. And while the tunnel mouths, protected from the elements by white canvas, were open on the Gaza side, in Egypt they remained concealed.

REGULATING A TUNNEL ECONOMY

When Hamas seized the Strip from Fatah in June 2007, its military wing, the IQB, appropriated the Fatah-run tunnels. From the outset, there was a de facto distinction between the factional tunnels, used for military and operational purposes and off-limits to government inspectors and customs authorities, and the privately owned tunnels, which were Gaza's primary source of imports.

Once in control of the commercial tunnels, the Hamas government set about formalizing the smuggling economy through regulation. In the wake of Operation Cast Lead, the Interior Ministry established the Tunnel Affairs Commission (TAC) to act as the regulatory authority for commercial activities. Among its first acts was to issue a list of blacklisted imports, including weapons, alcohol, and tramadol, a painkiller much used in Gaza. In response to public concern at a rising toll of tunnel casualties, particularly of child workers, the TAC issued guidelines intended to ensure safe working conditions. Over time, it fenced off the site and stationed some three hundred black-clad internal-security personnel at entry points to spot-check the documentation of persons entering and leaving the zone. Tunnel openings were patrolled on motorbike. The TAC introduced a tunnel-licensing system to prevent construction in areas deemed of national security (particularly near border fortifications where outside observation was feared, or in areas reserved for factional tunneling) and to regulate oversupply. Investors seeking clearance to build a new tunnel were required to provide proof of land ownership or notarized proof of authorization of the right to use the land. The TAC also intervened to arbitrate disputes between merchants and tunnel operators, and monitored the market for instances of sharp inflation or evidence of hoarding and price-fixing, particularly of fuel. Traders and consumers alike said they welcomed the price stabilization and removal of petty traders selling gasoline from the roadsides.

Violations were punished. In 2009-10, for instance, the TAC closed at least five tunnels for smuggling tramadol and two for nonpayment of cigarette taxes. It destroyed an additional fifty non-operational tunnels to prevent their use as safe houses or conduits to and from Egypt by "wanted" individuals. "We used to earn thousands smuggling small shipments of hand guns, grenades, bullets, and TNT," said a tunnel operator who first entered the business at the end of the Second Intifada, "but it is no longer worth the risk to be prosecuted by Hamas."

In a further sign of formalization, the TAC introduced an increasingly comprehensive customs regime, providing Hamas with a new revenue base that partially compensated for the Ramallah-based PA's monopoly on customs revenues collected at Israel's ports. Haulers weighed their trucks on an electronic weigh station buried in the sand near the entrance to the tunnel zone, obtained chits for their cargoes at an adjoining hut, and upon exit presented the receipts to guards. In September 2008, the Rafah municipality introduced administrative fees, charging tunnel operators a one-time license fee of NIS 10,000 ($2,850)/ tunnel and NIS 3,000 for connection to the electricity grid. Evaders were liable to tunnel closure and arrest, deferrable with a NIS 1,000 bail. Further charges were levied on heavily Egyptian-subsidized gasoline and diesel (about NIS 0.5/liter in Egypt), cooking gas (NIS 30/canister), cigarettes (NIS 3/pack), and generators. In addition, Gaza authorities levied a 14.5 percent value-added tax on all goods. A tunnel owner who raised a Fatah flag from his house had his license withdrawn.

Hamas's regulatory efforts did not go unchallenged, particularly after it taxed what had been a tax-free enterprise. Families and clans in the border area protested interference in their activities. In late November 2007, armed clashes erupted between Hamas government forces and members of the Al-Sha'ir family in Rafah after Hamas destroyed two of its tunnels. But for the most part, the rapidly expanding business opportunities available under Hamas rule trumped lingering resentments. With demand far exceeding supply, tunnel operators earned $50 for ferrying a hundred-pound sack through the tunnels.

A decade earlier, all but 1 percent of Gaza's total imports came from, or via, Israel. By the eve of Operation Cast Lead, the ratio had nearly reversed. Although the tunnels were often rudimentary, the trade cycle was generally faster than through Israeli terminals, and less laden with customs red tape. Normal deliveries arrived within three to five days of placing an order, faster than pre-takeover orders from Israel. Operators responded rapidly to demand. When Israel reduced gas supplies, smuggled canisters quickly surfaced on the market. Vaccines from Egypt entered Gaza following reports of disease sweeping chicken farms. Ahead of holidays, traders imported toys, live sheep, and fresh beef from Egypt.

Both Egypt and Israel had mixed reactions to the tunnel operations. For Israel, the reorientation of Gaza's trade to Egypt tempered the international outcry over the blockade and widened the divide between Gaza and the West Bank. For Egypt, smuggling offered copious opportunities for bribes (at both the local and national levels) from a hitherto unprofitable region. Yet both countries also saw tunnel growth as a security threat they could scarcely monitor, let alone control. In an effort to interrupt the traffic, Israel repeatedly deployed drones and manned aircraft to bomb Gaza's tunnels, while Egypt stepped up tunnel detection and demolition. Tunnel owners responded by improving their design and digging to depths of over twenty-five meters.

EGYPT'S COUNTERMEASURES

Israel's repeated attacks on Gaza culminated in the devastating Operation Cast Lead of winter 2008-9. Although Hamas's detractors in Gaza claimed the tunnels served as an escape hatch for some senior Hamas officials during the war, aerial bombardment of the Rafah border severely damaged the network, resulting in a temporary suspension of commercial traffic. Meanwhile, the land, air, and sea blockade remained fully in force.

As part of the internationally brokered cease-fire, Israel secured U.S. agreement to act against the smuggling routes supplying Gaza. Separately, Egypt committed to build (under U.S. military supervision) an eighty-foot-deep underground steel barrier along its border with Gaza aimed at blocking the tunnels within a year. By the end of 2010, it claimed to have sabotaged some six hundred tunnels by various means, including plugging entrances with solid waste, sand, or explosives, and flooding passages with sewage. Use of tear gas and other crowd-control techniques inside the tunnels resulted in several deaths. "The war marked a turning point in how Egypt's security dealt with us," remarked one tunnel operator. "In the past, they would look the other way when a lorry stopped to unload at a tunnel mouth, but since May 2009 they . . . raid the homes, sheds, farms, and shops of our Sinai suppliers."

But Egypt's countermeasures never quite matched its policy statements. From the first, Egypt cited logistical problems, such as difficulties hammering steel plates more than fourteen feet deep in stony ground. Tunnel operators cut through completed segments with blowtorches, nullifying the multimillion-dollar project for the cost of a few thousand dollars. Reluctance to forgo the bribes accruing from smuggling further compromised official resolve. Egyptian security forces often targeted the shallowest and most easily detected tunnels, leaving the more developed and profitable ones untouched. Tellingly, construction slowed where tunnel activity was most concentrated. Hamas's success in mounting a solidarity network to condemn the Mubarak regime for enforcing the siege further eroded Egypt's political will. Frustrated, the U.S. Congress suspended technical support for the underground steel barrier in mid-2011.

Motivated by family and clan unification, as well as economic benefits, Bedouin and Palestinians on Egypt's side of the border also resisted Egypt's security measures. "We're Palestinians working for the sake of Palestine," said a tunnel laborer in Egyptian Rafah. To foil Egyptian security, Bedouin operators sometimes tapped into well-armed clan defense committees versed in Sinai's topography from centuries of roaming. There were sporadic reports of clashes between Bedouin irregulars and Egyptian forces seizing contraband.

THE TUNNEL EXPANSION AND GAZA'S ECONOMIC RECOVERY, 2009

Meanwhile, the cease-fire at the end of Operation Cast Lead enabled Hamas to undertake repairs on the partially destroyed tunnels and to oversee a major overhaul of the complex, even reducing taxes to stimulate the work. Fear of Egyptian detection prompted operators to extend their tunnels to a length of one mile and to deepen them to up to 130 feet below ground. Operators reinforced tunnels first with wooden planks, then cement blocks and metal to allow sufficient widening for raw materials to pass through without risking tunnel collapse. Rope ladders flung down the shafts were replaced by electric elevators, while the thirteen-foot-long sledges (*shahata*) pulled by winches were replaced by carts running on rails, much as in coal mines.

Within two years, capacity had increased tenfold. By late 2010, large commercial tunnels were estimated to be shifting up to 170 metric tons of raw materials each per day. The number of tunnels transporting livestock rose from three in 2008 to at least thirty in mid-2010. There was also less loss and damage, since the longer tunnels were harder for Egypt's security to find, and conditions inside the tunnels had substantially improved. Economies of scale and diversified sources of supply lowered costs. By the summer of 2011, 60 percent of traders reported that prices had fallen to equal or below the pre-siege level for goods from Israel.

For example, a liter of fuel (initially sold in sand-riddled plastic soda bottles) cost four times more than in Israel in 2008; by 2009 fuel (pumped through three-quarter-inch pipes at a rate of 20,000 liters/hour) sold at a quarter of Israel's price. By mid-2011, prices for Turkish cement (Gazans snubbed Egypt's lower-quality products) had plummeted from $1,500/ton at the height of the closures in mid-2008 to the pre-siege price of $100. The cost of shipping a fifty-kilo sack of goods fell from $50 to $5. "There are at least 1,500 underground tunnels now," said an owner. "Most are bigger and better than ever before, and all of them are open for business. The result is more competition, more price wars, and less work for everyone."

Demand grew as capacity improved and prices fell to within a range average Gazans could afford. Between 2008 and 2010, traders of household goods reported a 60 percent rise in their import of goods via the tunnels. By mid-2010, Gaza's retailers reported that shortages resulting from Israeli restrictions had been reduced "to a reasonable extent or more." Wholesalers rapidly replenished their empty warehouses. By mid-2009, cars—hitherto cut into three and welded together in Gaza—were arriving whole, first dragged through the tunnels by bulldozers and then driven through expanded tunnels. To satisfy demand, tunnel operators tapped into contraband, particularly of cars, arriving from Libya after Qaddafi's retreat from Cyrenaica left his arms depots and ports open for looting.

Expansion also facilitated the import of inputs and raw materials, precipitating what has been perhaps the tunnels' greatest achievement: kick-starting Gaza's postwar reconstruction while donors remained on the sidelines. While world leaders promised billions at showcase conferences in Sharm Al-Sheikh's luxury hotels, but failed to persuade Israel to lift its ban on construction materials, the tunnels enabled Gazans to rebuild their enclave themselves.

Gaza morphed into a construction site. Roadsides were piled high with building materials from Egypt. UN Habitat estimated that, based on the materials allowed in by Israel, it would take eighty years to rebuild the six thousand housing units destroyed in Operation Cast Lead and accommodate the growth in population over five years of closure; tunnel flows reduced that lagtime to a more manageable five. Indeed so rapid was the pace of construction that by mid-2012 real estate agents reported that they were struggling to locate prospective buyers for the new apartments.

It was not only Gaza's housing stock that began to recover. Farmers resorted to tunnel imports to circumvent Israel's ban on seeds, pesticides, irrigation pipes, and basic agricultural tools such as hoes and buckets. The increased affordability of inputs helped factories resume operations: Hamas officials claimed that by October 2011, half the fourteen hundred factories destroyed during Operation Cast Lead were back in production. A food-processing plant resumed operations after items banned by Israel—including preservatives, plastic wrapping and packaging made in Egypt, and spare parts—arrived from Switzerland via tunnel.

All told, the tunnel expansion precipitated a recovery that rapidly reversed much of Gaza's earlier decline. From 2005 to 2009, Gaza's per capita GDP contracted by 39 percent in real terms, with the tunnels providing at best limited relief. After Operation Cast Lead, the tunnels facilitated what a September 2011 World Bank report described as "exceptionally high growth," notching 28 percent in the first half of 2011. Unemployment dropped from 45 percent before Operation Cast Lead to 32 percent by mid-2011. Rafah's markets bristled with shoppers and café-goers late into the night, its backstreet ATMs distributing $100 bills.

THE LIMITS OF A TUNNEL-BASED ECONOMY

Even as the World Bank was touting Gaza's exceptional growth, however, the structural flaws impeding Gaza's full-fledged reconstruction persisted. With few exports capable of generating sustainable growth, Gaza's consumption was capped. By 2010, the markets were saturated, with improved supply lines outstripping demand, while wages fell sharply, not least due to increased use of cheaper Egyptian labor. Intense competition pushed tunnel earnings and prices down even faster. With supply already exceeding demand, Israel's June 2010 decision to lift its ban on the import of commercial goods (following the international outcry over the Mavi Marmara aid-flotilla incident) triggered a market glut. Retailers hitherto limited to imports via the tunnels revived their former ties with Israeli counterparts.

By the end of 2010, operations at over half of Gaza's 1,100 tunnels had reportedly been suspended. Those that survived launched efficiency drives, reducing operating hours and cutting labor so as to remain commercially viable. Increasingly, tunnel activity narrowed to goods that were competitive because Israel either heavily taxed alternatives, such as fuel, or banned them. The latter included most raw materials, all items defined as "dual use" (e.g., construction materials, machinery, chemicals, and spare parts), and almost all export goods. "Israel's blacklist is the smugglers' green list," commented a prominent Gaza businessman who imports Egyptian cacti for his nursery through the tunnels.

By spring 2012, signs that the economy had reached the ceiling achievable through the tunnel conduits were increasingly visible. According to figures from the Palestinian Central Bureau of Statistics for the first quarter of 2012, unemployment had begun to climb, and the previous high rates of growth had fallen back sharply. Despite Egypt's acquiescence to increased passage through the Rafah terminal, most of Gaza's 240,000 refugee youth had never left the enclave, and 51 percent of them remained unemployed. Continued restrictions by the Egyptian authorities on the entry of tanker trucks bound for Gaza into the Sinai Peninsula left the enclave in darkness for much of the night. Israeli warships cruise on the horizon, a visible reminder of the three-mile limit Israel imposed on Gaza's seas. The claustrophobic feeling of being trapped by land, air, and sea has not disappeared.

Initially in the wake of Mubarak's 2011 ouster, the tunnel economy enjoyed a boom. As the internal-security apparatus took flight, Egypt's remaining impediments disappeared. Tunnel mouths placed deep inside Egyptian territory resurfaced close to the border, in the process taking an obvious toll on Egyptian Rafah's housing stock, where gaping cracks appeared even in recent construction. Construction on the underground steel barrier was formally halted. Tunnel owners reported next to no impounding of materials, only token destruction of tunnel mouths, and a marked decrease in demands for bribes. Many Egyptian operators who had been sentenced in absentia and who had paid hefty bribes to avoid arrest were granted amnesty. Heightened domestic opposition in Egypt to the ongoing Gaza blockade and increased activity by Bedouin armed groups offered tunnel traffickers additional protection.

In deference to Cairo, Hamas had from the start banned the use of commercial tunnels for passenger traffic, but reversed this policy after the Mubarak regime fell. Meanwhile, the new Egyptian authorities, with much fanfare, eased the restrictions on passage through the Rafah terminal. However, with restrictions still in place, the tunnels offered a viable fast track that circumvented much of the red tape of the overland crossing. To regulate passenger traffic, the TAC introduced a system of prior coordination that took two days rather than the two months required for applications to cross via the Rafah terminal. Moreover, while the Rafah crossing closed at five p.m. (later extended to eight p.m.), the tunnels operated around the clock. Male applicants ages 15 to 40, some 35 percent of whom were generally barred entry to Egypt on security grounds, benefited in particular, but all kinds of travelers, from Pakistani academics and Palestinian workers fleeing Libya to families on holiday, used the tunnel. Costs for the six-hundred-yard crossing, which previously reached hundreds of dollars, fell to NIS 100 ($30).

Relaxed controls also served to alleviate the ban on exports, the other grueling aspect of the siege. These included scrap metal (smelted in Sinai and re-imported as steel rods for construction and possibly also military use), dapple racing horses (which all but disappeared from Gaza due to high Egyptian demand), ammunition (which spiked in demand during Egypt's 2011 revolution), and surplus produce—watermelons, apples, and eggs—resulting from Gaza's drive for food self-sufficiency. That said, Egypt's lower labor costs and purchasing power rendered most Gaza produce uncompetitive, and Gaza's manufacturing base, traditionally geared to the Israeli and West Bank markets, was slow to adapt to Egyptian needs. Egypt-bound traffic comprised mainly re-exports of goods from Israel for which there was Egyptian demand, including heavily taxed items such as shoes, hair gel, and mobile phones.

Yet the political unrest following Mubarak's ouster in February 2011 destabilized the tunnel economy as well. Led by Hamas leaders, Gazans looked to Egypt's new Islamist leadership to dismantle the siege structures and open the crossing to overland goods traffic. Certainly, initial euphoria at the prospect of a new laissez-faire era in Egyptian–Gaza relations dimmed as Egypt's ruling military council, the Supreme Council of the Armed Forces (SCAF), consolidated its hold. In a sign of renewed leverage over Gaza, and reflecting a desire to cut their subsidy bill, the Egyptian authorities blocked tanker trucks en route to Gaza hauling heavily subsidized Egyptian gasoline. Although some fuel continued to trickle through the tunnels, the enclave again experienced outages of up to eighteen hours per day, as in the harshest days of the siege. The shortages not only rendered life uncomfortable, they deprived it of the dynamo to power more reconstruction. Inside Gaza, the Hamas government faced widespread charges of hubris for wildly overestimating the early benefits accruing from the Arab awakening.

SHIFTING POWER IN GAZAN SOCIETY

Seven years of Hamas rule over Gaza and sponsorship of the tunnel trade brought changes to the Strip whose impact could be felt at a popular level. Public infrastructure—including the parliament and other government buildings, police stations, and mosques—had been leveled or severely damaged in Israel's Operation Cast Lead bombardment. The Hamas government, armed with the proceeds from import taxes and an expanded tunnel infrastructure capable of transporting heavy goods and machinery, repaired and upgraded infrastructure. Hamas also widened the Salah Al-Din Road (the Rafah-Gaza City highway) to accommodate increased traffic from the south, and, in Gaza City itself, began beautifying prominent landmarks, sodding sandy areas, dredging the port, installing traffic lights, and rebuilding its coastal riviera to the south, which officials claimed would one day rival Tel Aviv's.

In an economy blighted by unemployment resulting from Israel's ban on Gazan workers, the bombardment of its manufacturing base, and the closure of export markets (above and beyond a significant slowdown in donor-funded development projects), the tunnels emerged as Gaza's largest nongovernmental employer. The tunnel industry attracted construction workers once employed in Israel from across the Gaza Strip. For a time, tunnel workers were the best paid in Gaza: in 2008, the average daily wage was $75, five times Gaza's median wage, according to official Palestinian figures, and more than West Bank Palestinians earned building Israel's Jewish settlements. The tunnel trade was also the largest overall employer of youth. School dropouts scrounging NIS 20/day as street peddlers earned ten times that much in the tunnels. Although market saturation and recourse to Egyptian labor later depressed daily wages to more like NIS 80, even this was quadruple a farmhand's wage. With each fully functioning tunnel employing twenty to thirty people, by 2010 the tunnel industry was estimated to employ some 5,000 tunnel owners and 25,000 workers, supporting about 150,000 dependents, or 10 percent of Gaza's population.

Such was the turnaround in the local economy that Gaza City had a surfeit of new hotels, restaurants, and beach cafés, which attracted not only the new moneyed elite the tunnels had fostered, but also exiles returning to the Strip (sometimes via tunnels), and even visitors from northern Sinai. Gaza's new luxury hotel, Al-Mashtal, optimistically bought cocktail glasses, while visiting businessmen from the West Bank complained that the latest-model sports cars and Hummers could be seen on Gaza's streets long before they surfaced in Ramallah. Real estate brokers said the multiplier effect of the increased spending power spurred a threefold increase in real estate prices.

Nonetheless, Gaza's macroeconomic growth figures disguised wide disparities in the distribution of the new wealth. In geographical terms, prosperity followed the new employment opportunities: the north languished, while the south boomed. Gaza's traditional mercantile elite, which had developed ties with Israeli and Western European suppliers, found its status and influence in Gaza increasingly sapped by a new generation of smugglers tapping into ancient informal trade routes that extended southward into Sudan, and who quickly diversified their supply sources to include Egyptian, Chinese, and Turkish suppliers. And while yesterday's commercial elite excelled in foreign languages acquired through travel and education, the new bourgeoisie of smugglers was less educated but had the benefit of cross-border clan connections and the backing of Gaza's Islamist rulers. Thus, the tunnels became a key driver of upward mobility and social change, empowering previously marginalized groups and spawning a class of nouveaux riches.

Further encroaching on traditional business elites, tunnel owners used their financial clout to diversify upstream into retail, developing their own networks of agents to increase their market hold. Spared the cost of tunnel fees and privy to market information gained from hauling goods, they undercut retail prices, prioritized their own goods over wholesaler deliveries, and even distributed their own catalogues direct to consumers. On occasion they flooded the market to suppress prices and push wholesalers to the point of collapse. "No matter what we do, we cannot compete with the tunnel owners. They have decreased our income by 70 percent at least," complained Ala' Abu Halima, a long-standing Gaza merchant specializing in agricultural inputs.

Western-backed NGOs and the United Nations, whose required funding criteria barred them from purchasing smuggled goods and therefore stymied their reconstruction efforts, vociferously campaigned to end Israel's siege. UN officials noted the paradox whereby U.S.-led financial restrictions, which prohibited the United Nations from accessing tunnel supplies, gave their supposed target, Hamas, a distinct advantage. Refugee families turned increasingly to Hamas rather than depend on the United Nations Relief and Works Agency (UNRWA), the organization charged with sheltering them (and three-quarters of the Strip's population). UN Special Coordinator for the Middle East Peace Process Robert Serry, fearing that the international community was hemorrhaging influence, complained in a May 2010 briefing to the Security Council that "the flourishing illegitimate tunnel trade permits smugglers and militants to control commerce," while "international agencies and local contractors who wish to procure goods entering through legitimate crossings too often stand idle due to the Israeli closure."

BUSINESS AND POLITICS

Armed with resources to govern from the tunnel proceeds, Hamas transformed itself from a nonstate actor with a social and charitable network, underground movement, and guerrilla force into a governing authority with a well-equipped internal security force, bureaucracy, and economy. The commercial tunnels and the Sinai population's growing economic dependence on trade with Gaza gave Hamas the soft power to project its influence into the Sinai Peninsula, even as the factional tunnels enabled its military wing to augment this "soft" influence by exercising its own leverage there.

Yet the tunnel economy has also tarnished Hamas's reputation for transparency, accountability, and financial propriety. "This is not the old style radical movement," notes a Gaza economist; "Hamas has acquired a business venture." The Hamas authorities were widely criticized from the outset for making tunnel

licenses conditional on appointing its members to the boards of tunnel cooperatives, often on preferential terms. The government's decision to wash its hands
of the pyramid scheme for tunnel investment mentioned above, which had been
endorsed by prominent Hamas preachers and had left numerous investors bereft
of their savings, marked the first major dent in its domestic credibility. Thereafter,
Islamist and secular opponents alike adopted the discourse of corruption that
Hamas had hitherto used to undermine Fatah. A Salafi jihadi from Gaza's Middle
Areas expressed it thus:

> Before entering government, Hamas acolytes focused on religious sermons
> and memorizing the Quran. Now they are most interested in money,
> tunnel business, and fraud. Hamas used to talk about paradise, but now
> they think about buying land, cars, and apartments. After the evening
> prayers, they would go to study, now the Imam looks at ways to make
> money. Before they prayed in the mosque, now they pray at home.

Hamas's lack of transparency about its use of its tunnel earnings compounds
suspicions. While Hamas officials said local revenues comprised half the government's $750 million annual budget for 2011, local businessmen calculated the
earnings to be higher, raising questions about where the funds go and why there
are repeated shortfalls in monthly civil-service salary payments. A similarly cava-
lier approach to child labor and tunnel fatalities damaged the movement's standing
with human-rights groups, despite government assurances dating back to 2008
that it was considering curbs. During a police patrol that the author was permitted
to accompany in December 2011, nothing was done to impede the use of children
in the tunnels, where, as in Victorian coal mines, they are prized for their nimble
bodies. At least 160 children have been killed in the tunnels, according to Hamas
officials. Safety controls on imports appear similarly lax, although the TAC insists
that a sixteen-man contingent carries out sporadic spot-checks.

The tunnels had been a mixed bag for Hamas. While its detractors praise—
albeit begrudgingly—its success in reducing the impact of Israel's stranglehold,
perceptions of corruption inside the organization have intensified. During the
renewed fuel shortages of spring 2012, there were widespread allegations that
Hamas leaders received uninterrupted electricity and that gasoline stations
continued to operate for the exclusive use of Hamas members. True or not, they
fed a growing mood of recrimination that Hamas had profited from the siege.

AN END OF THE TUNNELS?

The peaks and troughs of Gaza's tunnel economy came to an abrupt halt in July 2013, with Egypt's overthrow of Morsi and launch of its Sinai operation. Three years of exponential growth and even tentative development shifted into reverse. Construction ground to a halt; Hamas lost its revenue base, and Gaza its strategic safety valve from Israeli pressure.

Having geared its economy to the tunnels, Hamas struggled to finance its rule. Bereft of much of the $1 million per day it had earned in tunnel dues, in August 2013 the government put its 46,000-strong army and bureaucracy on half pay, and in early 2014 delayed paying even that, sparking rare public sector protests. Initially it sought to increase taxes on the trickle of goods that still managed to cross. Cigarette taxes tripled in a week; cement prices quadrupled. It also feared that the increased hardship could provoke rising discontent. Instead of the promised free-trade zone with Egypt, Gaza faced a buffer zone, or *cordon sanitaire*. Without fuel, Gaza's power plant shut down, increasing blackouts to some sixteen hours per day. In places, the sewage system collapsed, spilling into the street. In parallel with their disruption of passenger flows underground, Egypt's security forces closed the Rafah terminal. Claustrophobic Gaza was an open-air prison again.

At a time of such radical oscillations in the region, predicting scenarios is a hazardous exercise. But unlike previous shocks to the tunnel economy, which Hamas always managed to subvert, this latest assault felt terminal. Fearing potential unrest, Hamas's siege mentality revived. Only months after their triumphal tours feted on the shoulders of the faithful of the region's leading mosques, Hamas's leaders prepared for lockdown again. Despairing of their politicians finding an exit and determined to buck the region-wide Islamist downfall, the military wing flexed its muscles. The first Islamist movement to take power on the Mediterranean now speaks of making a last stand. Its forces erected night-time checkpoints in the center of Gaza City, closed news agencies, and detained a widening circle of suspected opponents. The head of a newly opened Egyptian community association in Gaza City was hauled in for questioning. The Qassam Brigades staged military parades, firing guns into the air, and giving the Muslim Brotherhood's four finger salute.

Whether or not Hamas can survive without the tunnels will largely depend on its ability to adapt. In a sign of its readiness to live with greater dependency on

Israel, its finance minister committed to introduce a tax on imports from Israel—
in effect promoting double taxation, since Israel already collected taxes on goods
crossing into Gaza to fund President Abbas's Palestinian Authority. Construction
materials began to sporadically flow again from Israel into Gaza. For the first time
ever, 400 truckloads passed over its Kerem Shalom crossing in day. "If demand
grows, we're ready to step in," said an Israeli army officer.

Such professed altruism had its limits. Following Morsi's downfall, Israel
reneged on upholding the terms of the cease-fire agreement with Hamas that the
Egyptian president had helped broker in November 2012, which had provided
for the phased opening of Gaza's crossings with Israel. Although trade rose, it
remained severely restricted. Israel continued to prevent the passage of raw materials for commercial use, and, after announcing its discovery of a tunnel from Gaza
into Israel that seemed to be for military use, halted supplies to donor projects
as well. With tunnel traffic all but terminated from Egypt, Gaza's development,
other than a Qatari-financed road project, largely ground to a halt.

Nevertheless, the common interests in preventing a Hamas's collapse and
Gaza's slide into its pre-2007 security chaos seem clear. Israel appears to share
Hamas's interest in perpetuating its rule. As noted above, Israel sought to maintain Palestine's divided rule and exclude Gaza from any arrangements it made
with President Abbas in the West Bank. And by acting as the aid conduit for
Gaza, it sees a potential benefit in improving ties with Qatar and Turkey, the
prime sponsors of Gaza's reconstruction.

Today, neither the Palestinian Authority nor the international community
sees an interest in reviving the tunnel economy. During a November 2013 visit
to Cairo, President Abbas commended General Sisi's efforts, perhaps hopeful that
Hamas's woes would be his gain. And the United Nations, while attempting
to ease the resulting hardship, welcomed the shift of Gaza's supply lines back
to Israel as a first step to its reintegration within the framework of the Israel-
Palestine paradigm. In its statements, the UN joined Egypt and the Palestinian
Authority in highlighting the illegality of the tunnels, and calling on Israel to
reopen the crossings. "The tunnels were an exception," said a UN official. "Israel
has to assume its responsibility for Gaza's needs."

Ultimately Gaza's rehabilitation will depend on its re-entry to the formal
economy. While the tunnels had prevented Gaza's collapse, they fuelled centrif-
ugal forces in the region, fostering the Bedouin uprising in the Sinai that threatens
to destabilize Egypt and regional jihadi militancy, as well as the erosion of central

authority through bribery and corruption. To this end, all parties—Egypt, Israel, Gaza, the Palestinian Authority, and the UN—might benefit from supporting the formalization of Gaza's economic relations, and ending the curbs and policies of exclusion which foster informal economies. As Gaza's economy normalizes, so might its politics. In short, while the tunnels served as a homemade driver of Gaza's reintegration into the region and a makeshift dynamo for regeneration, they did not equip Gaza with the tools required to rebuild and sustain a productive society.

Nicolas Pelham is a writer on Arab affairs for The Economist *and the* New York Review of Books. *He is the author of* A New Muslim Order *(I. B. Tauris, 2008) and coauthor of* A History of the Middle East *(Penguin, 2004), and has reported extensively on Gaza.*

V. PALESTINIAN DEMOGRAPHICS

The following statistical table is taken from the Palestinian Central Bureau of Statistics, which is administered by the Palestinian Authority. It represents projected head count in 2013. The figures used in this book are based on projected increases for 2014. Though the rate of growth has slowed over the last few years, the populations of both Gaza and the West Bank are expanding faster than the global average growth rate of 1.14 percent.

Total Population: 4,420,549
West Bank: 2,719,112
Gaza: 1,701,437

Rate of annual population increase: 2.94 percent/year
West Bank: 2.62 percent/year
Gaza: 3.44 percent/year

Percentage of (0–14)-year-olds: 40.1
West Bank: 38.0
Gaza: 43.4

Percentage of (15–29)-year-olds: 29.9
West Bank: 30.0
Gaza: 29.8

Percentage of (29–60)-year-olds: 25.6
West Bank: 27.2
Gaza: 23.1

Percentage of (60+)-year-olds: 4.4
West Bank: 4.8
Gaza: 3.7

VI. IN WAITING
by Riyam Kafri

The following prose poem was written by Riyam Kafri and is included here to stand in for sentiments expressed to us by nearly every one of our interviewees, whether their narratives were included in this collection or not. To read Riyam's narrative, see page 97.

Welcome to the land of waiting. People here are born waiting. Waiting to return to a homeland lost, and from the looks of it, in the most desperate moments, lost forever. Waiting to return to a home they still carry a key for in their hand and a memory in their heart, an image hidden in the folds of their dreams, that sadly and in the most realistic moments, they know no longer exists.

In Palestine you wait for Ramadan, just like you wait for a breath of fresh air in a crowded restaurant in NYC, you wait for a *tasree* (permit), you wait for the paycheck, or even worse you wait for the job.

You wait for schools to open, for the strike to end, for the checkpoint to be removed, for the accident rubble to be cleared. You wait for the Allenby Bridge to empty, you wait for the doctor to finally come in on time.

In Palestine you wait. You wait for your dreams to happen.

You wait to leave the refugee camp, you wait to leave the village, you wait to arrive to Ramallah, you wait for destiny to embrace you, but she really never does. In fact at the first stop she slaps you hard in the face and leaves her mark, and then you spend a lifetime waiting for that wound to heal. It never does.

In Palestine you wait to graduate, you wait to find a job, you wait for the next job to be better.

In Palestine you wait to get married, then you wait to have children, then you wait for them to grow, then you wait for them to become doctors . . . trust me they will not.

In Palestine you wait in line endlessly to receive permission to see Palestine that is yours. And after you finally get a chance to see her, you realize she looks nothing like what your grandparents described, and nothing like the country your mother cries over. You wait to see her, only to realize that she has moved on, and did not wait for you.

In Palestine you wait for the birth of a child anxiously with the hope she is not born on a checkpoint. In Palestine you wait for the hunger strike to end. You wait for sons and daughters to be released from prison, only to be rearrested again, at the next checkpoint on the next trip, on their way to find a job and start a life.

In Palestine you wait for your paycheck only to have it hijacked by hungry loan payments and red hot gasoline prices.

In Palestine, you wait endlessly in Qalandia to get home. Keep waiting . . . this might take hours . . .

You wait for the summer to end in the hopes that winter will bring more peace, and you wait for winter to end in the hopes that summer will bring more warmth.

In Palestine you wait for everything and everyone.

And in Palestine you wait for the next eruption, the next Intifada, the next incursion, the next war—which always comes.

ACKNOWLEDGMENTS

From the very start, this project has been blessed by a cavalry of people who helped us get the book off the ground and sustained it (and us) for the four years it took to bring to completion.

First and foremost, thank you to all those who shared their stories with us. The people in this book, and the dozens whose stories didn't make it in, have opened our minds and hearts and changed our lives. Thank you for letting us into your homes and into your lives for the last four years.

This book would not have gotten done without Luke Gerwe. Luke is not only an extraordinary editor, but also endlessly patient and never lost his sense of humor throughout many months of changes, rewrites, and endless pleas for just one more interview.

Big thanks mimi lok for her willingness to take a risk and fight for two young editors tackling very complicated and contentious subject matter. She not only provided her brilliant editorial eye throughout the project but also talked us through some of the trickier emotional aspects of working with traumatic stories.

We also want to thank Dave Eggers, first for believing in the power of the story enough to start an unlikely and inspiring organization like Voice of Witness. And second, for believing in our project and putting both the resources and name of his organization behind it. We love Voice of Witness, and couldn't be more proud to work with such an all-star group of people dedicated to real human storytelling.

Behind almost every word in this book is a team of multi-talented translators. To Jenny Baboun, Nidal Hatim, Amjad Alawi, Abeer Ayyoub, Iyad Ali, the Hebron crew, and Wassim and George Ghantous, thank you for not only translating, but guiding us, feeding us, making us laugh, challenging us, and cheerfully taking on every awkward situation we threw at you. We feel very lucky to have had the chance to work with you.

Thanks to Timothy Faust for twice coming to the West Bank with us and serving as a photographer, general assistant, and—most importantly—chai wallah.

We must thank all of our friends and family who have been listening to us drone on about this project for the past four years. We've missed weddings, births, birthdays, and holidays and your understanding has meant everything. We especially want to thank Doug Cosper, who was not only our friend and fundraiser, but the reason we fell in love with journalism and worked together in the first place; Nora Parr who provided us with endless amounts of both enthusiasm and criticism, whatever was needed most at the time; Daniel Adamson and Somi Cho, who made us countless meals and helped us work out exactly what this book was about; Ceil Malek, who not only lent us her expert editing and wise advice, but also put up with many missed calls; Abeer and Shadia, who alternately took care of us and made sure we never got too full of ourselves; Michael Hoke for his brief but expert counsel; Brian Sipsey and Jaime Lehner, for their love and support in the beginning; Nora Barrows-Friedman and Sari Andoni who provided some excellently timed advice and editing; and Thea Agape Lim and Rana Moussa for their friendship and expertise. Thanks to Julia Randall for early edits, and Cate's tarot deck for guidance and entertainment. And a warm thanks to Jesse Kipp, Branwen Cale, and Andrew Malek for helping with our Kickstarter campaign and so much more.

This book was originally supported by a Kickstarter project and we are grateful to everyone who took part in our campaign. A very special thank you to our donors at the publisher level: Khaled Dajani, the Mohrbacher family, Tom Duncan, Barry and Mary Hoke, Michael Hoke and Emmy Betz, Paul Malek, Jim Rees, Benjamin and Sas Hadden, Kathy Lehner, Brian Sipsey, Mark Eastaway, Branwen Cale and Kate Wright.

A hearty thank you to our Kickstarter donors at the editor-in-chief level: Taylor and Erica Pendergrass, Matthew Martella, Jaime Lehner,

Jenna D'anna and Aaron Wilson, Victoria Canty, Joanne Fattaleh, Heather Boronski, Ian White, Theresa Zordan, Jasper Malcomson, John Hoke, Sean Paul, Kim Locke, Valeda Scribner, Suzie and Steve Mckenna, Jim and Nancy Faust, Sean Paul, Patricia Kule, and Bill and Joan Betz. Thank you. And a huge thank you to everyone who donated—in any way—to our project and helped get this book off the ground. Finally, this project was supported in part by an award from the Lannan Foundation. Thank you.

ABOUT THE EDITORS

CATE MALEK and MATEO HOKE began working together in 2001, while studying journalism at the University of Colorado-Boulder. Their interest in human rights journalism began on a project in which they spent eight months interviewing undocumented Mexican immigrants about their daily lives. Cate now lives in the West Bank where she works as an editor and teaches English at Bethlehem University. Previously she worked as a newspaper reporter, receiving multiple Colorado Press Association awards. Mateo holds a master's degree from the University of California-Berkeley Graduate School of Journalism. In addition to his work in the Middle East, he has reported from the Amazon jungle and the Seychelles. His writing has received awards from the Overseas Press Club Foundation and the Knight Foundation, among others.

The VOICE OF WITNESS SERIES

The Voice of Witness book series, published by McSweeney's, empowers those most closely affected by contemporary social injustice. Using oral history as a foundation, the series depicts human rights crises in the United States and around the world. Voice of Witness also publishes a guide for teaching oral history called *The Power of the Story*. *Palestine Speaks* is the thirteenth book in the series. The other titles in the series are:

SURVIVING JUSTICE
America's Wrongfully Convicted and Exonerated
Compiled and edited by Lola Vollen and Dave Eggers
Foreword by Scott Turow
"Real, raw, terrifying tales of 'justice.'" —*Star Tribune*

These oral histories prove that the problem of wrongful conviction is far-reaching and very real. Through a series of all-too-common circumstances—eyewitness misidentification, inept defense lawyers, coercive interrogation—the lives of these men and women of all different backgrounds were irreversibly disrupted. In *Surviving Justice*, thirteen exonerees describe their experiences—the events that led to their convictions, their years in prison, and the process of adjusting to their new lives outside.

VOICES FROM THE STORM
The People of New Orleans on Hurricane Katrina and Its Aftermath
Compiled and edited by Chris Ying and Lola Vollen
"*Voices from the Storm* uses oral history to let those who survived the hurricane tell their (sometimes surprising) stories." —*Independent UK*

Voices from the Storm is a chronological account of the worst natural disaster in modern American history. Thirteen New Orleanians describe the days leading up to Hurricane Katrina, the storm itself, and the harrowing confusion of the days and months afterward. Their stories weave and intersect, ultimately creating an eye-opening portrait of courage in the face of terror, and of hope amid nearly complete devastation.

UNDERGROUND AMERICA
Narratives of Undocumented Lives
Compiled and edited by Peter Orner
Foreword by Luis Alberto Urrea
"No less than revelatory." —*Publishers Weekly*

They arrive from around the world for countless reasons. Many come simply to make a living. Others are fleeing persecution in their native countries. But by living and working in the U.S. without legal status, millions of immigrants risk deportation and imprisonment. *Underground America* presents the remarkable oral histories of men and women struggling to carve a life for themselves in the United States. In 2010, *Underground America* was translated into Spanish and released as *En las Sombras de Estados Unidos*.

OUT OF EXILE
The Abducted and Displaced People of Sudan
Compiled and edited by Craig Walzer
Additional interviews and an introduction by
Dave Eggers and Valentino Achak Deng
"Riveting." —*School Library Journal*

Millions of people have fled from conflicts in all parts of Sudan, and many thousands more have been enslaved as human spoils of war. In *Out of Exile*, refugees and abductees recount their escapes from the wars in Darfur and South Sudan, from political and religious persecution, and from abduction by militias. They tell of life before the war, and of the hope that they might someday find peace again.

HOPE DEFERRED
Narratives of Zimbabwean Lives
Compiled and edited by Peter Orner and Annie Holmes
Foreword by Brian Chikwava
"*Hope Deferred* might be the most important publication to have come out of Zimbabwe in the last thirty years." —*Harper's Magazine*

The fifth volume in the Voice of Witness series presents the narratives of Zimbabweans whose lives have been affected by the country's political, economic, and human rights crises. This book asks the question: How did a country with so much promise—a stellar education system, a growing middle class of professionals, a sophisticated economic infrastructure, a liberal constitution, and an independent judiciary—go so wrong?

NOWHERE TO BE HOME
Narratives from Survivors of Burma's Military Regime
Compiled and edited by Maggie Lemere and Zoë West
Foreword by Mary Robinson
"Extraordinary." —The Asia Society

Decades of military oppression in Burma have led to the systematic destruction of thousands of ethnic-minority villages, a standing army with one of the world's highest numbers of child soldiers, and the displacement of millions of people. *Nowhere to Be Home* is an eye-opening collection of oral histories exposing the realities of life under military rule. In their own words, men and women from Burma describe their lives in the country that Human Rights Watch has called "the textbook example of a police state."

PATRIOT ACTS
Narratives of Post-9/11 Injustice
Compiled and edited by Alia Malek
Foreword by Karen Korematsu
"Important and timely." —Reza Aslan

Patriot Acts tells the stories of men and women who have been needlessly swept up in the War on Terror. In their own words, narrators recount personal experiences of the post-9/11 backlash that has deeply altered their lives and communities. *Patriot Acts* illuminates these experiences in a compelling collection of eighteen oral histories from men and women who have found themselves subject to a wide range of human and civil rights abuses—from rendition and torture, to workplace discrimination, bullying, FBI surveillance, and harassment.

INSIDE THIS PLACE, NOT OF IT
Narratives from Women's Prisons
Compiled and edited by Ayelet Waldman and Robin Levi
Foreword by Michelle Alexander
"These stories are a gift." —Michelle Alexander

Inside This Place, Not of It reveals some of the most egregious human rights violations within women's prisons in the United States. In their own words, the thirteen narrators in this book recount their lives leading up to incarceration and their experiences inside—ranging from forced sterilization and shackling during childbirth, to physical and sexual abuse by prison staff. Together, their testimonies illustrate the harrowing struggles for survival that women in prison must endure.

THROWING STONES AT THE MOON
Narratives of Colombians Displaced by Violence
Compiled and edited by Sibylla Brodzinsky and Max Schoening
Foreword by Íngrid Betancourt
"Both sad and inspiring." —*Publishers Weekly*

For nearly five decades, Colombia has been embroiled in internal armed conflict among guerrilla groups, paramilitary militias, and the country's own military. Civilians in Colombia have to make their lives despite the threat of torture, kidnapping, and large-scale massacres—and more than four million have had to flee their homes. The oral histories in *Throwing Stones at the Moon* describe the most widespread of Colombia's human rights crises: forced displacement. Speakers recount life before displacement, the reasons for their flight, and their struggle to rebuild their lives.

REFUGEE HOTEL
Compiled and edited by Juliet Linderman and Gabriele Stabile
"There is no other book like *Refugee Hotel* on your shelf." —*SF Weekly*

Refugee Hotel is a groundbreaking collection of photography and interviews that documents the arrival of refugees in the United States. Evocative images are coupled with moving testimonies from people describing their first days in the U.S., the lives they've left behind, and the new communities they've since created.

HIGH RISE STORIES
Voices from Chicago Public Housing
Compiled and edited by Audrey Petty
Foreword by Alex Kotlowitz
"Joyful, novelistic, and deeply moving." —George Saunders

In the gripping first-person accounts of *High Rise Stories*, former residents of Chicago's iconic public housing projects describe life in the now-demolished high rises. These stories of community, displacement, and poverty in the wake of gentrification give voice to those who have long been ignored.

INVISIBLE HANDS
Voices from the Global Economy
Compiled and edited by Corinne Goria
Foreword by Kalpona Akter
"Powerful and revealing testimony . . ." —*Kirkus*

In this oral history collection, electronics manufacturers in China, miners in Africa, garment workers in Mexico, and farmers in India—among many others—reveal the human rights crises occuring behind the scenes of the global economy.

THE POWER OF THE STORY
The Voice of Witness Teacher's Guide to Oral History
Compiled and edited by Cliff Mayotte
Foreword by William and Richard Ayers
"A rich source of provocations to engage with human dramas throughout the world." —*Rethinking Schools Magazine*

This comprehensive guide allows teachers and students to explore contemporary issues through oral history, and to develop the communication skills necessary for creating vital oral history projects in their own communities.